Life

in a

by

Norman Finn

Green Ivy Publishing
1 Lincoln Centre
18W140 Butterfield Road
Suite 1500
Oakbrook Terrace IL 60181-4843
www.greenivybooks.com

ISBN: 978-1-945058-44-8

To Phil Barach who was the most
influential individual in every aspect of
my life.

"A friend is someone who knows all about
you and still loves you."
Ebert Hubbard

FOREWORD

I guess I would classify myself as a storyteller rather than a writer. I thought of setting down the events of my life a number of times over the years. I always thought it would just be a series of adventures and my experiences. I envisioned it as if we were sitting in a café and I was telling you my stories. I generally get asked the question: "How did you get into this business?" and the saga starts. It's always been that way.

About fifteen years ago when I was having personal problems I saw a psychologist who suggested I write down my history and the events surrounding it. I brought in my writings whenever we met. They were quite extensive for I traveled almost continuously and the flight hours gave me the time to write.

They were interesting, provocative sessions which gave me much needed insight into the issues that confronted me. These notes were the basis or, should I say, the impetus for this book. As I reread them, they took on a different perspective and additional meaning than when I wrote them. They served as an outline and made the project a priority. It amazes me how one's thinking and opinions change over the years. Some people call it wisdom. I would debate that. I call it just experience.

The opportunity to revisit my writing allowed me to come away with a different point of view and reevaluate my thoughts. I have vivid memories of my past for they are filled with the stories and memories of interesting characters and adventures. I call them adventures, for many of them were to new worlds for manufacturing and sourcing. These pages are filled with the personalities and situations and how they impacted me.

I thought about where I should begin and chose a turning point in my early career. My stories, for the most part, are all related to my creativity, artistic abilities and experiences. In a way, it's an unusual combination of artistic ability and business "smarts" that gave me the edge, this life, and this story.

They cover the individual entrepreneur and the corporate structures. It's all related to the shoe industry but has the familiar issues and situations found throughout the business world. There are lessons that one can derive from these experiences. They have helped me to understand the circumstances and ramifications of the events. They definitely made me who I am.

At the age of ten, you learn early. It was necessary to pay for the newspapers you delivered every week. I went down to face the dreaded "fat lady" sitting behind a look-alike teller's cage. I slid your four quarters, one group at a time, toward her. The desk had a large crack and when the quarters passed over, sometimes there were only three. I passed the next set of quarters over the abyss.

I tried to be at least accurate about whatever I have written. All the stories are true; all the events depicted happened; all the participants are real. Some of the names have been changed for obvious reasons but the facts are there. My thoughts are my thoughts.

"Some things scratch the surface while others strike your soul." *Gianna Perada*

Finally......A Chance

CHAPTER ONE

"And suddenly you know. It's time to start something new and trust the magic of beginnings."

Meister Eckhart

Where do you begin to tell your story of who and what you are? It's difficult to formulate....almost impossible to put into perspective. Events pour through your head. You start to focus on a timetable and begin the process by running your memory tapes. They are not in any order or sequence, but, they are there vividly. The years somehow tumbled into your lap. It is almost impossible to believe how they roll away. They are there before you, as you awkwardly trying to hold them all in your arms and psyche.

Somehow it is a jumble of family, friends, people, business, faraway places, loves and dreams. You begin to give them some semblance of order, but that lasts only a moment. There are too many events in motion, an endless array of your life's happenings rushing headlong to reach the surface.

Why am I doing this? Is it the need of men to bare their souls? Is it a way of paying homage to oneself? Is it the need to fill time that plagues those sitting and watching the day's light recede to darkness? Is it by chance a labor of love; a legacy to your children?

I'm really not sure. All I know is that I have always done what I set out to do....and made it my quest. Am I up to the task?

I know when I get into the nitty-gritty of paragraph after paragraph; Pandora's Box will be opened. Much more than I thought will come forth. Will I be truthful, most importantly to myself?

Am I willing to bend the truth or color events to paint the perfect response or landscape? That remains to be seen as it unfolds. Maybe what is real is too difficult to handle at this stage. I believe I am ready to start the journey armed with the desire to stay the course and tell it as it is...my thoughts...my life...my goals...my dreams.

I had just gotten the first real break in my business life as an assistant designer and pattern maker. I had been stumbling around trying to make it as a freelance shoe designer for two years while trying to keep my wife and baby in a decent living situation. I was just 23 years old.

After Clark University I really did not know what path to take in my life's work. My first love was art in all its forms and I realized this should be my career path. Unfortunately, I allowed myself to be talked out of going to art school.

How could a nice Jewish boy find his place in life as an artist? It was unheard of in my mother's eyes. My motivation to escape Worcester, Massachusetts, where I had grown up, was intensified when I fell in love with my college sweetheart. Judy was not Jewish and there was immense pressure brought to bear from my family. My brother-in-law offered me a position in his business if I broke it off. I was bombarded daily from every angle and promised the world if I stopped seeing her. Whatever the reason, all this pressure by the family created an even greater bond between Judy and me. We were, more than ever, determined to be together.

I packed my bags and silently slipped away to Boston. Judy left school and went home to Salem. She had gone to secretarial school before Clark and was able to immediately find work in Boston where she commuted. After a brief stay at the YMCA, I found a room on Beacon Hill and a job as a salesperson in a shoe store. We were employed two blocks from one another and we lunched on the Boston Common. Life was up in the air but we were together. We had no idea of where life would take us but we were deeply in love. Judy became pregnant and we married. Our honeymoon consisted of a lunch at Locke-Obers, a real splurge, and a movie, "The Pride and the Passion", starring Cary Grant and Sophia Loren. What could be bad?

We found an apartment on South Russell Street, the wrong side of Beacon Hill, in what you could possibly call a one-bedroom. It was bleak and run down but I painted and wall-papered to make it livable.

Judy got big and worked almost to the day Ted was born. She had to traverse the hill to get to the office, as both of us worked on the other side. We would laugh and giggle as she made the climb. I got my draft notice which scared the hell out of me, but I was deferred because of her pregnancy. When Ted was born, and we moved to Dorchester, a neighborhood in transition. Judy could not work and the living conditions were far better and cheaper than Boston.

I worked in the shoe store struggling to make ends meet. There was additional money at times from selling some designs and doing illustrations for retail ads. The challenge was before me. There is a line from "Fiddler on the Roof" that says it all. "They are so happy they don't know how miserable they are." I guess we were in that state.

Those early years before getting the Shain position were a blur. I just had to fight my way out of the situation that put Judy and I in a very tough place. We were two kids facing very difficult odds. I would not accept where we were. I believed our destiny was to build a far better life.

How was I going to get us out of this predicament? We had zero money and a baby. I was not a doctor or a lawyer or an Indian Chief, and my family was against the marriage. Was I destined to work in a shoe store the rest of my life? Did I have what it takes to fight through these obstacles? Could I achieve a better life for my family?

What saved us was my total focus on finding the answers. I explored every avenue. It was "a full court press twenty-four hours a day" to turn the tide in my favor. I knew my only hope was my ability to understand and be a quick learner in my footwear schooling and be able to put it on paper as a legitimate designer.

What I didn't know was how little I actually knew and what I had to learn. How does it go? "Ignorance is bliss, tis folly to be wise". I soldiered onward and kept the focus at a blistering pace. It was shoes and art. They were the only skills I had. Working in a shoe store since I was 15 years old after school and college were the only work experience I had ever known. Somehow or another, for some unknown reason I felt this was my future and focused all my strength on working toward a career in footwear and design.

These were very tough "innings" even with the break of getting this position. I worked in shoe stores, went to a technical shoe pattern school evenings and found odd jobs illustrating shoes for catalogues and retail advertising.

When I look back at those days, I realize I didn't have much of a choice. It was the only thing I knew. We had to eat! Shain Shoe Company offered me, not only a regular paycheck, but the learning experience I so desperately needed. I was extremely fortunate to get the position. The New England shoe industry in the 50's, 60's and more likely the early 70's was basically a closed industry; open only to family. In almost all instances, management positions were occupied by sons, sons-in-law, or possibly a cousin. It just didn't happen unless there was blood involved.

Shain was a big step up from the shoe store where I probably averaged $70 per week. After deductions, it was not very much. When I arrived in Boston I went directly to Tremont Street where there was an array of shoe stores of all types almost all in a row. I interviewed at two to three and chose the one based on the personality of the manager. Carl Berger seemed laid back and intelligent and I could feel that he really wanted to hire me. He was a handsome man, well-groomed and well dressed. Carl was soft-spoken with a personality and character filled with kindness and compassion. Both he and his wife, Maybelle were just wonderful to us. We were married in their home on a cold wet evening after Christmas. They were the only bright lights in our world for quite some time. Carl allowed me to sketch when there weren't any customers in the store. He encouraged me in every way.

It was amazing what you want to remember and what you want to forget. People can be cruel and the world follows.

Working in a shoe store brought me in contact with many of the New England shoe executives. One of them took an interest in me and offered me a position as his assistant. Just as I was about to start, he was offered a major position elsewhere. The question was: Do I still have the job? I was re-interviewed by the President and hired.

It was a strange situation. I had a company car that's primary purpose was to chauffeur the C.F.O. and myself to the plant located about one hour away. I picked him up every morning and was subject to his constant dissatisfaction with almost every aspect of his existence as well as everyone else's. I would classify him as the most negative person I have ever known. On top of that, he smoked the vilest cigarettes.

Three weeks into the job and just before the Xmas holidays, I was called to the President's office. "We are sorry but you're being let go, not for any cause. We really have no time to train you. It was a mistake hiring you." There was no severance.

I was out on the street. I had almost zero chance of landing a retail position going into the slow season. I was desperate, not knowing how we could get through the 2½ month period. I remember walking home from downtown Boston to Dorchester because I did not have subway fare. Those were dark days.

There's some form of retribution in this life. Many years later I had the opportunity to cast the deciding vote on a major program proposed by the President. I guess you know the answer.

I just got lucky. Ralph Shapiro, the sales executive, stylist, and line builder at Shain could not draw a straight line. He had a great eye for fashion and color, and an innate sense of knowing what would sell but needed someone to put it on paper. So there I was, a remedy, and a cheap one.

He interviewed me in his retail store which was known as the fashion stop for footwear in the Boston area. I was so nervous, dropping my sketches all over the floor. I was in awe of Ralph and his reputation in the industry. He liked what he saw and we seemed to hit it off. I became his right-hand for $105.00 per week. Actually, the salary was not open for discussion. Saul Shain just told me that was the salary. Working in the pattern room and designing enabled me to see how patterns were developed as well as the initial steps in making the product.

I had rudimentary pattern experience from taking courses at the Lynn shoe school and had gone nights and some days doing a year's course in three months. I now had the opportunity to see every operation in the factory and just soaked it up. I was now able to cut actual patterns and design. All this was beyond my expectations. The run of the plant was available to me and I took advantage of every opportunity to learn. Shain Shoe was a small better-grade business and learning how to make quality footwear was a great advantage.

I started at the source, the cutting room. We used expensive leathers and, if the materials were not used properly, all the profits would be on the cutting room floor. There was an art, or should I say expertise, on laying out the patterns on the skins to get the best yield and the proper stretch. Leather was a living entity and each skin had to be handled differently. It did not come on a roll as some young department store buyers thought. There was a high degree of proficiency needed to cut the material. The best skins had imperfections and defects that needed to be worked around or cut into areas not seen on the upper. You had to be an experienced operator. Each model was different and demanded a different approach to laying out the pattern on the leather. The cutters were the highest paid operators in the factory.

The stitching room represented a major portion of the process. The stitched upper, once completed, was ready to be put through the production process. The ability to put the pieces together to form the pattern demanded a number of skills, as it had to be precise. The cut pieces had to be stitched together within the limits of their allowances so they would fit. Depending on the pattern, the skill level on the part of the operator was key.

The initial pre-production preparation, folding and skiving of the pieces and the cementing of certain sections of the upper, were all part of the process. The number of individual operations in the stitching room was mind-boggling. It could be over 100 on certain patterns. There had to be great communication between the stitching process and the pattern department. There were, in many instances, no hard and fast rules for the make-up of certain materials and leathers had to be considered to make the upper correctly.

I was fortunate enough to be the go-between the stitching room foreman and pattern issues. I was able to pick up a wealth of knowledge. Our stitching guy was one of the best. He had originally come from a better shoe factory in New York and demanded perfection. He would say, "Kid...we vanna make them like pictures, not shoes...beautiful pictures," in his Yiddish accent.

Saul Shain, the owner, was in his mid-50s. He was slim, with a receding hairline, interesting features, and just about 6 feet tall. He was a master craftsman and shoemaker. There was nothing he couldn't do with his hands, as he had built a good portion of the house he lived in. Saul spent years working with his older brother, Cy, who had a volume plant in Newburyport, as the factory manager. He learned his craft well and, being entrepreneurial, got a break when two key customers wanted a better product. I believe Cy financed the operation to get it started.

Cy Shain was a customer of mine when I was selling designs. I believe he and some other manufacturers always bought two to three because I was a nice Jewish boy trying to make it, not just because of my talent. There were people out there who wanted to help and recognized that I had talent.

Saul called all the "shots". He bought the leather and set the production schedule. There was a factory superintendent but he was basically just a figurehead who jumped when Saul called.

The two accounts he was able to corral were what we called "anchors". Saks Fifth Avenue and Baker Shoes of California had the buying power to fill most of the production line. The factory was geared to make 3-500 pairs per day. Saks procured a brand for Saul which he used on a good portion of the product made for them. It was more of an exclusive. The label was Jacques Heim, a not so well-known apparel designer. It did, however, give him enough legitimacy to create the right fashion presence or aura for the product.

The sales, direct contact with the customers, and styling fell to Ralph Shapiro. He was one of the premier shoe men in the New England shoe industry. As far as I was concerned, he walked on water, could do no wrong, and was one of the most influential personalities I would meet in my lifetime. Ralph was just gorgeous; the best looking dude I had ever seen. He had "savoir faire" and used his looks as a tool to achieve his goals, personally and in the field. He had a wonderful sense of style and great merchandising skills.

His store in Newton drew the fashion crowd from all over New England. It was also the laboratory and testing ground for Shain Shoe. We could bring in short runs of avant-garde fashion and test it almost overnight. He came out of the pages of GQ and looked like Tom Cruise; slightly taller and better looking. Ralph captivated you with his manner and was the ultimate womanizer. There was not a close second. He charmed them, collected them. They stood literally in a queue to have him wait on them when he was in the store. Unless you were there, it was hard to believe.

All of the New England manufacturers made it their business

to shop Ralph's. He bought or made the latest, most stylish product. They wanted to "knock off" the most interesting, innovative and directional patterns and came to the store to find what was "hot".

When Ralph bought the stock he always added an extra one or two sample sizes. The manufacturers who came to buy the latest items wanted that size to copy.

Ralph was "king of the hill" in every way and I was his squire who picked up the pieces and carried the bags. Oh, sometimes I got two to three styles into the collection. Ralph gave me every opportunity to grow, giving me design themes to develop. I was involved 110% in the development of the collections. He was, in a sense, right out of the pages of Damon Runyon growing up in Revere with friends in the "good fella" classification. He found the right path; otherwise he could have gone in an entirely different vocation.

Ralph was full of stories and the one that sticks with me the most is the following: He had a group of boyhood friends who were the "wildest, craziest guys" you could ever imagine. They burned the candle at three ends. Wine, women, and song were their gods, and then they threw in gambling. They had made fortunes in the travel business developing the charter flight concept. They discovered Las Vegas and Hawaii and had made a fortune booking trips.

So here's the story! The boys invite Ralph to Miami for the Super Bowl. They have the longest limo you've ever seen and it is stocked with enough booze to float a ship and beautiful women. They proceed to bet over $75,000 (in late 50's dollars) on the game and were carrying on, laughing, drinking, and whatever all the way to the stadium. They even had a ticket for the driver. Well, they brought the booze and the women to their box seats and were having a hell of a time. The game is finally over and they lost, but they still are full of laughs and shenanigans. They all pile into the limo and Ralph ends up sitting in front with the driver. He turns to Ralph and whispers, "Tell me. The guys just lost $75,000 and are carrying on laughing and joking like I've never seen. What do they do when they win?"

Not only did I work with Ralph, but I sat in the pattern room and worked with Jim Whitman who made all the models. He was not the run of the mill pattern engineer in any way.

It was one of the key positions in the factory and the foundation of making fine footwear. Jim marched to the beat of a different drummer. He was a recovering alcoholic, pseudo-intellectual who believed his own press. I have to say, he knew how to make patterns. I was just out of pattern school and hung on every word. To contradict or offer comment was not in the cards. You lost a lot of "points" taking the other side or making a comment not to his liking. I had to live with him, as he was my ticket to understanding the real science of pattern-making. It turns out that he was more than willing to teach me as I was his bright light, willing to listen endlessly to his accomplishments. This "internship" and my schooling gave me a good working knowledge of pattern development and its application to design. I didn't realize at that time how important this step was in my overall development and how it would impact my future career.

My design ability began to emerge and Ralph pushed me forward. I do not believe I never enjoyed working with anyone as much as him. He allowed me to express myself and gave me the opportunity to be exposed to many elements of this business. My education took a great leap forward in every area. I was more than eager and he was more than helpful.

I worked in his store when he had his great sale. Ralph invented the 2 for 1 sale. They stood in line and a policeman would allow so many in at a time. It was absolutely amazing that a shoe store in Newton could sell almost 800 pairs on the opening day. I actually had to run up to Haverhill to get additional stock during the sale.

Ralph was inventive and had the uncanny ability to recognize a great new trend when he saw it. The great story is when a customer entered wearing a shoe she purchased in Europe (uncommon at that time) which had an unusual crocheted insert. He happened to be in the store at the time and immediately was drawn to the shoe. Charming as ever, he proceeded to give the woman two pair of her choice in return for what she came in with. The concept of the style became the major theme of the spring line and sold into the thousands.

Ralph sold 98% of the production and had a "salesperson" on the West Coast who was the brother of our second largest customer and handled the account. Lenny always dressed great and actually I never saw him without a fabulous tan. Ralph took me to the New York shows where I did all the detailing as he worked his magic with the customers. My eyes were wide open (also, probably my mouth) at his flawless presentations; the models, the beautiful fashion people, and the key buyers. Ralph had these crazy ideas. Well, maybe they weren't that insane. We lived in a fantasy shoe world making $100.00 product, which at that time was high price. His contention was, as he would say, "I'm selling orange and green patent leather stilettos. They have to be shown in the Presidential Suite at the Essex House and you drink champagne." It was all part of the show while watching the models walking the walk in the new collection.

Maybe I was learning bad habits, but it worked for Ralph. Everyone went about doing their marketing differently. In the years to come there were companies that made their mark using impressive marketing campaigns with enormous budgets. Most of them were successful. It was, in a sense, very strange. Four months later Saul wanted to hold back my $25.00 increase because expenses were too high. Everyone has their own agenda.

As I look back over these first experiences, I try to put them into perspective as my shoe life evolved. I think it was wilder in the early years. I learned from the master and it went on that way for quite a few years under different circumstances and different personalities. It seemed in the initial parts of my career there were more flamboyant, individualistic players that brought a very unique and colorful culture to the industry, especially in

New England.

Saul was ambitious and Saks wanted a low heel line that would be more contemporary and lower priced. It was the beginning of a whole new lifestyle look that was just getting started. The product was less structured; what I mean is softer, unlined leathers. It had a "cruder" look, not as finished as the dress shoes we were making. It was tailored and casual and was the coming trend. In retrospect, it was exactly the right direction with the right retailer but the wrong designer/line builder and program. The line was called Dee Scarpa and was priced at a volume level. Saul was shooting for the stars and wanted to compete with the big boys and raise the production level of the factory. Ralph really didn't want any part of the new project from a design/development position. He said he would sell some. I believe Saul and Ralph had a major financial difference of opinion over this new venture. Ralph wanted more control and Saul was locked into a situation he could not change. It's called the price of admission.

Saks wanted to buy them direct through the designer and Saul had a very "close" relationship with the buyer. The designer did not draw well. What I mean was her designs were drawn too stylized. They were not even done well for an advertisement. They needed to be redrawn so that a pattern maker could interpret them as the designer wishes. Her drawings could not convey this message. They left too much latitude to the pattern technician and, therefore, were never correct. Jim's interpretations of the sketches were poor. He had zero experience with this type of footwear. He was strictly a dress shoe pattern designer and did not have the "artistic touch" to work on a totally new concept without the proper sketches. It was an entirely new learning experience for Jim. Naturally, everything was new to me, but my ability to understand fashion led me to grasp the new looks when I saw them.

Hence, there was trouble in the glen. With Ralph bowing out of the picture, I was "elected" to get the prototypes and eventually samples done to her specifications. I can't truly blame her for the situation. I did not have the power to correct Jim's models nor was I totally capable of doing so. The corrections were also ridiculous. She would reject a prototype because she insisted on exact measurements which were impossible to achieve on any basis even for prototypes, samples or, needless to say, production. So we were all at war with her; all the departments could not give her "exactly" what she wanted.

I have found over the years that when designers "dig in" on millimeters they do not have confidence in what they are trying to achieve and "pass the buck" to the makers. This is a recurring story through my years working with designers and it runs from the most famous to the novice.

There are "designer" stories throughout the book. They range from the ridiculous to plain cruelty. Being the head of product development at U. S. Shoe, I came in contact with a whole series of influential designers who will go unnamed. Some were wonderful to work with and others as cruel and ruthless as could be. It was amazing at times to see household names in the fashion industry work, those with talent and those with just great P.R. ability, totally dependent on another's talent. I never could understand how it worked. The fashion world is a strange place when I see a talented designer get beaten down by people with little or no talent.

I offered to do the artwork and layout for the opening ads in Footwear News. It was a full page ad presenting Dee Scarpa to the trade. Naturally, Saul didn't pay me any extra.

It was a constant battle between her and the pattern staff. Unfortunately, I was in the middle as a facilitator and, as could be expected, both sides took their frustrations out on me. It was a great lesson as it became a political forum. I was not experienced and did not really know how to handle the gal from New York. She had Saul's ear and the experience of living through these types of confrontations and maneuvering to place blame in my camp. In Saul's eyes I was just a guy that ran the errands, kept a running account of the samples, and drew some sketches for Ralph; no one of consequence. My attitude changed and I just wanted to stick it up her ass, as well as Saul's, every chance I had.

As I said earlier, my review was coming up. It was just about a year and an increase was in order. This job offered me the most practical learning experience in every area from design to shoemaking. Most of all, working with Ralph, I had made somewhat of a breakthrough in the design area. Things were coming together and my design contribution was growing. I saw my first shoes in Saks and their ad in Vogue with my design. I was so excited. I had just jumped over the moon. I was so proud of myself!

Ralph was in my corner and tried to warn me not to expect much from Saul. When it came to money, you were dealing with someone who felt he could get along without you. He "discovered" me and I owed him my working life because he gave me the opportunity. I should wait until he was ready to say I deserved an increase. I started to get the message.

People have their own agendas and expectations that are based solely on their needs and their timetable with no concern for others. I had done significant business with Bill Richey from Australia when I was with U. S. Shoe in Italy. Bill was a great shoe man and controlled the better shoe business in Australia. When I went into business, Bill came to Taiwan to see the operation. He was impressed with the product. "Norman, the product is super. We want to use it exclusively, but we want it next year and we do not want you to sell to anyone else in Australia. You must wait the year."

"Bill, you're a great guy but if someone happens to walk through my door and lays down an order, he has my undivided attention now and next year."

The shoe employment network, mainly for those on the manufacturing side, was run by the component people, specifically those making lasts and production graded patterns.

Both these industries had constant contact with the principles or key executives and were carrying the message for whom and what was available. Naturally, there were benefits to provide this service from both sides. You would naturally want to work with the company that was instrumental in your search once you got on board.

I had formed a friendship with Harry Kennison who worked for a major last company. We first met at the Lynn pattern school. He was a director. He took a liking to me and followed my career. Harry was an excellent last salesman with good technical knowledge of the product. At that time the whole process of making lasts was a "hit or miss" process. The last was really the foundation of the shoe. It controlled fit and style. Made out of wood in the initial model stage and then turned on a lathe in plastic. It was the replica of the foot taking into consideration all the measurements, height, width, instep. The toe shape and heel height were the style factors.

Harry would present prototype lasts, actually promoting looks just as a salesman would push his product. You would look through his collection and see what toe shapes you liked and what heel height you wanted. Harry would run off to the factory and make these lasts for you. You then made a pattern to fit over the last to see the final toe shape. We call this process "lasting". Then the sole and heel are added.

Lasting was taking the finished upper and attaching it to the last. The last gave it shape, character and fit. You first attached an innersole to the last which served as the foundation for the upper. When the innersole was attached to the last, the upper was placed over the last by hand and then placed in the lasting machine. A counter was inserted in the quarter of the upper and activated during the lasting process to give it shape and fit. The operator manipulated the upper so that it would be "toe lasted" and "heel lasted". The machine would wrap the upper around the last anchored to the innersole. It was then "side lasted" laying the sides of the upper against the innersole and stapled mostly by hand. We then had a full lasted shoe which went through a series of heaters and drying machines. It was now ready to attach the sole and the heel. The whole process needed experienced operators and the right material to produce the right product.

At this point, with the prototype finished, you could try it on and either like it, throw it out or make a series of corrections. It could be a long, drawn out process and not very exact, but it was the way it was done in the American shoe industry. Once the model was OK'd for fit and look, the last could be turned in plastic and then graded to make the sizes if it was OK'd for production. You have to realize even today with all the advances in shoemaking the process involves close to 150-200 operations.

So Harry went to work looking at what was available and that's how I landed at Consolidated National with the American Girl Division. My interview there was what I would consider basic. They needed what I offered and I fit in with their program.

I went to Saul one last time and he wanted to give me a $20.00 increase in six to eight months' time. His proposal was not worth a rebuttal. Ralph was "pissed" at Saul for not anteing up to keep me and wished me well. Ralph did not put up a fight to keep me simply because he felt it was time for me to move on as there wasn't any real opportunity with Shain. We had developed a friendship that grew over the years. It was the classic story with Saul. He had given me my break and I "owed him servitude for as long as he deemed fit". Over the years I've seen this situation when young people have come to companies for employment and proceed to grow, but were still considered in the eyes of the beholder "indentured servants".

For me, the change was a major step up the ladder, at least I thought so at the time. Traveling to Haverhill from Dorchester was over an hour leaving before 5:30 am. I would be at my desk before 7 am when the factory came alive. The return at 4 pm was brutal. The town, even at that time, was bordering on being a depressed state. The milky red brick buildings were nestled between overrun empty lots filled with trash or abandoned appliances. They were remnants of days gone by one after another losing their individuality.

I had known Haverhill before Shain as I made the rounds of the better factories with my portfolio of designs. I was mainly dealing with factory owners or line builders in some instances. Most of the factories had offices in Boston and were there on Wednesday. It was market day.

Selling designs was an experience I would not like to relive. Factory owners thumbing through your designs, not having the slightest idea or ability to visualize what they would look like in a finished product were the rule, or those with a "feel for product" who would just want to steal your ideas. I do not believe I have been involved with a situation that was more frustrating. It was amazing and, at the same time, produced a lack of faith in my fellow man that someone would steal your idea for $10.00 a sketch. I did not have much of a choice. We had to eat so I had a lot of balls in the air; working part-time in a shoe store, going to pattern school, and working as a shoe illustrator for catalogues.

Haverhill represented a love/hate relationship, the town eventually faded from the shoe picture as the business became international and it was impossible to compete domestically in ancient mill buildings.

There was a combining plant in the building that put lining materials together. They employed a bright young guy my age. We used to eat lunch together and talk about our young families. I came in one morning to hear that Paul was killed in an automobile accident by a trailer crossing over the divided highway. Paul was a member of the TwoTen organization that was the philanthropic arm of the shoe industry. They paid off his mortgage and helped his wife and children through the difficult times ahead. I joined TwoTen the next day and through the years became a Director and a major contributor to the organization.

I seldom left the factory building, bringing my lunch and picking up a drink from the vending machines. Friends were few and mainly developed by visiting the component people in the building. I would be sent to find buckles, bows, ornamentation, generally metal, all in the neighborhood.

On the first floor of our building was Colonial Shoe & Ornament Company owned by Dave Berenbaum, who was a force in the domestic business. Dave was ahead of his time with great vision and talent to create new and interesting types of ornamentation. He was the major supplier to the trade in this category. He recognized my talent and over the years we not only became friends but worked on a number of projects. Ralph and Dave were great buddies and the reason why he became aware of my ability was through Ralph. When I came to look for a particular ornament, Dave would work with me and not pass me off to one of the staff who handled the customers. I actually would draw up designs for bows, etc. which he would make.

Years later, when my son, Ted, was five or six years old, I would be at Dave's house in Newton every Sunday morning to go over ornamentation and ideas while my son played "war" with him. It was that kind of a relationship. When Europe became an important fashion destination, Dave and Ralph would travel together, I would like to have been a fly on the wall. They loved the good life, and never missed a chance for a good time or interesting evening.

I was really struggling before I got the Shain job. What kept my head above water was working in a shoe store, hawking shoe designs, and doing any kind of art work that I could lay my hands on, and then I met Dick Herman. There was a group of retailers (3-4) that I came in contact with and one of them, Alex M., a good "shoe dog" (a great term of the trade to designate a journeyman in our industry) was about to open a shoe store in Mattapan Square, the last bastion for a Jewish shopping area. It was on the second floor and Al's wife, Shirley, was the brains and driving force for the store. Al was a wiry 5'8", good looking guy who in his early years was supposedly a great basketball player. At least, that's what they said. Shirley made all the decisions and she commissioned me to paint a fashion mural over the seating area. I think I got $125.00, an absolute fortune. Everybody loved it and the Dress Shop around the corner had me do a whole wall. I charged them $200.00 and was ecstatic.

Alex was part of the group and the leader was Dick. They bought together and had interest in each other's stores, but Dick, I believe, held the majority position in at least three units. I really do not know how to explain Dick. He did everything at "warp" speed. The word "impetuous" best describes him, well, a good part of him. Life had no constraints. Everything was fair game. He dreamed of conquering the world, his world first, and, in his own way, was getting there piece by piece.

He captivated me immediately and I became one of the entourage which met at least two to three times a week at Jack & Marion's or the Bagel Place. I was part of the pack; in a way it reminded me of the Frank Sinatra group. Dick was the Chairman of the Board. He set the agenda, called the shots and always paid the check, thank God!

They were interesting characters. Besides Alex there was John S. who was very Italian, not too smart but very willing. He owned a store with Dick and was developing a new unit in Winchester. There was another Al who was very slick and a good politician. He had a store in Stoneham and knew how to play the game. Again, I believe Dick held a major interest. When Dick spoke, they all listened and when he said "jump", they said "how high", including me.

Dick was the key salesman for Belle Mode Footwear. They were classified as jobbers, buying product to their specifications from a number of factories and stocking the product for small retailers. He had the New England territory and was a dynamic salesman, the type that, once he got you in his grasp, you had to buy. He was from the old school; relentless. He never accepted a "no" which reminded me of the story of the salesman that was working with his key customer. He had taken a hotel suite and had the whole collection laid out on the table. In comes the customer and the salesman starts his pitch. "This is my "#1 shoe," holding it in his hand. The customer looks at it, picks it up and gives a non-committal response. "Here is my second #1 shoe!"

Dick was about 5'8", just about 42, fairly muscular with a dark complexion. As far as putting himself together, he just didn't know how to buy the right suit. It was always too slick, too "wise guy", and the wrong body shape. I was brought into the mix to do store opening ads and he and I immediately connected. He respected my ability and recognized my talent as a designer and all-over shoe person.

First, he was instrumental in getting me into a positive financial situation. He landed me the Belle Mode shoe catalogue account, not only doing the illustrations, but the layout and the printing; the total job. This was a major coup. I was the new ad agency for them.

Second, he gave me a part-time job working in his stores according to my schedule so I could go to pattern school or sell designs. My salary was paid under the table, so I could collect unemployment.

Third, he co-signed on a Nash Rambler, my first car.

Fourth, eventually the Belle Mode's catalogue success generated a series of other major catalogues and I was on the map and a player.

Fifth, he brought me to the local shows and gave me the opportunity to detail his buy for the season and actually pick the styles.

Dick introduced me to Mike Davis who ran the company for his father-in-law. Mike was a different kind of shoe man; a Harvard graduate, soft-spoken, good-looking, with a pipe in place most of the time. He was tall, grey-haired, and had features that I would have liked to draw; a very sophisticated guy. I would classify him as a man of substance and character, not the typical shoe man, to say the least. Mike recognized my talent, not only as a catalogue provider, but my ability to put his ideas and thoughts on paper. I would go over to his house most Sunday mornings and he would describe the idea he had in mind or tell me about a sample he saw. I would sketch it out and he would take them to his sources to be made. I would be able to bill him $50 on most visits. Besides earning the much needed funds, it allowed me to learn how to create in a totally different manner. I never knew I had this talent and it served me well in a different time and setting.

This whole chapter with Dick and Mike not only gave me financial viability, it gave me a number of skills I didn't even realize I had. When the opportunity came up, I jumped even if I hadn't done it before.

I once worked my freelance designs with a factory and they liked what I was showing, a sale of 3-6 sketches seemed possible. The owner said that he liked what he saw but really needed some new looking sandals, which I had never done. I told him that I had a collection but left it behind. I immediately went home and stayed up all night to create 20-30 designs to show him the next day.

I am forever grateful to Dick Herman for giving me the opportunity to develop my skills through his generosity and faith in my ability. Many years later, I was able to somehow make the tables turn in his hour of need.

I found another advertising account. Bob Lubovsky had a small jobbing business and worked out of the shoe district. He was the "salt of the earth" type of guy; very conservative. His wife had relatives that owned a major shoe factory in New Hampshire and he was able to get dye-able footwear from them which he resold to the small retailers. He also bought fashion product from some of the importers for resale. Bob and I spoke the same fashion language. He came across as if he was void of fashion know-how but it was exactly the opposite. He had a marvelous eye for what would sell. He didn't look or dress the part, but he knew. I did his first catalogue and it was successful. When I was later involved with Shapiro Bros., Bob and I did very significant business together. It turned into a great relationship. We were friendly until his early passing, which was unfortunate.

So, Dick enabled me to live and develop before working for Saul. He allowed me to start an advertising business that payed the bills and allowed me to take the big step to American Girl, which was a salary of $150.00 plus a car. I was on my way, at least I thought so. The world was opening its door to a kid who wasn't a relative and there was a possible future in sight.

I had to make a major decision at this time. Was I going to be in the advertising business, mainly footwear advertising, or was I to chase my dream as a shoe designer/stylist. That was the call. By taking the position at American Girl, I had to cut back on the advertising work. There weren't that many hours in the day to do the job. The die was not fully cast but I had, more or less, made the decision to go for the design profession. I felt there was more opportunity in the design field and my proficiency was far greater as a designer than an ad man/shoe illustrator.

The whole atmosphere of working in fashion, whether I realized it or not, was intoxicating. I had seen the lifestyle of product people and it had satisfaction, fulfillment, and success. It was now part of my DNA. Advertising did not bring that feeling.

There was a level of confidence building in me for I had limited success stories with the situations that confronted me. It was a calculated risk, letting go of some of the advertising work, but I felt it had to be done. I had turned a page and, although I felt I could go back if needed, it really was not an option. I was ready for the next step. My horizons were, in my estimation, in reach. My financial situation was stable and I felt I had the wind at my back.

Not What It Seemed

CHAPTER II

"Expectations should not always be taken as reality because you never know when you will be disappointed."
Samuel P. Huntington

Consolidated National was the parent company, which was comprised of a branded business under the American Girl label with manufacturing plants in Maine and New Hampshire, a children's division located in Lawrence, and a private label factory in Ware, Massachusetts. They were a formidable organization. The corporate offices were located in East Boston as well as the headquarters for American Girl. It was good not having to drive from Dorchester to Haverhill.

American Girl had a priority position as one of the leading brands at an opening price point. The shoes were well placed throughout the country and had a decent following. The brand was well advertised and the potential, if handled properly, was limitless. I took the job because it was a significant pay raise, it came with benefits, and it offered me an opportunity to show my talents. It allowed me to "escape" Shain and prove myself. At least I thought so. I was hired to work as the designer for the line. Actually, I was hired to be an experienced sample expeditor with some possible design involvement. It didn't take long for me to figure it out, but I was here and had to stick it out. I could not be labeled a "job-jumper".

Ollie Sullivan was in actuality the President of the brand. His title was Senior Executive Vice President. One of the partners' sons held the title of President. Ollie was a phenomenon; an Irish despot in a Jewish company with complete, absolute control. His word was law and he didn't want to hear any other comments. The partners in Consolidated would not utter a word or opinion opposed to any of his methods or ideas. He was the Irish King in a Jewish Court!

I couldn't figure out how Ollie became that powerful and I finally came up with some ideas.

1 The families were manufacturing people and had little experience in marketing a branded product. They bought the name and turned it over to Ollie and his crew to sell. He knew what to do and they did not want to rock the boat.

2. They were afraid to challenge a winner and they just didn't know how to do it themselves

Ollie surrounded himself with weak people. If you wanted to work at American Girl, you better learn to say "yes". His lieutenants were Al Aronson and Harry Marchand and they fell into line one hundred percent. Actually, out of the office, Ollie was a super guy; great sense of humor. He was a different person even over the business dinner table. That was not the case with his lieutenants. They played the political game to the hilt.

I worked for Al Aronson in name only, because anyone in management took most or all of their orders directly from Ollie. "Al", which I called him once and was reprimanded for not using "Mr.", was supposedly Head of Product Development. Aronson had talent, but in plain English, no guts and no courage of his conviction. He would hem and haw and find a way to conveniently come around to Ollie's point of view. He could not make decisions unless he knew what Ollie's position was on the subject. In a sense, it was tragic because he knew his business and what strategies were needed to develop the brand from a product point of view. Years later I ran into him at a shoe show. "Hi Al," I said as I slapped him on the back.

Harry M. was more or less a sales manager and sold major customers. I really had very little contact with him. He was totally Ollie's boy in every manner, shape and form, always smiling, always political, always waiting for Ollie's commands.

So, how did the development work? Ollie would go to New York and visit with his favorite salesmen and buyer at Saks. At the time, Saks was the leading fashion retailer by far. They had great brands, and developed their own brand and the Fenton last, which stood for fit and comfort.

Ollie would buy at least 10—20 pairs. To him, these represented the core of the line. He listened to the opinion and choices of their people and bought into their opinions and sales figures about how well the styles were selling. The buyer was almost legend. If you were a better shoe manufacturer, you paid homage to him in some way. I must say, as I learned later in my career, that he was an excellent buyer with fashion skills that developed the business. Ollie would not shop any other store. As far as he was concerned, he "had seen it all", had visited Mecca and came away with the best of the best. In a way it was hard to believe since today we shop the world, study the internet, and spend considerable time making the decisions in the line building phases. He did it all in one trip to the city.

Ollie would have a meeting with Al, Harry, and me, laying out the original shoes and going over each and singing their praises and how they should be part of the line. No one said anything. Sometimes Aronson would make a futile and very political attempt to put his two cents in. In a way, it was pathetic. Sometimes one of the Shapiro partners in the corporation would sit in, never saying one word that was contradictory to Ollie's position.

At this meeting Ollie would lay out the program wanting all the styles copied virtually stitch for stitch. We were supposed to take the original shoes purchased that retailed at that time for over $100.00 to $150.00 and duplicate them for American Girl so that they would retail for $9.99 to $12.99. Needless to say, the ability to re-create the exact lines was a challenge in itself. What made it doubly difficult was the material issue, using very inexpensive leathers or synthetic patents which were poor quality with inexpensive components, coupled unfortunately with poor technical development at the factory level. This is the way it was done. The initial development was to be completed as outlined. There were a few styles carried over from last season that needed to be updated. That was my chance to contribute.

I got my marching orders directly from Ollie. It was my responsibility to deliver prototypes and eventually samples that were replicas of the original product. My general schedule was to accomplish this program by going to the factories twice a week. The factories were located in Sanford and Springvale, Maine; the first exit off the Maine Turnpike. I would go up on a Monday morning, stay in the company house, and return to Boston Tuesday night. Wednesday I was in the office and then the same schedule for Thursday and Friday. The towns were typical Maine communities, almost totally dependent on the factories we ran.

The main manufacturing facilities were under the control of Hymie Snyder. He had a superintendent running Sanford, but he "called the shots". He was in total control and a partner in the corporation. How much he owned, I don't know. He was a disgruntled old man who always seemed to sing a negative song with the glass always being half empty. He would complain whenever you brought a new model to make. You had to walk on eggshells every time there was new development. God forbid you by-passed him and went directly to the pattern department. You were playing with fire and the wrath of God. Most times his bark was worse than his bite, but it was his constant negativity that made the whole process tough to handle. Nothing was ever right. The factory was doing you a "favor" to make the prototypes. Hymie would be in the Boston office every Wednesday and did not say one word about the samples to Ollie. It really was something to see.

Part of the problem was he never could handle the passing of his daughter who died of pancreatic cancer leaving one child.

It was tragic. His son-in-law, Lloyd Davis, ran the Springvale plant. He was in his early 40's and knew his business. Lloyd had this "hungry and tragic look" to him. It was quite unusual. You could see the expression etched on his face. I really couldn't explain his demeanor for he seemed to be in constant pain. There was the impression that he had x-ray eyes that penetrated your thoughts. It was a weird feeling. Lloyd was always at odds with Hymie, for he wanted new machinery, new methods, and wanted to expand the production; all points that were not in Hymie's wheelhouse. They just did not get along. Lloyd was not the easiest guy to live with and they just rubbed each other the wrong way. I got along with him extremely well...in fact we were friendly outside of the business. My wife and his girlfriend got along famously and we saw each other socially on a regular basis. Lloyd made my life palatable at the factory level and went along with my ideas for development.

Getting back to Hymie...he had a sidekick by the name of Joe Davis. Joe was to Hymie as Aronson was to Ollie Sullivan. A complete "yes" man who picked up all the pieces Hymie left behind. He wrote the specification sheets for production and he made it a major undertaking as if life and death hinged on his actions. He would triple check every detail which avoided mistakes but just took it way beyond reality. What made it so frustrating was our detail sheets just had to be transposed... they were the factory details from the final OK'd prototype for production.

Joe was in his middle 60's, well-groomed, knew how to dress, and probably had an executive position in the shoe industry at one time. Something happened and he ended up with Hymie...not an easy way to live.

They were all in the Boston office every Wednesday and really didn't have any particular function there. I shouldn't say any reason...Hymie had a meeting with his partners, the Shapiro's. Lloyd always stayed at the factory and only came home weekends.

I had my work cut out for me, trying to bring Ollie prototypes that would "replicate" the Saks original. What made this project extremely difficult was the pattern department. They were just not capable, well-schooled or talented to make patterns. It was always 7-8 trials before they were even in the ballpark. The head pattern maker did not have the style sense, the feel for fashion or the technical skill. As most American pattern makers, they were not schooled but picked up pieces here and there. So it became a hit or miss situation. What I did not realize at this time was the method they were using and the one taught to me actually was antiquated. I learned later in my career how it should be done.

Ollie did not want to hear any stories. He wanted those prototypes, as I said stitch for stitch, and with the same exact look as the original. It was not only a question of pattern making and material. The factory did not want to put in new lasts and would want to make these styles on lasts that were currently in production. It was a war to get Hymie to buy a new last that replicated the original Sak's style. Nothing went smoothly. You had three camps, Ollie, the factory and me. The process of getting the job done was difficult enough, trying to please Ollie. But the combination of the factory not willing to go along with the development made the work extremely difficult. Creativity was supposed to be enjoyable and turned out to be the direct opposite.

There was little chance of using my creative ability. I was a glorified sample chaser and messenger. The opportunity occasionally came when I was able to put on the table prototype samples that I designed and made up at the factory controlled by Lloyd. If I did not have a sample to hold in their hand, it was meaningless. The problem was that you were dealing with Ollie and, in some cases, Aronson. If they did not have an original shoe to hold in their hand...my sketches were meaningless. They had zero sense of what they wanted unless it was a finished shoe which they could identify with. So, I could push some new models into the pattern room that were my designs. Most of the time those styles were rejected by them because they had not seen similar ideas at retail. I had come from where fashion product was a necessity. I was now at American Girl and what we made was totally in contrast to what I was taught or believed in. It was not my world.

They sent me to the shows...first to New York which was a national show. We had the ballroom at the Sheraton 34th Street Hotel, which was the heart of the shoe district at that time. The big hitters, U. S. Shoe and Brown Shoe Corporation had permanent showrooms around the corner at 32nd Street. The best volume retailers in the city were all located in this area. All the wholesalers had offices in the Marbridge Building at the corner of 34th. Wednesday was market day...and all the retailers would come and see what was available from the vendors stock. Within a three—four block area you could see some of the best collections in the country in New York.

It was my first branded show and it was exciting to meet the key customers and hear their comments on the line. It was always Ollie who worked with these customers. It was always him giving direction on what styles were to be in stock. There were salesmen and the sales manager but it was always Ollie who ran the show.

I have to say, it was a learning experience in a number of ways. One of the salesmen took me to lunch and ordered me a vodka martini and then a second. I never had a martini before and, needless to say, after the second I was three sheets to the wind, absolutely done for most of the afternoon.

I had made points with Ollie because low heel footwear was now becoming important and I had the experience level at Shain. The 2-3 styles that I managed to get into the line were well received. It was my first real "win" at American Girl. I thought I had made a breakthrough and I was now a design person they would listen to. It really never fully happened. Ollie had his system that was tried and true and he was not about to change.

Aronson was a non-factor but continued to be a pain in the ass to anything I would like to do. He could not make a decision and his game was always to punt the ball to Ollie.

I went to the Syracuse Boot Show and it was an interesting experience. The Fair was an important event for it opened the selling season for cold weather boots and heavier footwear. The results of this Fair had a direct influence on what merchandise we would stock for the season. Our #1 salesman had the New York state territory as well as parts of New England. He was a powerhouse kind of a guy and knew his business.

I remember arriving early evening and went to the hotel where I was staying and where the show was located, just dropping my bag in the room. Then I went straight to the ballroom where we were showing to see Dan. The show was over for the day. He was sitting at a long table covered with sheets and the whole line displayed. He was writing orders from the day's customers, trying to catch his breath and sighing. I could not figure it out until I realized there was someone under the table giving Dan a considerable amount of pleasure and it seemed to becoming in waves. The crazy part was that Dan, true to his endeavor, never stopped writing orders. He was unquestionably focused on the job and the situation. It reminded me of someone getting a blow job while driving, unable to take his eyes off the road or pull over. Both parties were committed to staying focused. This was really the first time I was exposed to sex in a business situation of any kind. Naturally I was amazed and then a little bewildered when Dan offered me to partake.

Consolidated was nepotism in its highest form. There were a number of partners...the two Shapiro brothers, who were the original partners who had sons in the business...a total of three. There were the Isenberg's...totaling two, Abe and Milton...and Hymie Snyder. As far as I was concerned, two of the three were fish out of water and contributed very little to their divisions...in some instances creating a negative effect.

There was Bernie...the oldest who should have been an

academic and was actually President in name only of American Girl. I really did not know what his duties were. He lived under the huge shadow of Ollie...as everyone else. Bernie was a tall, good-looking pipe smoking, Ivy League type. I believe he went to Harvard and was well spoken. He was the only one who actually had the courage to counter Ollie on any matter. The problem was when it came to playing in Ollie's ballpark; he could not get to first base. What was so unusual was that Bernie thought everything was open for debate and that he had an opportunity to sway Ollie. He just did not understand. It was Ollie's way or the highway.

Ware Shoe was strictly a private label factory, making for the low-end chains at the time...Burt's, which was part of Edison Brothers, Montgomery Ward, Sears, etc. Bobby Shapiro ran the manufacturing and was extremely capable. The sales were run separately by a very experienced salesperson who knew how to handle the buyers. I had the occasion of going to the Ware factory for we were going to make a construction there. Bob Wodin, the vice president who sold the production of the plant and really called the shots, seemed to be interested in me. We had lunch and he asked what I would be interested in doing if I came to work with him. I told him I would like his position. He chuckled and that was the end of that conversation.

The youngest Shapiro ran the branded and private label children's division. He was an enigma...a fish out of water trying to be a marketing guru but did not have the tools to get the job done. Looking back at the situation, he just couldn't make a decision and his sales manager played the political game to the hilt...totally second-guessing and always creating doubt on any of his ideas. I knew him fairly well because he was in the office on Wednesday and would ask me to draw up some ideas.

There was Milton Isenberg who ran the Portsmouth, NH Continental factory which made most of its casual product for American Girl. Milton was extremely bright and industrious and, as did Lloyd Davis, wanted to expand American Girl product lines and price points. But he could not buck Ollie. He was not a marketing person...but understood the need for American Girl to move forward and not stay as an opening price point line.

Milton and I got along famously. He made my ideas into prototypes. He lobbied for more stylish lines and a totally different approach for the entire company. I actually spent considerable time in Portsmouth on the way up to Maine twice a week. Some of Ollie's originals had to be developed at Continental. That's where Milton and I were on the same page and realized this was not the way to develop American Girl. He believed his factory was held back by the mentality of the "A" Street office. Although Aronson in reality had no power, he was a hindrance to getting the product development side more current and Milton used to take it out on Aronson.

Consolidated, as a total group, had the opportunity to be a major force in the industry. It had a brand that had national recognition and the power to make it almost invincible to competition. They had the manufacturing base and total control of costs. They were diversified. What they did not have was vision. It had great opportunities to buy and develop brands that arrived on the market. Management didn't recognize either the opportunity or the need to expand their horizons.

Ollie's decision to keep American Girl in the basement signaled its fall. It took two to three years after I moved on to make the brand a non-entity. In order to maintain a basement line, you had to keep the price points, which naturally was harder and harder to do as the world started to change. Profit margins became thinner and thinner. Probably the most important factor was that other brands moved up to the first floor and brought style and a fresh look to the product lines. Basement business was trending down and American Girl was trapped in this cycle.

As I said, there were voices within the company that knew change was needed but none strong enough to rock Ollie's boat and make him change his course. The sons of the partners were without power when it came to influencing the course of the business, partly through their ineptness and their complacency, as the profits were still significant. But the die was cast and it was only a question of time until the holes in the "armor" appeared too late to repair.

I didn't know all this as a 25 year old kid struggling to make a name for myself. What I did know was that Consolidated and American Girl were not the place for me. I could see how Ollie manipulated the owners and his key staff. Actually he created a "fear-factor" and he intimidated me in trying to achieve his goals. He made me pretty miserable and, in a sense, made me feel inadequate trying to make "diamonds out of glass". He really was a bully at times...but it was his show and he wanted to control every aspect of the business. It was his style and as a sensitive artistic kid, I was extremely unhappy...to the point I spent less time in the office and more time in the factories. It was not a happy time and I "wanted out" in the worst way. It was Ollie's style and as I look back, I believe it evolved because he actually had no one to "talk to". The partners didn't know how to run a brand and Aronson and Marchand were just "hangers on" and were not prepared to go that extra mile or stand up and be counted. So Ollie took total command but he just didn't have the vision. Maybe I'm wrong but that's the way I saw it as I look back.

Consolidated had the opportunity to become a real competitor to Brown and U. S. Shoe. There was a major opening which never materialized because of many of the factors that I mentioned. They had the opportunity to buy additional brands at bargain prices with talented staff which would have changed the culture and vision of the entire company. I believe their manufacturing mentality caused them to pass.

Companies lose their position or fall off the grid in this fashion business because they lack vision, the courage of their convictions, talent, and financial status...to name a few. If you really analyze Consolidated, they lacked all three.

Vision...they could not see the need to take American Girl to the next level. It's the old story: if you stand still, you go backwards. The basement philosophy was a yesterday concept and they got just too comfortable. In the fashion business, comfort equates to disaster. It is a trap we all fall in. Success does not necessarily breed success. It needs great skill, knowledge of the market and the feel to read the situation and have the courage to pull the plug and move on. There was the need to rethink the basic concepts of the company. They needed to be a marketing entity, not a manufacturing group.

Courage of Conviction...This is a very difficult concept to interpret. I know of executives that knew exactly what to do to either reconstruct or build their business...but did not move forward. They couldn't pull the switch one day or another. Credit it to personality or their psyche; they were totally indecisive when it came time to make key decisions. I experienced it at Consolidated and later at U. S. Shoe. I never had that problem...my issues were at times being too big a "risk taker". I learned it from Ralph and later on with great shoe men I worked with and for. My philosophy was centered on the following: "If I'm going to hang, I want to put the rope around my own neck." If anything, I had too much courage of my convictions...sometimes during my career it worked both ways...to the heights and to the depths.

Talent...It doesn't work without talent...plain and simple. You can't replace it with B.S. You can't replace it with poor product whether it is in design or manufacturing or both. It wasn't exclusive to the product but to those who will set the course. It is tied to the concept of vision whether it's design or sales or overall strategy.

Product...It doesn't happen unless the product is right. There are two elements that are essential: quality and fit. All the marketing and advertising and P.R. are meaningless if these points are lost. The ability to engineer and manufacture a consistent level is the key. It is generally the reason in any industry why companies get into trouble. Somehow or another they take their eye off the ball. They presume or cut corners in the process. It just doesn't work. These are hard lessons to learn.

I can attest to falling victim during my career. Our ventures in Asia put us to the true test. We finally figured out how to proceed; we were then successful. This only happened when we built the finest product team and paid our dues.

Financial...Without finances, it becomes almost a certainty of failure. This was not the case with Consolidated. They had a great balance sheet and unlimited credit. They just did not use their assets to their fullest extent.

We wonder why our domestic industry disappeared and we try to piece together the causes for its demise. It started here in product development. Our people were never trained properly and many were "fish out of water" when it came to sheer aptitude or ability. The whole mentality in the industry was archaic. We were trying to make footwear with equipment that should have been discarded years before. We were competing with others who were light years ahead with manufacturing methods and equipment. Our plants were inefficient, trying to make production lines work that were set up on multiple mill floors transported by wooden racks instead of conveyors. The component industries supporting the factories were light years behind in many instances.

Our whole approach was defensive. We were never on the offense. We were always followers and, as a whole, lacked innovation in many or all areas. When Italy came on board followed by the others, it was the beginning of the end.

So I now had a number of sources that could put out their "feelers" on what was available and where there were possible leads. It was still the same situation. The same rules applied. The industry was engulfed with nepotism and this limited the opportunities

Again...luck was with me. The stars were aligned and the gods in agreement and opportunities appeared that changed my life.

I first met Phil Barach at American Girl. He was representing a fabric company that catered to the shoe industry. As the "designer" for the brand, I used to meet with all the suppliers for new products and accessories for possible sampling, etc. Naturally, everything had to run through Aronson and Ollie.

Phil was a great-looking guy, tall, 6'2", porcelain white skin, even then greying hair. What set him apart were his personality and his uncanny ability to completely focus on what you were saying. He looked like a Wasp but was Jewish as could be in his Ivy-League suit and tie. He knew his product and presented it in an interesting way. We went to lunch and during the conversation I learned he was a Harvard MBA. I almost choked on my sandwich and asked him why he was "schlepping" a fabric sample case? He told me he was being groomed to run the company.

We liked each other from the start and when he saw my sketches and design work, he thought I was very talented. Phil had that quality of bubbling over with excitement when he saw creativity and the ability to build product. The glass was always half full for him. He was the most positive person I ever met. He had that quality that drew you to him. You wanted to be in his company, you wanted to be his friend...hoping he would be yours.

There was a natural bond from our initial meeting. Phil was six years older than me, had been in the service and was married to a girl from Newton whose family had hoped she would have done better. Little did they know what success lurked around the corner.

We both came from similar backgrounds...poor to low income families, losing our fathers early, learning the need to fend for ourselves. I believe we both learned to compete whether it was as athletes in school or getting that job after school. We were cut from the same cloth with similar values and dreams.

I saw him a number of times during my tenure at American Girl. We never got together outside of business but we were extremely pleased to see and work with one another.

When I left, we more or less went our separate ways. A few years later, I learned he had gone to U. S. Shoe Corporation and was running the Jumping Jacks children's division. I was pleased for him and knew this guy was going places.

Norbert Gallagher owned Gallagher Pattern Company and knew and worked for most of the major factories in the New England area. The function of the pattern shop was to "grade" the sizes for each pattern for production. You needed a high level of expertise for grading patterns was an art. The patterns were used to make metal cutting dies which were costly. If the patterns were graded properly, you could eliminate a fair amount of cutting dies. All the factories used pattern shops to have what they called "blue board" patterns bound in metal for dies and actually to hand cut from these blue boards.

If you were making better priced footwear, there were times you did not have sufficient pairs to amortize the cost of dies. So, you hand cut the sizes from the blue board patterns. This could not be done in lower priced volume factories as leather costs or experienced cutters were not financially feasible.

Norbert was the kind of guy everyone liked and wanted to give him their pattern business. He was a wonderful conversationalist and always with the stories and aimed to please. He was always there for the "little" people like me for he knew they someday could write an order. A down-to-earth Irishman! He told me about a possible opening at Shapiro Bros. Shoe Co. in Auburn, Maine, a volume producer for the better chains and specialty stores. He thought the position was perfect for me for there was opportunity and the Shapiro's (not related to Consolidated) were the salt of the earth.

Originally I balked at the idea for Maine. To me, it was the end of the world. I did not want my kids going to inferior schools or being raised in the "boondocks". Norbert was insistent, "Go talk to George. He's a great guy and I believe what he's after is someone like you who can create, design and possibly help him with the accounts."

A Place in the Sun

Chapter III

"A wise man will make more opportunities than he finds."

Francis Bacon – "The Essays"

George Shapiro and his three brothers, Arthur, Lou and Saul, had the plant in a massive brick building on six floors. The factory and offices comprised four levels. There was a leather cutting business on the second floor. George's brother-in-law ran a retail shoe operation at street level. Sam was a pretty lucky guy. He had an in-stock department for he had the run of the factory and he took full advantage of it. If it wasn't for George's sister, he would not have been there. It was the classic mill building, more than likely used as some sort of knitting mill or machine shops before its conversion to a shoe factory.

The Shapiro's were originally from Haverhill in the 40—50s. The father established the factory there and its functions until he died early in life. George took over the business as the oldest and eventually moved it to Maine. There was pressure on pricing in their grade and labor costs were rising for low cost producers.

There were the twin cities, Auburn and Lewiston, and they were called "L.A.". Lewiston was the larger town and more industrialized. There were shoe component plants as well as both genders of shoe factories. The major women's plants were in Auburn...Lown Shoe Co. which made a fashion women's brand "Troylings", Clark Shoe Company (no relation to Clarks of England) and Belgrade Shoe Company which made "Moxees", a casual brand. Actually, none were in direct competition with one another for they made different grades and categories. All the factories were situated in one area of the town. There was a rather secluded residential area where George and his brothers and son-in-law, Steve Passerman, lived.

George was about 5'6" and 225 pounds, greyish curly hair that was very distinguished. He had a regal look about him, immaculately groomed...always with shirt and Countess Mara ties. He loved good clothes and wore them well for a man his size. His style and demeanor was very deliberate and he moved slowly with a certain level of confidence. He was more than the CEO. George was the head of the family and the brothers would never ever consider challenging his decisions. There wasn't a question that he was the heart and soul of the business. The brothers were "inside people". They had zero contact with the marketing, sales or strategy of how the business functioned in these areas.

George's word was law and in his soft-spoken style, he conveyed his message. The factory was his life along with his lovely wife, Eve, and family. His daughter, Harriet, was married to Steve Passerman, who worked with Lou Shapiro as a time-study person in the stitching room as well as in quality control. Steve came from a wealthy New York family who had made their fortunes in the parking garage business. I could never figure out why he wanted to work in a shoe factory. I think he liked Maine.

George had a son with special needs who was institutionalized. Robert came home for short periods for the holidays. I became the son he never had.

When I made the trip for the interview on a Saturday morning, it was the start of an almost magical experience. I knew I had the talent to succeed. The problem was getting the opportunity to perform. My training came at a price, even though I still had a long way to go...the drive, the creative energy was there...and now, hopefully, the opportunity.

When you turned off the Maine Turnpike at the Auburn exit, you passed the Holiday Inn and turned left. You started down the secondary road for about a mile...the dense forest on either side. Staring you in the face as you got closer was the Shapiro factory. Whenever I drove there, I would always contemplate the day's events when the brick façade started to appear and grow.

Here I was in Auburn...a 3½ hour ride from Mattapan. I had left really early, not knowing the way and nervous as hell. I didn't have a resume to hand out. I had my sketches. I imagined Norbert had given George a full rundown. I had no idea what to expect. Did I really have a chance for the position? What did it entail? Did it require me to move to Maine? What was the salary? What was the opportunity? All these thoughts were in my noggin as I drove the 200-plus miles.

I finally arrived and took the freight elevator to the sixth floor. The operator gave me "the once over" as I was wearing my blue blazer, bought in Filene's basement, grey flannels, white shirt with rep tie. My "spit shined" shoes were picking up the dust from the factory floor. The plant was not working on Saturday except for a small office staff. Morris Schiffer, the office manager, gave me the "look-over" as he brought me to George's office which was surprisingly small but with lots of light. There were piles of papers and shoes on the tables surrounding his beat-up desk, the windows needed washing and I was nervous as hell.

I don't know if you can call it an interview. George did all the talking. He took me through the whole history of Shapiro Bros. and their move to Maine. It was extremely detailed and then he moved on to tell me about his brothers and their functions in the operation. He then gave me a detailed rundown of the business, how it functioned, the account structure and the types of product they were producing. He explained the entire setup. There were two plants, one that handled the volume accounts and the second that was higher-priced. He had this way about him...very deliberate and when he told you a story, it was the whole story with all the detail, every word, all the dialogue.

I had arrived at 9:15 am and it was now twelve o'clock and I had not said three sentences. He was a story-teller and you could see that he was in his element telling me all. We went to lunch across the street in the local diner and he continued to give me more information. I was getting nervous...because he had not asked me a single question and it started to make me crazy. It was not a hot day but I was sweating. Eventually we got around to me and I seized the opportunity to say my piece. I had brought a portfolio of designs and he leafed through them, stopping for a moment here and there to study some of the sketches. He took me out to the factory although it was not working and walked me through the plant. Again, he did all the talking on how it functioned.

George had, more or less, made up his mind about me when I walked into his office. As I said, Norbert and some other sources had given him a good idea of what I had accomplished. But, looking back at the whole interview, George saw a nice Jewish boy who was supposedly talented and willing to get the job done and hired me. I almost fell over when he told me it was not necessary to live in Maine and that I could do the shoe man's commute...back and forth on Tuesday, returning on Friday. I would be assisting him in sales which meant selling the production of Shapiro to basically two to three customers located in St. Louis. That was one of the major reasons for being based in the Boston area. My expenses would be paid and I could have the car of my choice. The salary was $250.00 per week with a possible bonus based on performance. That was $100.00 more than I was making! He asked me to think it over and get back to him on Monday.

It was about 4:30 when I left. George walked me to my car and insisted on paying for my tolls and gas. The interview was roughly seven hours of which George spoke six and a half; I am not exaggerating. If you knew George, you would understand how he told it all. I was, in a sense, dumbfounded. He had introduced me to his brothers who just said hello and then disappeared. I stopped on the road to call Judy to give her an idea of what went on and an estimated time of arrival. She didn't believe my rendition of what transpired. What had happened was beyond my belief and my wildest hopes and dreams. Was it real...was this another American Girl deal where I was told that I would have a real design position and became a runner? I could not pass it up. I was extremely unhappy where I was and going nowhere. American Girl, in my estimation, was being run by management who lacked vision and was not gearing up for a new way to compete.

I called Norbert on Sunday and wanted his opinion. I was just looking for confirmation. Judy could not believe what had been offered. The $100.00 increase in salary meant we could leave the changing neighborhood of Mattapan and move to Needham for a better life and educational system for our kids. It was a no-brainer.

My life changed dramatically. We moved to Needham into a brand new townhouse that to all of us was heaven. Judy was ecstatic. We had arrived at Mecca. There wasn't any question we were on our way. There were drawbacks. I now spent 3—4 days in Maine away from the family.

When we moved to Needham the whole world was brighter. I was making an excellent salary at Shapiro Bros. and we were in an all-new condo unit with great facilities. My next-door neighbor was Bob Efferson, a great guy and sportsman like myself. Bob loved to gamble on the football games, specifically the pro games on Sunday. We would go over the line every Sunday morning...I was sort of hooked. It wasn't "serious" money but it was not "chump" change...a few hundred dollars. Bob's wife, Barbara didn't want Bob gambling at all so Bob would sneak across the way to our house and place the bets. Well, what cured me was the following. We loaded up on the Giants vs the Bears and played the points. The game was close and we were starting to count our money when the ball was tipped by a receiver and into the hands of a defensive back and, sure enough, he ran for a touchdown, putting us in jeopardy. The Giants came back and could have given us the win but the field goal hit the crossbar and we lost. Bob and I figured we would give it one more shot and bet the Bruins game at night. We lost when the puck bounced off the goalie's mask into the net. That was it and I never bet another nickel on a pro game since that day forty-plus years ago. Bob went on gambling. I enjoy the games much more.

The job was interesting from the start. George took me to St. Louis almost the second week on the job. We traveled first class. He wanted to introduce me to the major customers and we went on what I would call a "P.R." trip. We did not have any samples or any development they had given us.

George had a special relationship with these customers. It was built on his integrity, consistency of product and willingness to develop their ideas and programs. We started at Wohl Shoe Company, which was a division of Brown Shoe Company. At that time, Wohl was the "tail that wagged the dog"! As a division of Brown, it was their largest and most profitable entity. Wohl leased the major shoe departments in most of America. They had Macy's, Famous Bar...all the shoe departments owned by Federated, Dillard's, May Company. They had separate groups that controlled the merchandising, advertising and, in some instances, all the personnel besides key management. They also developed a number of brands that not only supported their leased departments but they marketed it to all retailers as "wholesale business". Wohl was close to being "kings" of the retail industry and were noted for their top personnel. It was a totally different culture than Brown...much more aggressive and definitely more talented.

Every major brand came through their doors wanting to sell their departments. The Wohl team saw every new idea, theme, material as the top brands flocked to St. Louis for business. It was a tremendous advantage to have all that information at their disposal. They divided the company into two divisions.

Retail was run by Jack Schultz with key merchandisers. One of them was Wayne Weaver who later became part of Nine West and later owner of the Jacksonville Jaguars...a Horatio Alger story all on its own. Wholesale, which was our key customer, was run by Joe Cramer, who in my estimation was one of the smartest shoe persons in the industry. Joe not only understood marketing and fashion, he had a remarkable grasp of manufacturing and production. He bought into George and developed us into one of his major resources. George loved Joe and they both complemented one another, developing the business. Joe and I maintained our friendship over the years and were constantly in touch. He was a great sounding board and I used his great experience level many times. He played an important role later on in my life.

There were three buyers for the whole business. Dress: Tim Hitsman; Tailored: Ben Alper; Casual: Seymour Feinstein. They were not only buyers but they were line builders, a term the trade used for putting together the styles that would make up the collections, not only for the brands but what Wohl retail would buy for their leased departments.

Wohl was a well-run organization and the key positions were held by some of the most talented people in the industry. They had a totally different culture than the parent company. Brown just did not have the personnel to match Wohl. Brown at that time was controlled by manufacturing people who dictated what type of product they would make. They "watered down" new and interesting design to conform to their methods of production. They would not make certain constructions that demanded excess stitching and complicated constructions. On top of these rules, the design staff did not have the creativity and know-how to devise patterns that could fit into their schemes. The combination of the two gave companies like ours an opening to compete for the business.

It was my job as part of our presentation to bring interesting and unique product to the table that could price extremely well and compete with the basic product from Brown. Our production and profit depended on achieving these goals

Brown's culture was manufacturing and their marketing and sales strategies were dominated by the shoemakers in top management.

George did his business with Wohl in the following manner. He would come to St. Louis and work with the buyers. They would give him original shoes to copy or some sketches to develop and make in various materials. They would give him ornamentation to acquire or copy. Everything was handed to him. It was an easy way to do business. The entire creative process was done for him. All he had to do was make the prototypes, return to St. Louis for their OK and corrections and get the sample details on the specific styles they picked to sample for their branded lines or for their retail outlets. With these details, they would give you "target pricing" for they had total control of what they would give you to develop. In one way, life was easy for George. He had his entire development handed to him. If they wanted Shapiro to make a specific construction or certain groups, George really didn't have any other option. He was totally dependent on what they wanted him to make. It was not necessarily the best "mix" of constructions and patterns for the factory. Wohl was under the obligation to give the basic production to Brown which meant that more difficult constructions always ended up with George. In fact, it was the only way to compete against an in-house resource. Your ingenuity was key and it went from design to the finished product. We made what Brown/Wohl could not produce, mainly in the fashion area. Our ability to move to new constructions and product and adapt to the ever-changing fashion picture was much quicker. It was the reason for our being a key resource. It was the reason for our being.

Ben Alper was our key buyer. His responsibilities were mainly to develop the tailored and semi-dress collections. He put together the Jacqueline and Connie Collections in these areas. Ben was a little guy, about 5'4" on the roly-poly side and shuffled along almost like Charlie Chaplin's walk. He was in his late 50's or early 60's with a pipe as a permanent fixture in his possession. He was a very affable guy who was not a political animal. We seemed to hit it off from the very beginning. Ben was not that creative but was extremely well organized and was open to suggestions. He enabled me to use my ability to develop the programs. Ben loved hot food...very hot food. We went out to lunch together with his assistant and ordered barbeque. We made the mistake of letting Ben put on the sauce. When we took the second bite, we were on fire. We ran across the street to get ice cream cones and Ben finished the rest!

Ben presented us with the perfect situation. We had a buyer that had no aspirations to be a designer. All he wanted from us was to put the right product on the table. Unfortunately many of us have that designer gene and it comes out in many ways. In my experience, most of the time, it's detrimental to the development of the product. Ego is difficult to understand and control. Everyone has an opinion...many after the fact. When it mingles with the designer virus, it can be deadly. What is this virus? We all have some of it in our systems. Many of us feel we have the ability to create and design. It becomes a real issue when the buyer feels he no longer just has to make the decision on what to purchase...but the need to design it. It becomes even more serious when he rejects everything except what he as "designed or styled".

I have had more than my share of these situations and you are at times just stymied by the virus. You want the orders... and you know better...so you bend. In some instances, some of these decisions in which you knew better but went along with came back to bite you...especially in the pocketbook. It's a Catch 22. Every situation is different...many of the results are the same.

Sometimes there are funny incidents which I experienced years later. My right-hand gal in Taiwan came to me giving me notice. "Norman, I'm leaving because I am getting married and my fiancé is a lawyer and we will live in New York." Bernard arrived to see her and would come to the office before she was finished for the day. He frequented the facility and spent time wandering around. One day he came to me with shoe in hand. "Norman, don't you think this style should have a bow on it?" "Bernard...you have now arrived. You are one of us, designer extraordinaire!"

It is not only happening in the fashion business. It happens in industry in general in many ways. It is a reoccurring problem that at times becomes extremely complicated.

There are probably a different set of complications today because the designers, in many instances, are without a shoe background and are void of the boundaries needed to avoid in the process. It can become a major issue and without someone guiding them (if they are willing to listen), it becomes a constant battle. It is hard to escape this syndrome or virus with all these existing conditions. The necessity for a strong, well-experienced design head is vital. I used a different strategy which seemed to work. Human nature became our ally. I spell it out just a few paragraphs forward.

I took to the job immediately and realized what and how to proceed in working with these buyers. The key was changing the system. That meant presenting new, creative product to the buyers that Shapiro developed for their lines. The advantage was building innovative product that not only filled a fashion void but was designed to work in the manufacturing process. In this manner we would have the opportunity to be in control of our destiny and not beholden to the customer. It would enable us to show product that would price well for all concerned. In this way we could influence what we eventually would make and at least have some control over the process. I knew that if we could create a reason for the buyers to depend on us to bring creativity to them, they would be, so to speak, "more in our corner" when it came to which styles and pairs went to Brown or to us.

Naturally this didn't totally happen overnight...but the strategy began working from the very first season I started developing new product. So...when George and I went to St. Louis we had at least two bags of new styles which we felt were great prospects for their lines. I spent considerable time researching their brands and formulating a program.

The line builders were very receptive and slowly and surely they became dependent on our development. I had the ability to sit with the buyers and sketch out what they felt was missing. It paid great dividends. Psychology was on my side as they "automatically" became the "designer" as they told me their thoughts and I translated them into viable ideas. After 2-3 trips George didn't need to go and I was left to make the program. It was an unusual situation for I was a designer with the shoe experience to bring saleable new product to the table. Our business began to grow and at the same time they became more dependent on our ability to bring new product to their collections.

Their buyers were quite interesting. The dress buyer was Tim Hitsman. He was 6'4" and exceptionally well-groomed, dressed to the nines daily. Tim was the type who could be in a room where the temperature was 100 degrees and would look perfect...not a hair out of place nor a wrinkle in his shirt. His style sense was superb but very dress oriented as he was perfectly positioned by Joe Cramer. We started to do significant business together and Tim invited me home for dinner to meet his wife, Dorothy. She was a fashion person. It was the second marriage for both with no kids. She was definitely in command. Tim showed me around the house and opened his closet in the master bedroom. I never saw anything like it. The suits were lined up equal distance from one another as if they were soldiers at attention. His shoes seemed to be all spit-shined and set on the floor perfectly placed. It looked like the Marine Sergeant was about to give a full-blown inspection. Tim was ready.

Seymour Feinstein was the low-heel and casual buyer. He was older in his early 60's and always struck me as a very complex person. Seymour always held his cards very close to his chest. The relationship was very cordial and even somewhat friendly, but there was always a wall that you could not penetrate. He asked me if I was on commission and, naturally, I answered that I was not. He wanted to know the inner workings of Shapiro Bros. and always asked a ton of questions. I was naïve and never got the message.

We were becoming a very key resource and my designs were being accepted by all three buyers. With the trend toward medium height styling in the dress area and casual area, there developed problems.

The buyers' responsibilities were divided by heel height. Tim's dress category started at 15/8, roughly two inches. Seymour's limits were zero to 14/8, slightly less than two inches. War broke out between the two and I was in the middle. I would build new ideas for both and bring the styles for working sessions to St. Louis. Both buyers would want me to take one of the styles I had developed and either raise or drop the heel height so it would fit into their category. It became so nasty that I laid out the prototypes on the table and told the two to come to a meeting of the minds. I walked out of the room.

There was bitter rivalry and I believe both buyers really didn't like one another. I could not be the umpire and eventually I brought Joe Cramer into the picture to settle the situation. We had reached a point where we had a significant voice in what Wohl showed in their branded lineups.

I was ecstatic...the shoes were nationally-advertised and some of my styles ended up in Vogue and Cosmopolitan, etc. I was, in a way, part of their organization. They invited me to their sales meeting in Colorado Springs. They put on fantastic fashion shows, using a whole set of top-ranked fashion models.

The great story I remember most was during the Chicago

Shoe Show where they put on a major fashion show at the Hilton. I was walking down the hall with the model who was wearing an over-the-knee boot as part of the show. She was Asian and a knockout in anybody's vernacular. Wearing these great looking boots with a mini skirt, she was prancing down the hall toward the ballroom. There were showrooms along the way and one of the salesmen gave her the head-to-toe treatment and asked, "Honey, where did you get those boots?" She looked at him with disdain and uttered, "I did not get them fucking!"

We were involved with Edison Bros. as our other major. In fact, at one time Edison took the entire production of the factory. It was not the best situation for George...the pressure was on constantly for price. He was a "captive" factory or, should I say, an exclusive one. The factory was losing money and George went to Joe Cramer and struck a deal.

George had a long relationship with the Edison brothers and more than likely would never have decided to diversify to other sources if Mark Edison had lived. George and Mark were more than a business relationship. They were dear friends. There were four brothers and Mark was the brains, the visionary, and had that ability to solve the issues of the day. Edison was never the same after his death. Simon, who took over, was a shadow of his brother and did not understand the factories and how to deal with them. He was the absent-minded professor. This was all long before me and George, in his own way, gave me the blow-by-blow of how the relationship with Simon was never the same when Mark was no longer around.

At dinner with Simon one time George brought up the question "Should Edison change its pricing ending from 95 to 99? Simon almost had a seizure stating, "Why George, those four cents can buy a pack of gum, etc., etc."

The long and short of it was there was a different mentality running the show. The Mark Edison philosophy was gone and if you could remember the date, it was the slow demise of the company. It was never the same.

Simon was something! One night at the Show, George and he had dinner. Returning to the Plaza, they were looking at Bergdorf's windows when a "lady of the night" approached George. Simon was in another world looking at the windows. George turned and said, "Get the fuck out of here now! Simon wandered over, "My, George, you know everyone!"

Simon made the rounds of the show "selling" his resources and giving them the pep talk. I was there when he came in and gave us the spiel, "You have to hold the line. We cannot raise prices." He then turned and walked in to the john as if it was a Groucho Marx sketch!

Joe Cramer wanted to do business with Shapiro for he knew their quality and versatility was what he needed. What transpired was Shapiro Bros. was able to diversify and sell the two giants with equal production at 4,000 pairs per day. George was able to pull it off...diversifying the production between the two giants and gaining some leverage. What we were able to do going forward was make them slightly dependent on us.

They had two entirely different approaches to the business. Wohl understood the branded business and the need for stable resources. Edison approached it differently. They had three major groups, Chandler for higher-priced better footwear, Bakers...the major division and Burt's as a low-end retailer. They also had leased departments. They did not have a manufacturing mentality in any way. They wanted key factories but, in reality, only on their terms...which meant a one-way street. The only way you could "win" this game was to become a key resource through your creative styling ability. It was the only road to travel. They expected and paid for creativity.

Baker's was the backbone of their business. Their price points were $7.95 to $12.95. Sam Demoff ran Baker's with Harry Archiries as his administrative sidekick and "hatchet man". Sam was probably the smartest shoe buyer/developer that I ever knew. First of all, he was as smooth as silk. He reminded me of Roland Coleman with the pencil-thin mustache. He had all the moves of a great politician and leader but, most of all, that uncanny eye that recognizes what product would perform and at what level. He had the courage of his conviction for if his group of merchandisers that covered each region voted against a strategy he laid out...he would say, "You have eight votes and I have ten."

I was probably biased because Sam loved me. He had a huge pad on an easel that he used for meetings with the merchandisers. I would sketch out his ideas as he spoke. No one that he did business with had that ability. I played to his ego and he just ate it up. The results were amazing. Ninety-eight per cent of the salespeople that serviced Edison were owners of the factories. My competition was 50-60 year old sales executives. I was a 25 year old kid that sold Edison 4,000 pairs per day because of George's ability to produce this product and my artistic and design ability to give them what they needed. Doing business with them was not a walk in the park. They were hard bargains. Sam would lay out the programs and Harry A. would "negotiate" the prices. That was George's department and was always a difficult chore. We did have a slight, but distinct, advantage because we brought them new and interesting product and they were willing to pay us slightly more for our creativity. Eventually, I would spend a week or a month in St. Louis working with both Wohl and Edison. There would be two to three evenings a week that I would entertain the buyers from both organizations. I would stay in Clayton, which was the town where Wohl and Brown had their offices.

George no longer came to St. Louis for he had developed some health issues that kept him not only from traveling but needed time at home to recover. I took on more responsibility as the business was expanding. There was greater demand for Shapiro product through the volume factory and the better factory, LoSarge Footwear.

The factory supervision and programs were run by the brothers. Lou Shapiro was the "real glue" of the operational process. He bought the leather and upper materials, negotiated the prices with the suppliers and made the price list for George and myself. He calculated labor costs and actually did all the scheduling. Lou was a workaholic and lived a different schedule. He worked seven days a week, arriving at the office around noon to one o'clock and worked until midnight. There's a reason for everything and I suspected Lou was not happy at home and the schedule eliminated many issues.

Lou and I worked closely for I would sample materials and give the details to Lou so he could follow through. He knew leather better than anyone I have ever known. He had key suppliers like his pal, Chaffy, who could come to the office after 8 pm with a bottle of cognac and they would "negotiate" the prices. Chaffy was the classic "entrepreneur". He was no more than 5'3" with a cigar stuck in his mouth like a beacon. He had a full head of the whitest hair you ever saw and carried the biggest case filled with swatches of all the leathers. He must have had some kind of throat condition for he would have to clear or cough every twenty seconds. He could not sit still and would continually circle Lou's desk, pleading his case and sipping the cognac. He was the only one I knew that would go to India and Pakistan, buying the material, mainly calf and goatskin in very significant quantities. He would peddle it in the States. Lou would buy black calf whether he needed it or not if the price was right and would "hundle" with Chaffy for hours. Chaffy knew if he was overloaded with materials that Lou, at the right price, would take it off his hands. Since a good portion of what we sold was in black and calf, we had a distinct advantage pricing the goods based on Lou's buys.

Arthur was the factory superintendent and manager. He had help, a so-called assistant who was really the shoemaker and answered to George and Lou. Arthur was a dedicated worker and walked the factory floors during production. He really didn't have any relationship with me and always seemed to be very helpful and willing to rush samples or prototypes that we needed.

Saul bought components, heel, soles, shoe boxes, corrugated and buckles, etc. but Lou gave him the quantities. He was a very likable man who seemed to have a lot of interests out of the building. I never really knew where he was.

George told me a story about Saul's two sons that was a classic. There was a very decent Italian restaurant in Lewiston called "Steckino's" which had a special once a month where there was an antipasto array of appetizers and lots of main dishes. The cost was $10.00 per head. Well, Saul's boys were, I believe, 15 and 16. Each weighed at least 200 pounds and had appetites that ruptured the Richter scale. When the owner of Steckino's saw them coming for the event, he stopped them at the door, gave them each $5.00, and told them to go to the Chinese restaurant around the corner.

There were "interesting" times. George was a practical joker and loved to find his prey. Norbert Gallagher appeared for his usual P.R. trip to the factory. We all went out to lunch across the street and George gave me the high sign and started. "Norbert, are you going down to New York for the show in a couple of weeks?" "Of course" Norbert said, munching on his sandwich. "Well Norbert, I don't know if you realize this but American Airlines and the New Yorker Hotel have a new deal. If you fly American you automatically have a room for the Show. It's a no-brainer." Norbert took the story hook, line and sinker. We all forgot about it and when we went down for the Show we saw Norbert just by chance in line at the New Yorker waiting to check in with his American Airline ticket in his hand. We were hysterical and luckily had booked extra rooms so Norbert was not shut out.

There was always something going on. George loved the ponies (as well as Lou) and there was always something going on back and forth in a shoe box.

I was with George during a New York Show and we went

out to lunch at the same deli which was made famous by Damon Runyon's hangout. George knew Maxi, the owner, quite well and Maxi came over to our table. After the pleasantries, Maxi was in rare form. "George...I was really pissed off at one of my waiters and I beat him up for doing a lousy job...the next day I gave him a raise. Three days later I fired him. The waiter came to me and asked me, 'Maxi, why...a raise and then you fire me!" "It's very simple", he replied, "I wanted you to lose a better job!" in his wonderful New York Jewish brogue.

The second factory, LoSarge Footwear, (Lou, Arthur, and Saul) made better grade product and marketed to a different classification of customer. They had a common cutting room with Shapiro but a totally separate factory style lasting room to packing room. The factory's production was primarily sold by Johnny Flout, who was almost a legend in the industry. He developed his own line and sold a list of customers which were the key independent retailers throughout the country. He probably earned more than any other salesman of his type. There were few people that had similar situations as Johnny. He had found the perfect "niche", interesting, mid-range fashion, a management team and factory base he could trust to support him. He had a cost structure that made him extremely competitive. Johnny lived on the edge, almost every day of his life. Everything he did was to the extreme. He burned the candle at three ends. He sold shoes any way he could. There was no question wine, women and song were his specialty. Johnny was the only guy that I ever saw that could party until three or four in the morning and be at breakfast at 7:30 a.m. as if nothing ever happened. He drank more whiskey, screwed more women and gambled more than any ten people I knew. When Johnny had four to five drinks in him, he became very mean and ended up in a fight...sometimes a very serious one. I once saw him in Chicago at the show. He turned around and punch the living daylights out of a guy who was three sheets to the wind and leaning on him. He warned him once and just beat the hell out of him. We had to pull Johnny off him.

When I met him he was in his mid-60-s and still going strong. I must have been working at Shapiro at least five to six months before he showed up. Johnny had received his samples just before I joined and was out selling and then staying home in Arkansas. He was a hillbilly at heart. When he showed up he took me to dinner that night. The sulkies were running in Lewiston so we went to dinner at the track and Johnny looked over the race card. He reached in his pocket and took out some bills and had me go up to place a bet on #6. I'll never forget the number. It was five one hundred dollar bills and I couldn't believe it. The guy at the counter couldn't believe it either. The tote board at the Lewiston Roadway went crazy. We now had a minus pool. Naturally, he lost.

Johnny liked me and was pleased that I could design and develop new product. He started to lean on my design ability or would bring in an original shoe and ask me to expand on that theme. Johnny had a group of customers that were real characters. They all came to the show to work and play with him. There was Carl Robinson who had stores in Nashville and was one of Johnny's drinking partners and a vocalist in his choir. Carl was bald as a billiard ball and had the most outlandish toupee ever made...ever seen. It seemed to have a life of its own. I couldn't figure it out whether it was supposed to go east/west or north/south. Well, Carl got loaded somewhere and came stumbling into the hotel show room and his toupee was half over his eyes and he tried to fix it and hold onto to his rye and ginger at the same time. Needless to say, it was a performance that happens once in a lifetime. George and I could not stop laughing and, when I think of it today, I still can't believe it. There were wonderful personalities in these years and the stories were memorable.

One of the leading leather companies in the industry was Fleming Joffe. They were, without a question, the fashion leaders in the industry. They produced a variety of articles from wide collections of exotic materials...snakeskins, alligator and wonderful prints.

"The Clipper"
A domestic product that retailed extremely well

Arthur and Teddie Edelman were the driving force and would give full presentations of the line at the leather shows and would come to Boston and work out of their office on Lincoln Street in the shoe district. The key material in the collection was a type of leather they called "Sweet Kid". The leather was extremely versatile for many types of footwear for it was soft, flexible, well-priced and used in large quantities by volume factories. All the New England manufacturers would come to their show room to view the presentations for each season. They were the leaders. The show room was packed and Teddie was going through her routine, showing the entire line. The presentation was long. All of the sudden, Jake Isenstadt, who owned a factory in Norway, Maine stands up and in his Jewish accent yells, "Cut the bullshit, I wanna see the Sweet Kid."

Arthur and Teddie had their moments and more or less vacated their shoe business and concentrated on leather furniture. They did raise a son, Sam Edelman, who has made himself into a major brand in our industry.

George had developed a great account in Hahn's, a Washington DC based retail operation with 50-75 stores throughout the Southeast. It was the only customer at this time that we sourced product for in LoSarge and Shapiro. Johnny did not call on Hahn's and ceded the customer to us. They began by setting up a dye-able pump business with us which we stocked for them. It was not a major deal but they were extremely appreciative they could pull single pair sizes and have them shipped the same day. Their buying staff was easy to work with and extremely professional.

Hahn's was purchased by U. S. Shoe and part of their retail division. It was a fine company and headed by Steve Heller, who had married into the family, and was a pleasure to work with. They had additional stores in the Houston area under Krupp & Tuffly and they were run by a young buyer my age, Roger Lewis. With the design programs I had instituted, we began to do "serious business" with all the buyers. Our prices were extremely competitive and we were able to hit upon some fantastic items. We made a new-looking moccasin on a low heel in a patent material called the "Clipper" that became a 75,000 pair shoe in a multitude of colors and materials. We were on the board big-time and the news was resonating through to U. S. Shoe and their corporate and divisional people.

Roger and I became great friends and maintained that friendship over the years until his death recently. It was a great loss. Roger was the sole Christian in a Jewish company and I swear he would have converted if we asked him. We spoke the same language for the other two buyers were thirty years older than us.

This is where I met Kenny Diamond, who we nicknamed "Mr. Rhinestone". Kenny was truly brilliant in every way. He could do anything. Roger Lewis needed an Amex card for his trip to Europe...Kenny got it for him in a day. He was one of the first salespersons to sell European product. He represented a Belgium fashion company that gained a major presence with better retailers, with great styling and pricing. He could keep you in stitches with story after story. We all stayed at the same hotel when we worked with Hahn and spent many a fun evening with the buyers. Coming to Washington and working with Hahn's was a pleasure in every way. They were reasonable, professional and great personalities. Checking out of the hotel I had three sample cases plus my personal bag. I needed a taxi to the airport. Somehow or another, the porter put my cases in the wrong cab and I was off in another,. "Follow that cab!" Years later, Kenny showed up at the Park Palace Hotel in Florence where we were staying waiting to find our apartment. He was fun there...as before.

There were two major sources for Hahn and we were one of them. Imports were a word that really had not entered our vocabulary. You heard stories about Italian sandals but it was only rumblings. U. S. Shoe Corporation showed more interest in Shapiro and in me.

I was very involved in the pattern development. Our pattern department was fairly sophisticated...light years ahead of the Consolidated American Girl group. Our patterns were done well and we seemed to be able to move at a fairly decent pace.

Then... there was a disaster. Our head pattern person went out hunting when the season opened and got killed. We were in deep shit. We needed someone quick and we had Norbert scouring the industry for the right guy. He came up with a young German pattern maker who had been in the country for a short time working in Pennsylvania. He was unhappy there and wanted a change. We brought Dieter Mueller to the factory and I interviewed him. He was my age, spoke English quite well and seemed to have the right personality for our operation. I needed him to show us what he could do and gave him a sketch and an original shoe to copy. I had been trained as a pattern maker through the Lynn Shoe School and was taught a system that made patterns on a one to two dimensional process. Dieter opened his case, took out a wide roll of masking tape and proceeded to cover the last with the tape. He then started to draw the sketch on the last. My eyes could not believe what I was seeing. The light bulb went on...all the lights! It was the European method... far superior to what we were doing...making more accurate patterns. When the sketch was finished, the tape was cut off the last...made flat and a paper pattern was made from the draft. We advanced light years overnight! I hired him on the spot. He brought a totally new method that changed the way we made patterns and created a system that made the process simpler.

I had a wonderful relationship with Larry Schwartz and his Dad, Sid Schwartz. I was introduced to them by Ralph Shapiro, who had a very close, longstanding relationship with them going back to Shain Shoe Co. When I was at Shapiro Bros., we became major suppliers. Larry and his Dad were just wonderful customers, but more than that, it was wonderful to spend time in California with them. They had a very unique operation called Standard Shoes. They sold tons of merchandise at great price points. They had three great stores and one day I got a call from Larry, all excited, and his voice was filled with trouble. The warehouse had a fire and he was desperate for merchandise. I flew out to the coast the next day to see what he needed. We delivered the merchandise in two weeks for we had the material. Lou Shapiro had the materials in our warehouse and we were able to move quickly.

The Schwartz's were in a class by themselves. It was impossible to buy them dinner. All they would do was give the high sign and there wouldn't be a check on the table. A year or so later Larry called me and asked me if he could tag along on one of my style trips to Europe. It was a five-city trip and he had never been to Europe. Every night he wanted to pick up the check in Florence, Milan, and Dusseldorf. I would say, "Larry, we are saving you. You will have the opportunity." Finally, we got to Paris. We went to La Serre and had a fantastic meal. "Larry, it's now your turn!" The check was $650.00 for three! We continued to do business and I believe we were a resource when he just had the outlet store. I believe it spanned 45 years. Larry died young...a great loss.

While working for George Shapiro I went to Los Angeles to work with our key customers. It was a two to three day event for we had significant business in the area. One of my favorite people was Marty Lieberman who ran the stores for Genesco. He was a brilliant shoe man and a mentor my whole life. We were good friends. I usually went to dinner with him at least once or twice while I was out there. We used to go to lunch at the deli around the corner. The owner knew Marty very well and when he saw a nice Jewish boy he wanted to marry me off to his daughter and set me up in the pickle business. I told him I had a previous commitment! I'll never forget many years later Marty came to the Las Vegas Show in a wheelchair and we embraced and told the old stories of days gone by.

One evening while I was there I was free and looking in the paper saw that the Ahmanson Theatre (1967) was opening, playing "Man of La Mancha" with Richard Kiley. I decided to give it a try for I was just looking for one seat any place. Luck being with me, I ended up in the orchestra sitting between Gregory Peck, Robert Taylor and their wives in formal attire. Somehow someone didn't show and there I was sitting between and around the stars. I loved the show. It just had special meaning to me and when I heard Kiley sing "The Impossible Dream", tears were in my eyes for I felt the words pounding at my heart. I had come so far in such a short time. I went from the brink of disaster to a point where I was on my way to a great career and life with my bride and children. I never forgot that moment. The song has always meant so much to me for at one time I was scorned by family and felt covered with scars and now able to reach that unreachable star and to dream the impossible dream. The song just hit home in every way. We remember certain times in our lives and those memories will never fade. The words will always reach home whenever I hear them. One should never forget where one came from and this song has been a constant reminder. I'm a hopeless romantic anyway.

The Impossible Dream

To dream the impossible dream
To fight the unbeatable foe
To bear with unbearable sorrow
To run where the brave dare not go.

To right the unrightable wrong
To love pure and chaste from afar
To try when your arms are too weary
To reach the unreachable star.

This is my quest to follow that star
No matter how hopeless, no matter how far.

To fight for the right without question or pause
To be willing to march into Hell for a Heavenly cause.

And I know if I'll only be true to this glorious quest
That my heart will lie peaceful and calm
When I'm laid to my rest.

And the world will be better for this
That one man, scorned and covered with scars
Still strove with his last ounce of courage
To reach the unreachable star.

Dieter Mueller, now our established German pattern maker and slightly "Americanized", came to me with a question. "Norman, I do not understand this game of American football. "What do you not understand?" "Well, these players first hit one another and then have a meeting... then it happens again. I do not understand." Everything at some time or another needs an explanation.

A friend out of the past appeared...Phil Barach. I had heard how he had the incredible rise from head of the children's division, Jumping Jacks, to becoming CEO of U. S. Shoe. There were two factions, actually two families that controlled U. S. Shoe...the Sterns and the Stix's and they were literally at war with one another. Joe Stern was the CEO and everyone was unhappy with his performance, including the Board of Directors. They were looking for a new CEO who would be acceptable to all concerned. Enter Phil Barach...a Harvard MBA, young, 34, capable and a candidate all the factions could sign off on. They were under the impression they had a candidate who was acceptable to all and controllable by the factions and the Board. They underestimated their new leader.

I had not seen Phil since our meetings at American Girl as seller and sampler years earlier. There was a lot of water under the bridge for both of us. I had found a home at Shapiro Bros. and Phil had hit the jackpot rising to CEO of a 70 million dollar company. I was happy for him and sent him a note reminding him that he was not that far removed from making sure the pickle barrel was stocked in his father's store.

The course of events dictated changes. Johnny Flout got sick, very sick, and I took over the sales and styling of the LoSarge line. He never returned. I hired a sales person to help me...a buyer that I had met who was working for Streichers, an independent chain out of San Diego. Gary had a flair for product and a great personality. He had a strange relationship at home and loved the freedom of the road. He was a player constantly in motion. His wife once called the office and Maurice made a major faux pas re Gary's whereabouts. Gary came back to me saying, "You can only call me at home on Thanksgiving and Christmas."

Shoe business was good. Johnny's customer list was added to and we expanded the product lines. Our business with Hahn's was sensational. We had now started doing business directly with one of the U. S. Shoe Divisions...Joyce.

Roy Bowen leased the shoe department in Jordan Marsh Miami and throughout Florida as well as the other major departments. Roy was the ultimate shoe man. He had the greatest eye and a very big set of balls. He also had a "lock" on the better shoe business in Florida.

I first met Roy with George at a New York leather show. He wanted to meet with us as soon as possible. He loved the idea of detailing a wide variety of colored patents with matching snakeskin. We had brought down a number of samples but he felt he needed some with a more opened feeling. I took out my sketch pad and sketched him a new looking sling (open back) that used both materials. Roy loved the idea and in five minutes he detailed six combinations and gave us the quantities...the total was over 20,000 pairs. I told Roy that we would rush the samples so that we can have him confirm the pattern and material for he wanted quick delivery. Roy turned to me, "Norman, you OK the pattern, etc. and make the goddam shoes yesterday." It was unheard of...totally amazing.

Roy owned horses...serious ones that he ran at the best tracks in the country as he owned the better shoe business in Florida and he was a major customer of Herbert Levine, which was the premier women's fashion shoe brand of its day. Herb loved the horses and when Roy was in New York for the shoe show, it coincided with the racing season. Roy knew George loved the ponies and called and invited him to go out to the track with him and Herb.

Herb was quite the guy...cigarette holder, dressed in the very best and made very expensive shoes. He and his wife, Beth, were the aristocracy of the shoe world. Well.... Herb came to pick up Roy and George in his Silver Cloud. George had never met Herb. On the way, Herb asked George about his business. George sheepishly gave him a quick story of Shapiro Bros. "George...what price do the shoes leave the factory?" "Well, they are sold on a volume basis and they are 4-6 dollars." Herb looked at George and said, as only Herb could have done, "George....I can't make out my tags for that price."

I took over Johnny's schedule...the Dallas Show where he had major customers. It was a time in the business where it was a seller's market and we were fortunate to have the product and the production space. I was now going to Cincinnati to work with U. S. Shoe retail and the Joyce Division. Whenever I went to work with the buyers and line builders, I always had the opportunity to spend time with Phil.

Bob Stix, head of U. S. Shoe manufacturing, visited Shapiro Bros. and was impressed with our production quality and our ability to make fashion product that was applicable for mass production. Phil and Bob were Shapiro fans and asked me to come to Cincinnati to feel me out if George would be open to a sale. U. S. Shoe had bought the Foot Flair plant in Manchester, NH and needed additional production on fashion product. They could not get it done in their factories in Ohio, Indiana and Kentucky.

George was flattered with the proposition put forth but what I did not understand at that time was George was not interested in selling...or the money. He loved the independence for him and his brothers and he wanted no part of the corporate bullshit. He realized that it would change his lifestyle and that was not in his lexicon in any way. Phil, unable to make a deal, wanted me to join him. He had rejuvenated U. S. Shoe, bringing in talent from the shoe industry. Most of the key divisions were now led by a whole new team. Phil was a dynamo and slowly, but surely, started U. S. Shoe on a major breakthrough. He was in the office every day at 6—6:30 am and was on top of every issue.

On a trip to Cincinnati I met Phil for an early breakfast. We then arrived at the building around 7:00 am. The security guard was there and Phil knew his name and greeted Stan. "Oh, Mr. Barach, I'm finishing up this week." "Why are you leaving?" "Well, I'm really not getting any respect around here and the money is not great. The guard on the other shift was made a sergeant and I was passed by." Phil went upstairs and made a call to Human Resources. He then went back to the lobby and made Stan a lieutenant with a $5.00 increase! Stan would probably still be there is there was a U. S. Shoe.

The "Bowen" Sling
snake w/ patent combination

The most unbelievable sale of my career

Phil would call me every Sunday morning between 8 and 8:30 to sell me on U. S. Shoe. We would be in bed and Judy would say, "It's that bastard Barach calling again. Doesn't he know it's Sunday morning?" I was so flattered that he was pursuing me...but Shapiro was my home, my place to create. I had carte blanche. George just stepped back and allowed me to run the show. I was developing an industry-wide reputation. The sun was certainly shining in my direction and I loved it.

I had offers from other companies that were tempting but the ability to be my own person was the element that kept me on board. George knew of these offers and came to me with a program that made me a partner. I had come full circle. I was to have a stock purchase program that would eventually deliver all the stock. The Shapiro's had an agreement among themselves that was set up that upon the death of one of the brothers or partner, the remaining partners had to buy the deceased's stock. I also got a significant raise and a cash bonus that allowed me to buy a house in Newton.

Steve Heller, President of Hahn's, called and wanted both of us to come down to meet the new general merchandising manager...a new position which was usually his duties. We arrived and Steve introduced us to Lyle Burrows. He had worked for the local department store in Baltimore, short, opinionated, very smart, and in his late 50s to early 60s. We had lunch, talked about the business and received a vote of confidence as a key resource. George and I walked out and were about to get into our rented car. I was driving and George looked at me across the roof and said, "What do you think?" I looked at George and said, "This guy will be trouble as long as we know him." I didn't realize how true that statement would be in the years to come.

It was 1967 and our business was booming. At the Chicago Shoe Show, Wohl came to us and asked if we could work Saturdays. They needed the production. I shall never forget that date for, almost a year to the day, the world started to change and it changed rapidly.

Italy arrived...mainly with sandals. They were made beautifully at low prices. That was only part of the problem. We were shoemakers and not sandal makers. Our production, our facility, our machinery was geared for shoes. Our overhead was based on closed footwear and did not equate for sandal production. The biggest problem was we just did not know how to make them. Sandals were not made by machine. They were lasted by hand and we just didn't have the hands or expertise to get it done. Fashion trended toward open footwear and Italy had the tools to get it done.

Brazil emerged in the late 60's and brought a whole new dimension to the shoe world. They had leather, skilled labor and German mentality and organization. Brazilian footwear was made in an area close to Argentina in Novo Hamburgo, which was settled by German immigrants in the 20's and 30's. They had built a domestic industry that was sophisticated.

When the American importers arrived, they had a thriving industry with excellent skills. I will never forget the first time I saw a Brazilian sample. I was at the offices of Bernie Marcus who owned Wilbars, which was a chain of high fashion footwear. We sold Bernie a few shoes each season. I had laid out my samples and was giving him my sales pitch when he opened the drawer in his desk and pulled out a sample. It was a well-made burnished leather tailored sample with a genuine stacked leather heel, leather lining and leather sole. The product I was trying to sell was synthetic lined with synthetic soles and upper material that was not in the same class. The price was $3.00 less than mine. I asked Bernie where they were made and who was importing them. I scoffed at the whole deal...said they would never deliver. It was the start of one of the most successful shoe companies... Nine West.

Our business started to get tough. The combination of Italy, now Spain and Brazil, was taking its toll. We fought the best way we could. Our strength was quick delivery and we changed our production methods to shorter lines with quicker reaction times. I started to design very forward-looking product to compete against the imports.

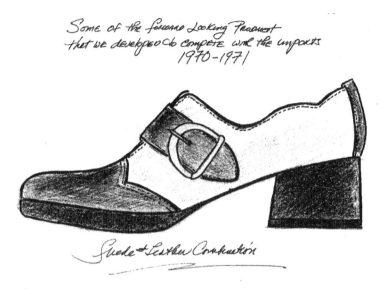

Some of the forward Looking Product
that we developed to compete with the imports
1970-1971

Suede + Leather Construction

    I came up with a unique hinged wedge construction and a new lightweight burnished cork-like material. They did well for what they represented. We were now in the item business, the bread and butter going to the imports. We sought areas where the imports were vulnerable. Believe me, there weren't many.

    I had been to Europe for a style trip for the first time. Ralph Shapiro took me by the hand and showed me the ropes and where to shop. My eyes could not take it in quick enough; the Milan Fair, Florence and Paris. The clothes, the stores, everything was exciting and my mind was going 100 miles a minute. I wanted to buy a suit and almost every store I went into they did not have my size. Finally, in Paris I found a sensational corduroy suit that came in my size and I couldn't wait to try it on. The salesman slipped on the jacket and it felt and looked great. Standing and looking into the mirror, I was congratulating myself...what a handsome dude was there. I slowly peeked down at the price tag that was on the sleeve and quickly did the calculation from francs to dollars. It was $900 and I almost fell over. I had already started singing my praises of the garment to the salesperson. I was stuck. I looked in the mirror and pushed my shoulders back and stated, "It is a wonderful suit but it is too tight under the arms." I quickly took it off and sneaked out of the store.

By late 1970, I could see the die was cast and if we were to survive, we had to bite the bullet and think of new alternatives to exist. It was not going to happen sailing the same course. George and I were not on the same page. It was one of the great lessons of my life. My interests were not necessarily someone else's. I proposed the following:

1.   Build a new factory on one level with new modern equipment

2.   Junk the factory and go into the import business.

3.   Go out of business.

I told George about what lay ahead if we did nothing. If we closed the factory we could have a viable import business. We were well-financed and had a reputation second to none. There weren't many companies that had made the transition from manufacturer to importer. We had an organization and I felt it could be done.

The idea of building a new factory was not my favorite for the domestic shoe business would have ever increasing difficulty competing with the importers. For me, it really was not an option nor was going out of business.

I did not know "diddly" about the import business but I saw the products rolling in and knew this was the road to travel. George sat there quietly and listened to my pitch and took it all in. He was quite philosophical and understood completely my point of view. I'll always remember what he said, "Norman... you and I are at different stages of our lives. You are in your early 30's and my brothers and I are in our early 70's or late 60's. We have different goals. I have to say, if I were in your age group, I would be thinking as you. My brothers and I have had the good fortune to become well off through this business.

Our lives are here in Auburn and to change this equation is not in our best interests. So we shall keep the factory going until it reaches a point where it becomes unprofitable. We will then close...pay our bills and severance to the employees and retire." This was his reply paraphrased. I asked him what of me? "You are entitled to your percentage of the business as we outlined and are more than welcome to stay as long as we feel the factory is viable." I just didn't know what to say. This job was my life. George was the father that I never had. He treated me as the older son. I was devastated realizing that my wonderful world was no longer a haven for me. Everything that bred stability was in flux and I felt fear of the unknown...a feeling I had forgotten from my early years.

I was with George for nine years and thought it would be that way forever. I was doing so well in every area of my business career. I had major health issues with Judy that were pressing, but I had my escape to Maine and the wonderful shoe world that I had developed. It was not a happy time for my world was coming apart. I picked up the phone and called Phil Barach. He had been lobbying me to join U. S. Shoe for the past two years. Phil had me come out to Cincinnati and presented two scenarios. I could move there and become the product person and senior vice present to Joyce...a premier division of the company. The second option was quite different. Their Bandolino division was not performing as it should and they wanted to make a change. It meant living and designing the collection in Florence, Italy. There was a travel schedule that had to be addressed and going through an interview with Arnold Dunn and Walter Marx.

Bandolino was a division of Marx/Newman which Phil had purchased from Walter Marx and Otto Newman, the owners. They were still involved in the business, at least Walter was, but Arnold ran the business and originally worked for them and stayed on when it was acquired. There were two brands, the second one being Amalfi, which Arnold directly oversaw with an assistant. Amalfi was doing unbelievably well. They held a priority position in the better sandal market and actually had little or no competitors.

Phil said, "The job is yours; all you have to do is say yes." It was Phil who pulled rank and hired me. I then went down to New York for an interview with Arnold and Walter but it was a "done deal". I had come from a totally different world of private label sales or working with Wohl or Edison Bros., who had different mentalities than the likes of Marx & Newman and department store buyers. Arnold and Walter welcomed me, because they needed someone with my talent to fix the leaking Bandolino boat. But I was not their man...I was Phil's guy and they never forgot it.

They had this "thing" with U. S. Shoe. They were part of it but they wanted no part of it. U. S. Shoe people were not allowed in their showrooms. They wanted, not only to maintain their independence but they felt they were "special"...a sense of aristocracy which was the mantra of the higher priced branded lines of the fashion world.

Arnold Dunn had been with Marx & Newman before it was acquired by U. S. Shoe. He was Otto Newman's assistant and spent most of his time in Italy with Otto developing the line. Arnold carried himself well, about 5'10", 59 years old, fairly handsome with little hair, but it served him well. He had become the CEO when U. S. Shoe took over. Walter and Otto basically were consultants and Otto left after his contract with the corporation ended. Arnold never had much to do with Bandolino. He had always hired a designer.

Joe Famolare had started as the first designer and left to start his own business. I knew Joe well for he had come from my world, the domestic shoe business. Arnold's talents were not in the styling needed for Bandolino. He did not understand the "Junior" concept of the line.

Arnold's whole personality, demeanor and lifestyle were

geared toward Amalfi. We called Arnold "Digger O'Day" and teased him relentlessly. He had a collection of the same black, ill-fitting suits in New York and Florence which he wore every day. White shirt and black tie were there daily. When he traveled back and forth to his apartment in Florence he only needed his briefcase. Arnold thought of himself as a financier, more than a shoe man and would have liked to have been a Swiss banker in another life. He did manipulate the company's money, playing the currency game quite well. He had a good heart and left me alone to do my job. Arnold needed that drink at 5 pm. It wasn't an absolute necessity but when things got tough, he had an eye on the clock.

Walter was no more than 5'3", full head of white hair and always dressed in his Brioni suits and ties. He had his Viennese accent with him at all times. He didn't have any real title except as a consultant to the corporation but he had major influence with Arnold and even with Phil. Walter was always in the office. He regretted selling the business to U. S. Shoe. He had gotten slightly over $1M (his share) and now saw the company prospering beyond belief. He could be a tyrant at times, but we never had a bad word or any issues. He realized his expertise was Amalfi and he stayed away from Bandolino. Everyone in the office was afraid of him. He walked around looking here and there...never saying much. I believe he reported his findings to Arnold and the office manager.

He was the salesman in Marx & Newman and the product person was Otto Newman. Otto was the brains and built the business and was just leaving the company when I joined. The legacy he left behind was memorable in every way. Otto was a flamboyant character. He was sophisticated, generous, brilliant, and what we would call "a man of the world". He always had a black pilot case with him at all times and would become paranoid if anyone moved it. He and Walter had escaped the Nazi's by hours and left penniless or close to it and he swore it would never happen again. If he had to leave, he would not go poor for he had gold and negotiable securities in that bag. Otto loved the girls. He was a confirmed bachelor and really didn't want to date anyone over 25...he was in his 70's!

I was in the driver's seat and worked out a marvelous deal that included a great salary of over $150,000 with a bonus arrangement, car expenses, a furniture allowance for Italy, a per diem when we returned to the U.S., full tuition for the children at the American school and a very good expense account when traveling. The deal was unbelievable for a poor kid from Worcester. I went back to Phil and told him the details which I expect he had signed off on. The only real issue that possibly stood in the way was the family. I told Phil that as far as I was concerned I was on board, but the family had to sign off on Italy. That meant taking them to Florence and seeing what their new world would consist of. They had to sign off.

We all sat at the kitchen table one night and discussed this move and how it would be the adventure of our lives. I had been to Italy before but never to an Italian shoe factory. The kids went off to see the sights and spend time at the American school. Judy went to see living situations and a general tour.

Arnold picked me up and we went off to visit the major Bandolino factory. It was located on the way to the sea near Lucca in a town called Massarosa...also the name of the factory. The owner was Sr. Lunadini and it was run with his son-in-law, Antonio Bianchi. As we came over the mountain into the valley, we could see the factory. It was two large Quonset-type constructions on either side of the road. We were greeted by Lunadini and entered the office section of the building. The showroom was filled with the product of the past seasons and the administrative offices were quite different for they had these large machines that had tapes whirling. I asked what they were and was told they generated the "tags" which listed all the components needed in the production process. Essentially, it was the first computer I had seen. In the first building was the warehouse and we looked at some of the new sandal product rolling off production lines. There was a conveyor that was situated under the road connecting both structures, bringing the finished product to the warehouse.

We entered the factory building, which had five to six production lines. They were all automated with a fantastic conveyor system. I had never seen one before. I was just mesmerized by the process. The cutting room was our first stop and was totally fitted with the newest hydraulic cutting machines which were called "clickers" and they were state of the art and much faster. We went to the stitching room which also was automated and followed the uppers to completion. There the uppers were then moved to a staging area for lasting. The sandals came off the production conveyors and were packed using less people than I believed possible, making the process cleaner and faster.

I had a hundred questions and didn't want to seem that dumb so I only asked a limited amount. We then went back to the office complex and we had coffee from the bar in the show room. It was May...a beautiful day and Antonio suggested that we go up to the roof garden so I could see the view. I shall never forget looking out at Viareggio and the sea beyond. How could one compete against this type of technology, ability and labor pool? It was impossible. How could we compete in an old mill building on four floors with wooden racks that move the shoes vs conveyors and modern technology? There was no choice... you had to join them or leave the industry. It was a defining moment in my life.

I said "yes"...if the family said "yes". Everyone loved Italy; the school, the food and the adventure. It was a go. I shook hands with Arnold and made plans to join the company.

It was probably one of the most difficult days of my life. I drove down Maine to give George my decision and settle the financial matters. I gave him an unlimited notice and offered to find a salesperson to replace me. I had someone in mind that was excellent. He was a salesman but not a designer/line-builder. George needed the former first rather than the latter. Larry Litvak was a real pro who knew the customer base and needed the job. He was the best candidate and I worked with him for a few weeks...spending time to develop a new group of samples for the coming season. It gave him a running start.

When it was time to leave, George walked me to the door and hugged me. I started to cry...it was just too much to handle. I was entering a new phase of my life. I was leaving the security and warmth I had known.

The Experience of a Lifetime

Chapter IV

"The biggest adventure you can ever take is to live the life of your dreams."

Oprah Winfrey

There was a lot to do, and actually not much time to do it. We wanted to be there for September; school opening and actually the start of working on the fall collection. We were fortunate. I did not want to sell the house...who knew what could happen? What if we needed to come home? The best scenario was to rent it and we found the best possible situation. Being in Boston, there were many professors who came for teaching positions at the major universities. We found a family that lived the exact opposite lifestyle as we were about to start. The family was from Hong Kong and taught at Harvard. They had grown kids who were accepted at Boston College which was right down the street. Their year was September to June and then they would return to Hong Kong. We lived the opposite cycle and were able to return to our home in the summer. We could not have asked for a better situation.

I would commute to Florence during June and July for August was the Italian vacation month, Ferragosto. It was the perfect solution for it allowed us to keep the house, stay in touch with our family and friends and commitments in the States. Their rental fee paid the mortgage so it was not a burden to keep the house. It was probably one of the best financial decisions I ever made. Newton real estate eventually went to the moon. It was a great deal...we had a significant deposit to cover issues. But, most of all, these people wanted the house for three years. Our friends were real estate agents and they were set to take care of all the details during this period...mortgage payments, etc. The situation could not have been better.

The offices of Marx & Newman were in New York...they had just moved from the Empire State Building to 9 West 57th... the new tower that was just opening. We were the first tenants on the 40th floor. There was an express from the lobby directly to our office. The building was magnificent and the space just as grand. When you exited the elevator and opened the office doors, you were greeted with almost a 180° panoramic view of Central Park. Nothing matched it for there wasn't an obstructed view. It just captivated you. We had almost half the floor with showrooms for the lines. The administrative offices were in the rear but every office had huge windows with great light. I went down to New York to meet everyone and start a small project for an interim line.

The Bandolino organization consisted of Norman Zeichner, who was the President and Sales Manager. He was an ex-ball player in the 50's, still in decent shape, greying distinguished hair and a salesman's smile, even if someone kicked him in the balls. Norman knew how to handle the customers. He dined them, screwed them if it was necessary, and gave them markdown money when the shoes didn't perform. This "markdown money thing" was a whole new game for me and it took me awhile to understand the whole process. It was all tied to gross margin that was more or less guaranteed by the brand. It was a great deal if the line performed for the profit margins were sizable. It was not the case when sales were off and you had to ante up. Norman was helpful and willing. The problem was that he was not a style person and this was a problem since I needed him "buying in" on the styling and direction of the line. Norman, as most sales managers, only wanted to be a partner when the line was hot. We shall discuss it again. I had to learn to live with Norman over the years. He sold the shoes and had the ear of Walter Marx and, at times, Arnold's.

I understood the situation. There were two factions; those

in New York and those in Florence. It was always a situation...a crisis...a plan gone astray that was the cause of one or another. The problem was that New York never wanted to own up that they had a part in it. It was a source of discontent...growing or receding, depending on how the business developed.

Zeichner had a great second in command, Marilyn, who knew the business from every angle. She had a good eye and knew the customer base. She actually handled the house accounts. She swore like a trooper and, at one time, would screw anything decent that walked in the door. I liked her from the start, she was my kind of people for you always knew where you stood. She was my eyes and ears in the office. I valued her opinion and listened when she requested certain styling for the line. Marilyn was 35 pounds overweight and 5'5" but to me she was a princess.

The controller and office manager was Howie Glick. He answered to Arnold and at one time was a salesperson for the company. He was our "money man" and checked our expenses. It was almost unbelievable how we spent money. I had what seemed to be an unlimited expense account covering all expenses in New York and a per diem in Boston. I had come from a totally different world where every nickel was accounted for and expenses were held to a minimum. This world was unreal. Howie was also the "house spy", conveying all that happened to Walter and Arnold. It was his job, in a way, to keep the peace between all factions.

Everyone was more than cordial and willing to help me get acclimated. Bandolino had suffered a series of 3-4 seasons of lackluster business while Amalfi was on fire. Norman was complaining and was one of the voices wanting a change. I was supposed to be the new hope.

It was early July and I made my first trip to Florence as a Marx & Newman employee. Arnold was with me and he wanted to give me a better idea of the factory setup for I had only spent time at Massarosa. There were two other factories involved.

Delia was owned by Sr. Mori but Simoneta, his son, ran the factory and marketed the product. Delia had an "artigiano" flavor to its production. It was not the industry type plant as Massarosa but it had the ability to make product that had a handmade look. The styles they were making did not fit the character of the plant. Simoneta knew it and he and I were automatically on the same page. It was too late to do anything serious for the season which would need a new collection for August. We tried to put a Band-Aid on a bleeding wound by building two to three styles but it was really too late.

Simoneta came across as a jolly, happy-go-lucky fellow. It was the exact opposite. He was a "type A" and knew exactly what to do. Over the period of time that I was there, he built a great business with the Delia brand throughout Europe. He eventually outlived Massarosa. His product development ability was excellent. The story I remember most still brings a chuckle. Simoneta has a new BMW with a radio that you could remove from the car. Sure enough, his radio was stolen and he replaced it, only to have it stolen again. He was so pissed. He had enough and brought the radio up to his apartment each night. Unfortunately, someone broke into the apartment and robbed him...by the way, they took the radio!

The other factory was Cassi, the weakest of the three. It wasn't entirely their fault for Bandolino, not known as a strong dress line, used the factory in this area. It was located in Pistoia and I remember the factory was located in a cluster of trees which surrounded the concrete structure. In the winter the factory would be freezing as once the cold penetrated, it never dissipated. We would go outside to warm up. The factory needed a re-vamping of its product lines and it was to be a very difficult project for its overhead had been based on a dress product. The restaurant near the factory had the best zuppa di panne, bread soup, in all the world. There was definitely a need to visit the factory for this reason alone.

Cassi was an odd duck. He seemed resigned to his fate

as a second rate resource. He had real estate interests and the factory was not his emphasis. He was sort of a half-ass shoe person which was so unlike the owners we dealt with. His days were numbered in my estimation and, to be perfectly honest, he felt the same way. Arnold did not want me to cut the cord until we tried once more.

Amalfi was a great label and it was made by Ugo Rangoni who was somewhat of a legend in the Italian shoe business. His organization was second to none and not only produced fantastic quality, but knew how to style the product. They had a group of modellistas that were exceptional and presented Arnold with an exciting grouping of sandals to choose from. Rangoni was in the leather business and was in control of a great Napa calf that gave Amalfi a unique priority position. Amalfi became a brand in the U.S. when Walter Marx and Otto Newman joined with Rangoni and became the agents for the label in the States. They ended up in the States and when the war was over went back to Italy and founded Rangoni/Amalfi.

Werner Marx was the nephew of Walter who founded the company. Werner was the President/Sales Manager of Amalfi and carried out the daily duties. The real head of the division was Arnold. Werner was a likable fellow, his shoe experience was limited and everyone realized that he carried out Arnold's program. He was a good soul and extremely well-liked by the staff and the customers. If there was a situation or an issue, Arnold was there.

The Amalfi factory was right in a Florentine neighborhood less than two miles from the center and Marx & Newman had an office around the corner. I now had a fairly good idea of the Bandolino factory's capabilities and I discussed the whole situation with Arnold. He was open to any new plan that would turn around the trend for the line. Arnold was a pretty clever financial person and played the exchange market extremely well. He brought some huge profits to the company over my tenure. One year we made 17%. It was exceptional.

I met my head technician on the trip. Arnold was not completely sold on his performance and gave me carte blanche to make a change if I wanted. He was a pleasant guy...Swiss national with an American wife, who seemed to have the desire to get the job done. I spent most of the week with him and decided that, unless he was a complete screw-up, I needed someone who knew the factories, the personnel and where the bodies were buried.

We were in tougher shape than I thought. The lines they were about to show in August were just ho-hum. No one would be jumping up and down over this collection. We would be starting out for fall, not on the starting line, but with a slight penalty which we would need to overcome. My analysis was pretty right on. We held the business because Zeichner had plenty of markdown money and had the opportunity to take back slow product.

I was spending the week in New York in late July and August and one of the projects was... Parla Italiano. The factories and our Italian office were almost without anyone who spoke English. So I signed up for Berlitz. There was lots to do to get ready to go so I would take lessons for an hour or two most days. When I got into the workload, there was little time for lessons. I had taken romance languages, French, Spanish and German, with a base of Latin. I thought there was headway but I soon realized when I landed in Italy the lessons did not give me an everyday knowledge of the language. I could say, "See the yellow pencil" but not much else.

I attended the New York August Show, mainly as a spectator, and gave some presentations of the line which I had nothing to do with. There were a few styles that we rushed from my week with Arnold which were received without much fanfare.

There was another American involved in the product

development who worked under Arnold as an assistant line builder for Amalfi and lived the same schedule that I was about to do. He had a family with two children and had been at it for three years before I joined Marx & Newman. He was extremely helpful and both families became friendly. We gravitated toward one another, there were not many of us. We traveled on styling trips and to the Europe fairs. We were both from the New England shoe business and had similar roots. He spoke Italian and was very helpful in the early days of our arrival.

We went to the Semaine de Cuir, which was the largest shoe and leather fair in the world. It was a Sunday and we made the mistake of staying to the end. When we came out, the taxi line was from there to Florence. We said the hell with this and figured if we walked five to ten blocks we would find a taxi. You cannot flag a cab in Paris. You must wait at a taxi stand, there is no other way. We walked and walked, stopping at taxi stands...nothing. Finally, he said, "I'm not walking another step. I want to wait at this stand, if it's all night." About ten minutes later, two couples came walking up to the taxi stand. They are Italians and one says to the other in Italian, "These two asshole Americans don't know from shit; let's jump ahead of them and grab the cab when it comes." He and I said nothing. When the taxi finally came, the Italian made his move. I grabbed him by the neck and said, "Senore, questa es nostro taxi? Capito!"

The office found a temporary residence where we could live until we found a permanent apartment. The Park Palace Hotel was located on the road to Piazza Michelangelo. It was a small hotel with a villa adjacent that was available. The accommodations were very satisfactory and it was our home for almost four months. The office had an old, somewhat broken-down Alfa Romeo which served my purpose until a new car could be delivered. Things were in place for the move.

We were all excited for the end of August was almost upon us and we wanted the adventure to start. Ted was thirteen years old and Rachel was ten. They had loved the original trip to see what it was all about and were more than ready. Judy was recovering from a near devastating illness and was in the best health in two years. It was a major concern, but she voted for Italy.

We sent a few things ahead, but mostly everything would be purchased there for our new home. When we left for the airport, we had thirteen suitcases, two cats which Judy and the kids would not leave behind, and two coils of rope. Thank God, for we needed it in Rome. We flew Alitalia non-stop and arrived early morning. It took us a while to round everything up and get the porter with a huge cart for the trip through customs and immigration. When the customs agent saw us coming he, in predictable Italian style, threw up his hands, "Is this all yours? Do you have papers for the cats? Go, please go."

I had rented a Fiat 130 which was the largest car in Italy with a roof rack. It was hot as hell and it took me more than an hour to get everything loaded and tied down. We did not have additional room for a magazine when we finished loading everyone in. I was exhausted, but running on adrenalin for the three-plus hour trip to Florence. I had never driven the Autostrada north with a load piled high. It was truly an adventure and I was scared shitless. I did not speak, did not understand and did not know the way to the hotel. How I managed to get us there is still a mystery. Florence is a maze of one-way streets and zones where cars cannot enter.

The staff at the Park Palace was fabulous. We adjusted quickly to the villa and hotel service daily. The Kraft's, who were Swiss, were the owners and Luigi ran the dining room where we had our meals. The kids were in ecstasy eating pasta and bongo-bongo (profiteroles) every night. I believe I gained twenty pounds after four months. I ate everything, including the tablecloth. Everyone settled in and after the first week I went off to Bologna for the shoe fair.

The kids were in ecstasy for the soccer team from Florence would stay at our hotel whenever they were playing at home. Fiorentina was a Class A team and we used to go to the games. We became soccer (calcio) fans almost overnight. Ted was the portiere (goalie) for the upper school. Rachel became the captain of the boy's lower school team. She was born before her time for she could have played for Team USA at a different time.

It was the start of the development season and I needed to get to work on the interim collection and finalize a plan for the fall collection. My technician and I traveled daily to the factories. I would meet him on the Autostrada around 7:00 am and head out to the factories which were anywhere from five to sixty miles away. We were on the road every day. He was extremely helpful with the language and knew what had to be done. We would grab a cappuccino most mornings and the place was loaded with truck drivers as the Autostrada was the major road north and south. They were drinking café correcto... espresso and grappa. One morning I tried one; what a jolt. My eyes were burning up. It was fire water. Once was enough!

One of us would leave our car there and pick it up in the evening. We always shared the driving. We spent all our time driving the Autostrada Firenze Mare, which was the main road to all our factories, the tanneries and component people. We could travel on the average 100-150 miles per day.

I spent very little time in the office. I met with the factories daily and my briefcase was my office. The Marx & Newman office was run by Mrs. Vanini. She was an American who married an Italian and worked for Walter Marx from inception of their business. When U. S. Shoe bought the business she stayed on. Mrs. Vanini's daughter, Anna, and two to three non-English speaking employees made up the staff. It serviced both divisions. Arnold and the assistant were there most of the time although they had space at the Amalfi factory.

I was shocked at the way the office was set up. There wasn't a telex machine. Everything was either conducted by phone or telegram. It was the dark ages. I went to Arnold and demanded a telex. He agreed but his excuse was he didn't need the ball scores or chitchat from New York. Arnold was content with being isolated from New York.

My major problem was developing the interim collection. The collection they showed in August was not a blockbuster; far from it. Yes, our basic padded sock sandal business was more or less intact, but our directional, fashion segment was not well received. It needed a real shot in the arm as soon as possible to salvage the season even at this late date.

The sandal story was changing and a whole new technology was being developed. Polyurethane, a light, durable material, was now being developed by the Italian sole industry. The new material opened up a whole new concept for footwear. It could be used for both closed and open product but for us the sandal option was the course to take.

The industry was in its infant stages and development was difficult to generate. We needed to find a way to make the models to cast the molds. I started working with a urethane supplier and realized that we were on our own to develop the prototypes. We started searching for a model maker to work on the project. I asked if there was a zone in Tuscany where they made furniture. We came up with an area around Pisa in the town of Pontedera. We found a shop where a father and son were carving lamp models. Senor Lannini and his son were master carvers as we soon discovered. They were working on a full scale model for the Alfa Romeo dashboard. It was something to behold. They did not speak English so my technician was the translator early on when necessary. My hands and gestures told part of the story to them.

We brought them the lasts as the basis for the unit soles and started the development. First we made clay models to simulate the soles from sketches I had designed. Corrections followed. We gave them a quick course in last technology to maintain toe spring (the correct amount of height of the toe) and the dimensions and circumference of the sole. They proceeded to carve a size 7B model so we could make the molds.

This whole process took weeks to get to this stage. It was going slow, but we were on new ground. We were one of the few tackling this new technology. We then had to work out the proper filler to give the heel support and a shank for stability and support. We were novices and it was trial and error. I felt this was our only avenue to simulate this look in leather which would be way out of our price range.

I had seen these looks in leather at the fair from the fashion leaders. We needed to find the answer to simulating these ideas in our own way for our price range and customer profile. I began working on the finishing of the soles. The effect that we wanted had to be hand cut into the molds. To tell the truth, we didn't know the fuck what we were doing. I didn't have the foggiest idea of what the finish would be. I knew what I wanted but it really was a crap shoot at this point. We worked with the poly factory and trials were made and remade.

Our whole fashion program was based on these soles. I had rolled the dice and things were not looking good...at all. In the meantime, the rest of the line was being developed. Arnold came around occasionally and looked at some of the development, said very little, and just asked if I would have everything ready for the sales meeting and show. He was nervous for he knew this was all new and a recipe for disaster.

I started second-guessing myself. What if we can't get the soles right? I guess I better think of two alternative plans... first, a back-up sole which would be a disaster or second, living back in Newton in another house. I had rolled the dice, and it was getting "dicey".

Each factory has a major sample program and most of the trials were "lookin' good". The major program dependent on the soles was the bone of contention.

We rented an apartment on Via Della Robbia #20. It was off the Viale Mazzini near the English cemetery and only a few blocks from the synagogue. The area was upscale about two miles from the center and the Duomo. One of my leather suppliers lived right across the way so I knew it was the right area. At that time, you had no trouble parking your car on the street. It really filled the bill for it was a great area and building. We rented that they called an "attico"...two levels with bedrooms, living, dining room, kitchen on the first floor and a bedroom suite above. We had a marvelous terrace that had a fantastic view of the Duomo. There was Santi and his wife, the portiere for the building.

We had the furniture allowance which we used to create a wonderful living space. The apartment had panoramic windows leading out to the terrace. We went to Ilum, the fantastic lighting store, to see the fixtures. Italian apartments do not have closets so we bought guardarobas for the three bedrooms. It was fun to see the whole apartment come together. The family seemed to be adjusting to the new life.

The terrace was huge and, off to the right, Florence was visible in all its glory. Every night we had a sunset that was memorable. We bought an arc lamp that Ted has in his house today. Some of the furniture we took back to the States and is now in our children's homes. Actually, one of the guardarobas ended up in my office as a storage bin. It's as functional now as the day we bought it.

Naturally the language was an issue for all of us. I was learning on the job and it seemed to come fairly easy. Most of the people I came in contact with did not speak English, so there was no alternative. We found Marietta, who came every day to cook, clean, etc. She made "Marietta's chicken" with roasted potatoes that was amazing. The kids were having a great time. Everything was different. Someone delivered water and wine weekly. A whole new life was upon us.

We had leased the apartment from a Spaniard married to a Florentine whose family owned half the street. It was a great deal for he wanted dollars deposited in the States. We obliged and worked out a very favorable rental.

When Marietta wasn't cooking, we would walk to the other end of the street to Trattoria Ada. Their food was marvelous home-type cooking at prices that could not be duplicated with the ingredients in your kitchen. We ate there two to three times a week.

The American School was a haven for us all. The kids loved it, made great friends and we became friends with the parents. It was quite a mixture of expats, professors on sabbatical, shoe people as myself, pharmaceutical executives, long-term vacationers and residents, Italian and American. The school was situated in what they called Bellosguardo, which meant beautiful view in an old palazzo. If you had an Art Book on Florence, more than likely it would have a close-up of the Duomo. Well, that photo was taken from the schoolyard.

Ted was becoming a young man. He had the attico to himself and his friends flocked to the house all the time and stayed on weekends. What was interesting was that the school brought a need for everyone to help one another and no one was left behind. There was a sense of making sure everyone came along. They all needed one another and recognized that fact from the outset.

There was excitement. We had the two cats, Sheba and the mother, Tippy. One morning we could not find Sheba for she had climbed out of Ted's window onto a very steep roof. When we finally located her, the situation looked impossible. We tried everything. Santi came up with poles and ropes but to no avail. This wasn't the States where you could call the fire department. We just couldn't get her down. The next morning... we found Sheba lying in her favorite spot. How in heaven's name she managed to get back into the house only the good fairy knows.

The big problem was the water pressure. We were on the top floor and it was a trickle at times. I would make sure I took my shower at 6:00 am and, even then, it was a trickle.

I had some wonderful experiences. The weather was starting to turn cooler and I needed a warmer jacket that was somewhat waterproof. I went into town and found a shop right on the Arno that had what I wanted in the window. All the shopkeepers spoke English and I struck up a conversation with the owners, man and wife. I told them that we just moved here and that we were adjusting to Italian life. They were extremely friendly and were more than eager to help me. The jacket was great and I reached for my credit cards. They were not with me as I left them in the office. I told Roberto and Anna that I would return tomorrow and pick up the jacket. They made me take the jacket home and told me to come back on Saturday to pay. We have been dear friends since 1971...we have made special trips to Florence to see them.

Four years before we moved to Italy, Judy developed a brain tumor and was fortunate to have come out of the operation whole. The surgeon gave us no guarantees and we were ever thankful for the results. However, it was not over. She had a rare children's disease that only showed up in 2% of the adult population. She grew tumors in different parts of her body that had to be removed by surgery. We were fortunate they did not appear in the vital organs. She survived because we lived in Boston and she became a patient in a research program at Children's Hospital. The cure was almost as difficult as the disease. There were only short periods of the day when she had the strength to be out of bed.

I was father and mother during this period. I was fortunate to have the funds for additional help. She slowly recovered and started to be the vibrant person she once was. Judy voted for Italy and we were ever watchful of her health. I bring this up for when we were preparing to go home for the Christmas season, she had a relapse and we left her in the States for roughly two months. It was always on my mind whether I had made the right choice of coming. She never wavered and I will always remember how her courage was beyond what you would expect. It all worked out for she beat the horrible illness and spent the majority of our time in Italy together.

The factories were very willing and extremely helpful in every area. We were building sample collections in each of the factories. Massarosa, as the main plant, was my main concern. The polyurethane program was to be made here. Antonio and his modellista staff were working on all the sketches I had given them for the uppers. We needed to finalize the soles. We had developed the new material that was burnished and simulated the look of leathers at couture prices. We were, hopefully, on our way.

The material was a breakthrough, for it not only looked great, but the pricing was competitive. I had a sigh of relief; two-thirds of the puzzle was working. All I needed was to get the soles right. Antonio, my technician and I made a trip to Milan and Vigevano to see how the soles were coming. The finishing was key and we still did not see the actual sculptured molds to simulate a stacked leather finish. This was the crucial step and I was not sleeping well. I was second-guessing myself for putting so many eggs in that basket.

Massarosa was our basic fashion bootmaker. His factory was also geared to make sandals and moccasins; sandals being the major thrust eight to nine months of the year. I had developed an interesting program for both the boots and moccasins on a crepe-type synthetic substance that was new to the market. They looked great and eventually sold much better than expected. Actually it became a major construction as we developed future lines.

Italian pricing had started to climb and the way to combat it was using unit soles, which cut the labor cost dramatically. The labor laws in Italy were geared to full employment. When you hired a worker, it was almost impossible to fire him. You owned him, literally, for life.

The development really started with making new lasts

for the program. I had never worked in a last factory to develop the styles. The best last factory in Italy was located on the way to the Adriatic, which was about two hours from Florence, north on the Autostrada to Bologna and then heading east, entering the Marche. This was all new to me. My education in last-making was almost nil. The whole system was light years ahead in Italy.

The last is the key factor in the development cycle. The entire concept of what you wanted to create hinged on making it right style and fit-wise.

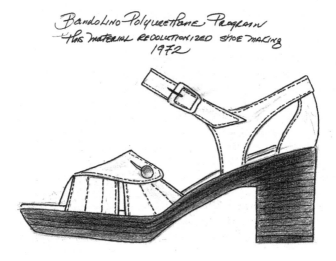

BandoLino Polyurethane Program
—this material redolutionized shoe making
1972

Formificio Romangolo was state of the art. It was the largest last factory in Italy with the key plant in Forli and satellite factories scattered throughout the shoe area. You went to Forli to work with the best. We were the largest customer for Romangolo between all the factories. We worked with the best last makers and the service was exceptional. You worked with a modellista who built the last to your specifications right there. Giving him what heel height you wanted, the type of shoe or sandal and toe shape needed, he would then proceed from there to bring it to fruition. He would then turn rough models in wood that were approximately the heel height you wanted. We then could work out the shape of the toe and look.

I had come prepared with technical sketches. We went to their library to see certain types. All these elements helped you and the modellista arrive at a last that filled the requirements you were after. During a number of visits, we developed twenty new lasts.

The trip was well worth it for Senor Rossi, the major principal, would take you to lunch. This was an experience, always interesting, for there were at least two to three other designers, mostly Italians that were working there at the same time. Some seemed to be on the same schedule as myself. We became sort of friends...Jerry Ferragamo, Sergio Rossi...famous names in the fashion world. It was not a lunch, it was a feast; at least twelve courses with the great wines of that region. It was a late lunch, for there was not a whole lot of work done upon returning to the factory.

Most of the time we were able to take a number of the models we made with us. They would turn them in plastic quickly upon completion. In the initial stages we were there five to six times in two to three weeks. Franz was our modellista and a master craftsman as he fashioned the wood model. I was there...at every step...mainly to check the character and the basic look. It was a whole new learning experience. We leaned on Franz's talent and experience. Our only real contribution was toe shape and heel height, both crucial in achieving the right proportions and style.

Things seemed to have fallen into place and slowly we began to see the results of months of work. The finishing of the soles was still an issue. Everything was so new; the language, the personalities, the new systems. I was pressed and it resulted in long working days from early morning and then at home correcting or designing the next day's needs. Unlike Amalfi, half our day was travel and it made for a long work day and the need to be super organized.

It was already November and we were in a sprint for the samples not only had to be OK'd but we had to produce sample lots...six pairs in each color, each style for the office and salesforce. Everything had to be signed off on as soon as possible to attain delivery.

We finally saw the completed molds with the finish we were shooting for. It was not perfect, it was just OK in my estimation, but there wasn't a choice. We had to go forward with what we had. Starting over at this late date was not a possibility. Maybe my expectations were too high. Maybe I was asking too much for a new technology to achieve? Maybe I should have taken an entirely different route? I still think about it today. What if?

Part of the problem was that the style concept was new. Bandolino had not stepped that far out in the fashion world and our sales force did not understand the styling. We sold the sandals pretty well. they performed B+ but they were not A's. I was not a happy camper. The rest of the collection was an A and carried the day.

We had a wonderful Thanksgiving with three families at our house. It was truly a time to be thankful. My wife was well, the kids were more than content and I survived the first development season. My Italian was getting better and I could carry on conversations but I would make mistakes. The Italians were great; they would speak baby talk to me. I was once in a conversation in the factory trying to explain a problem with transportation of the goods in Italian. I kept saying communista instead of cammunista and they were hysterical, for I was saying communist instead of truck driver.

In all my years in this industry there has always been the classic "struggle" between the design team and sales. Living in Italy you depended on the sales manager to feed you with the trends and retail developments in the States. It was Zeichner's job to do so. In retrospect, he just was not a fashion or style person. The information he sent over was often too generalized or off-base. It was a major bone of contention between us from the very start. He was not a Ralph Shapiro who took a stand on what he perceived was the right direction. It was the old proverb, "You can lead a horse to water but you can't make him drink." Fashion was not an equation and when you don't have that instinct in your fingertips, you stumbled or made excuses.

Arnold, with all his conservatism, bought into the program. He was committed and supported my efforts. He held his cards very close to his vest, but he voted with the design team over sales. The problem was selling these new concepts to the salesforce and mainly to management. The classic take is wanting to sell "old faithful". Even if it is slightly tarnished, it's a security blanket. Zeichner nodded and smiled (it was a winning one) but he did not believe or didn't know what to believe. I was new and young and did not have the track record nor could I give the guarantees that all would be wonderful. Actually, I spoke well and gave them all the style reasons why they should climb aboard. They only were willing to take half a ride. It's the old story, "You can't be a little bit pregnant!" You have to be all in or all out.

So...we did not get along. Zeichner was used to having things his way. The former designer did not rock the boat in any way. He knew the power was in New York. I guess I was dumb enough not to realize it.

My problem was I was a lousy politician. I never had to be one. My years with George were more or less politically free. There was some with Wohl but very limited. Marx & Newman was a different story. It was an everyday occurrence in New York and the ramifications found their way to Florence.

I came to New York about a week before the shoe show and the sales meeting. All the samples were shipped in A, B, and C groups. The "A" group was a single pair for the showrooms. They divided them in that manner because many years before, they shipped all the samples on by sea on the Andrea Doria which went down. It was a different time. All samples were now shipped by air.

Arnold had a rule. The new samples were put into each showroom and were not to be opened by anyone except the designer. I stayed at the Warwick Hotel and had been a regular customer there all summer. I expected to be there about two weeks before returning to Florence. I had to get ready for the sales meetings. I was present at the August meeting but the collection was not mine and I had limited involvement. I had met some of the sales force but only a limited amount. We had reps covering the country and one in Canada. The key reps were from New York, the Southeast, Texas and the Northwest. They were a diverse group, a good portion in their late 30's, looking at me as the guy who might bring Bandolino back to its glory. There were big shoes to fill and I hoped they would buy in to what I was selling.

I opened up the collection with Marilyn and she was more than pleased. I was looking at the samples and thinking how I could have improved them. I was excited and nervous at the same time. I sat for a day or two with Marilyn and Zeichner to go over the merchandising of the line before the meeting. Zeichner seemed pleased, but you could not read him for if someone kicked him in the balls, he would give you one of his famous smiles. We threw out some of patterns that we felt were not needed. The line sheet was finalized with the colors and the details for the salesforce were completed.

Everyone, Arnold, Walter, Howie Glick, even the administrative staff, was at the presentation. It was an incredibly interesting meeting, the way it started was amazing. I came to the meeting dressed in a new casual suit and a silk shirt that were just off the fashion runways and conducted the meeting. The salesforce was in suits and sport jackets with shirts and ties. The meeting went well. I gave the presentation and went over a portion of the line. Things seemed to be going fairly well.

On the second day, I again was dressed very casual; new suit, new silk shirt. The salesforce came in and they were now all dressed in casual clothes. When the meeting was about to start, Walter walked in and, in his Viennese accent, spoke: "Gentlemen...pointing to me. This man is the designer. He can wear anything he wants. You are salesmen and you shall wear shirts and ties. So go back to the hotel and change...NOW!" There wasn't a sound as the salesmen filed out the door.

I had learned quite a bit that first season. My Italian was getting there. I seemed to understand the factories and had a very good relationship with them all. Our sandal business was always superb and I had done a good job designing this segment. Massarosa alone was making close to 10,000 pairs per day. We had somewhat of a priority position in the department stores.

Things were fairly smooth. Zeichner was off selling and the fall line was generating decent sales figures. We would soon be thinking of and planning spring for it was our major season.

The major problem facing us was rising costs in Italy, especially leather prices. Our sandals were all leather and the initial cost sheets did not look good. There would be a significant price increase. I was involved in the pricing but the final decision was Arnold's and he negotiated firsthand with me. Actually, as I look back in retrospect, I would wish in my next lifetime to come back as a Marx & Newman factory pricing the product for Arnold. He was a pushover.

Arnold traveled back and forth at least two to three times a season. He really preferred to be in Florence and believed he could run the business from there. In retrospect, I know he made a major mistake believing he could do so. We were a marketing company, whether he thought so or not, and the action was in New York, not Florence.

We had a continuous round of department buyers coming to Florence. Federated, Associated, May Company and Dillard's had their own private label programs and came to Florence twice a year to build their packages. They came to our offices to see what we were doing. What they really wanted, besides some information, was dinner. During the season, there was a steady stream of having to entertain the buyers. It actually became a pain in the ass; it would be a new buyer every few days. We were busy in the factories and had to run back to Florence for dinner dates. I would take Judy and she would throw up her hands and say, "enough...go alone!"

There were company dinners. Arnold and Debbie loved to entertain and invited us to his favorite restaurant, Oliviro's. We were always with Arnold's assistant and his wife and the wine flowed. Dante ran the restaurant and made sure Arnold was able to play a few tunes on the baby grand. We were a small community and depended on one another for not only entertainment but a sense of being a community.

There were reality checks. I used to go down to the corner bar when I was heading to the office. One morning I saw a horrific accident when a young boy on a Motorino tried to beat the bus around the corner. When Ted came home from school, I laid down the law. "If I catch you on a Motorino with Michael Brasini, who drove one to school, you are going off to military school...no second chances."

I finally got my new car and it was really new. Audi had brought out an experimental model called an R080. It had a double Wankel engine and was capable of easily doing 200 mph. The car was magnificent, a full, sleek sedan semi-automatic. You did not hear a sound from the engine. There were two issues. You needed to change spark plugs often and it never missed a gas station. The gas tank was situated in the middle of the chassis, which is the reason I am writing this account.

My technician and I had to go to Vigevano to check on the production molds for the poly soles. It was fog season, and the north of Italy was the home of the densest fog that I had ever seen. At times you could hardly see beyond the hood of your automobile. We were trying to figure out the best route to take. We decided to take the main Autostrada from Florence to Milano and then turn off for a short ride to the plant. All went well and when we were leaving we decided to return on a different route. Hopefully, the road from Vigevano to Genoa and then down the coast would be fog-free. We then could take the new road right to Florence.

I drove from the factory through to Genoa and down to Viareggio, which was near Massarosa, and stopped for gas and a bite to eat. We were fortunate the road was clear and we were only sixty miles from Florence. He wanted to drive and we turned on to the new spur that would bring us home. We were moving along...the road was a series of gallerias and bridges, quite a feat to build, and we were making excellent time for the road was clear. Unbeknownst to us, up ahead there were a series of about twenty accidents. The road dipped down and created an immense fog bank that made it impossible to see three feet. We came out of the galleria and he started to brake as the wall of fog engulfed us. He managed to get the car down to about thirty miles an hour. I was starting to brace myself with my hands on the dashboard. As we braked and slowed, we were hit and the car went up in the air and fell. All I could smell was gasoline and turned to find the technician, his head covered with blood. He had gashed his head, more than likely on the seat belt bolt on the roof. I immediately pulled him across and got both of us out of the car. There was no question that I thought the car was going to be an inferno. I pulled him to the side of the road. I just could not believe that I was unhurt.

Then I heard someone moaning and turned to find someone trapped under the front wheel. His shoulder was pinned there. Another person and I lifted the car and pulled him out. The red Fiat 128 that hit us had been going over 100 mph; they never braked. There were no skid marks and both died upon impact. My technician had a concussion and the ambulance took us both to the local hospital. We were sent to a ward and he was put in bed just the way he was. I couldn't believe it and walked out. My friend, Manny, came to get me.

If you saw pictures of the R080, you would not believe that anyone could survive. We lived because the gas tank was in the middle and the cabin was designed to fold to absorb the shock. The force was so great that it split my metal Samsonite attaché in half. My back was seriously bruised but that was the extent of my injuries. It took about ten days to recover and our work just went on.

Three months later I received an official letter in Italian from an attorney. I read the letter twice; my Italian was not that great but I had tried to read the newspaper daily and looked up words. I gave the letter to Mrs. Vannini and asked her if it said what I thought. "Yes, the person you pulled out from under the car, who had no reason to be out on the road, is suing you because he lost his sense of taste."...end of story. I bought another R080.

Judy was not feeling well and I brought her back to Boston to see her doctors. The prognosis was that she needed complete rest and a return to the medication that cured her, but only for a limited time. It played havoc with me and the kids, who were nervous over their mother's departure. We were extremely fortunate that her recovery was quick and she returned to Florence in six weeks.

We were in a routine; building the lines and watching the production. Phil came over and I showed him the factories and what we were developing. He was excited and asked a million questions. Arnold wanted to keep him under wraps. He didn't want him to know the operation. It was that way from the outset when U. S. Shoe bought Marx & Newman. Phil wanted to expand Marx & Newman and, when we were in the car heading out to the factories, he told me that he just acquired Capezio and wanted to give me the line to design and have Marx & Newman market the brand. I flipped; I wanted the project and Capezio was just the right venue.

Arnold was furious; he actually did not want any additional contact with U. S. Shoe proper and he felt they would get "their tentacles around us". Phil was the boss and his philosophy was to use the Marx & Newman vehicle to expand the business. It was diametrically opposed to Arnold's philosophy. What Arnold did not want was to live under the U.S. Shoe umbrella. It was not to be. He was part of the corporate structure and it was a bitter pill to swallow.

Capezio was mine. It meant that we would be sourcing the brand, not only in Italy but in Spain. Spain had come of age and could price items far better than Italy. Arnold didn't like it because we had to use the U. S. Shoe office in Spain. He didn't have a choice. The line was to be marketed through the Bandolino division sales team who would add a number of sales people where it deemed necessary. Zeichner was in command of the marketing.

We had to re-organize the marketing arm to support the new brand. It was not my area but I was involved. We had a major "pow-wow" in New York...Arnold, myself, Norman and Walter Marx. The outcome was, more or less, the same. The major difference was actually on the development side. Spain had to play a more important role because of the price points that were needed. Zeichner was lobbying for an additional line builder for Spain. Arnold killed it at that time.

There were developments along the way. Bandolino's padded sock sandal program was in a tough position. We had to make a decision in regard to pricing. The product was all leather and we had a priority position in the marketplace. Every major department store carried this program. It was a major decision whether to continue an all leather product or consider a new synthetic lining and sock.

There was new innovative development in the marketplace. A new lining material appeared from Coronet, a Milan-based company, that was breathable and simulated leather better than anything we had seen. I ran trials for wear-ability on the material and it actually stood up better than leather. The material had a nice feel and, naturally, was considerably cheaper than leather. Zeichner was not sure what we should do. I could not blame him for being indecisive. There was a lot riding on the decision.

Our key customer was Nordstrom's and we wanted to get their reaction to the possible change. I suggested we make up a group of sandals with the new lining and show them how they look. Zeichner asked me if I would go to Seattle and present the shoes and give them the technological information on how well the lining performs. The ball was in my court and, although the Nordstrom buyers were not overjoyed with the change, they OK'd the new lining. They wanted the prices to hold and that was the only way possible.

Basic Italian Padded sock Sandals
by Bandolino
1972

We had made the break from all-leather product; actually never to return in any Bandolino product. In the long run, it did not affect the sale of the basic program. What affected it was the style change that was happening.

It is always a difficult decision to change a winning combination. No one wants to get off the successes. The entire salesforce did not want to cut back on this program. They wanted updates and updates which we gave them. At the same time, I brought in new constructions that were part of the answer to the declining sales in our basic program. We were in a transition period and we were not transitioning as we should have been. The new product was never really given the stage that it deserved.

Timing is everything in the fashion business and we just couldn't synchronize the change-over. I cannot blame Zeichner. We had a large inventory of basic sandals and a major markdown would not be in the best interest of the division. We were on tough ground and we were not playing from our strength which made it more difficult to combat. I was feeling the heat, for it's always design that takes the fall. How could it be anybody else's fault? The culprit has been and always will be the designer. That's the way it works in the fashion business.

Arnold had this weird idea that we should be making sandals in Mexico. He had found a factory in Leon that wanted to work with us. They were substantial people and were willing to do whatever it took to duplicate Italian sandals. Arnold loved the idea...no duty into the States. Lead times would be cut by half to two-thirds, transportation would be two to three days or less, instead of two to three weeks. We would only be hours away and in the same time zone. We would import the leather as we did in Italy. The idea was sound except that it was Mexico and it just was not ready to make sophisticated footwear.

Arnold asked me to go with him to check out the factory, etc. We flew from Paris non-stop to Guadalajara and then drove to Leon. Leon was the center of the Mexican shoe industry and, without a question, the asshole of the world. I had not been to India at that time, but it remained a close second. The poverty was beyond belief but what made it even worse was this magnificent cathedral that stood in the center of the city, surrounded by the squalor and dilapidated structures. I don't want to get into that discussion for it was appalling to see this situation.

The Emyco factory which we visited was a modern plant producing well-made basic- styled men and women's footwear. The people were exceptionally nice and very willing. Arnold wanted me to come because of my pattern and shoemaking skills. We had brought lasts and finished sandals for them to copy. Their pattern department had a lot to be desired but we worked together to develop patterns for trials. Actually, we had brought the Amalfi calf to see if they were able to finish it properly.

We spent four days there, making trials and looking at additional factories. The accommodations were atrocious. The best hotel in town was a dump. I was afraid there were bedbugs or lice or whatever I could pick up. The crowning touch came at dinner one night. We ate with the Emyco people most of the time as their guests. One night we ate at "the best" steakhouse in town, just Arnold and I. We ordered steaks and they seemed to be just fine. I proceeded to cut a piece and lifted it to my mouth and, glancing at the plate and saw the biggest cockroach I had ever seen on my plate under the steak. Arnold said he never saw anyone turn green before and I almost heaved.

Arnold decided that he did not want to take the long drive back to Guadalajara and wanted to rent a private plane for the trip. Great idea! It was the second time in my life that I almost died. The one-engine job took off and we were just fine for about ten minutes. Then the thunderstorm hit us and we were thrown up and down like a yoyo and also sideways. I thought it was all over. My hands were welded to the arm rests. I couldn't speak and I was just praying. We had that turbulence for at least thirty minutes; it seemed like eternity. We barely survived. I looked at Arnold and said, "No more bright ideas!" and had to change my underwear.

The project never got off the ground. Mexico was not going to happen. It's only happened for a few people in very casual, crude young footwear.

There was a significant period where we were at peace; sales and product had a truce and we went about our business. Arnold did not like confrontation and found a way to stay out of the issues that cropped up.

Capezio had been developed mainly in Spain. I would go to the U. S. Shoe office in Elda and develop the product. Spain had great soft nappa and kidskin and we built the line around these materials. The office was run by an ex-line builder of Marx & Newman and he was perfectly cast to head the office.

The first show with Capezio was well received and we seemed to be headed in the right direction. The meeting went well; the product looked good and our key accounts wanted to put the line in. I was staying at the Warwick Hotel as I usually did when I came in from Europe for this trip. It was November again; I had bought two new suits and sports jackets for the show. The designer had to look the part. I was in the office the week before the show to open the samples and run the sales meeting. I came back from the office and went to my room, threw my coat on the bed and saw the message light was on. I went to the closet to hang up my coat and jacket, opened the door, and nothing was there. My first thought was, "Did I send everything out to be cleaned?" I could not believe it...everything was gone, even my shirts, socks and underwear. They packed up my suitcase and off they went. The police came and smirked when I asked them about the possibility of getting anything back. Next morning I took the plane to Boston and went to Louis and got a suit and jacket.

I felt I had accomplished quite a bit in my stay at Bandolino. We had made the transition from just a basic padded sock sandal line and created more of a fashion image. There was more order and substance to the business with better quality control and shoemaking. We had learned to compete on a different level than we did in the past. I had learned to live in a different environment than Shapiro Bros. I was far from understanding the political game but I was on my way.

I had replaced Cassi with Ramas, an excellent tailored

factory in Castel Franco. The owners were young and ambitious and we got along very well. It's funny or, should I say ironic, how things develop. Ramas, years earlier, worked for the original Joan & David and Martini Osvaldo brands. Their lines were exceptional and I would venture to say that production from Ramas, as well as others, put many nails in the coffin of the American shoe business. I found the old samples they had hanging around and was thinking back to when I saw these shoes at retail when I was with George. It had come full circle...they were struggling to keep their heads above water. They hoped we would be their saviors for the Joan & David's were long gone. Strange how the world turns.

My technician came to me and gave me his notice. I couldn't believe it and questioned him why he wanted to leave. He was doing a good job, but the problem was he needed constant direction. I didn't mind for if anything went wrong, I was to blame for the quality or the failure in the manufacturing area. He told me he had bought a shoe store in Connecticut and wanted to return to the U. S. "My God...you haven't the foggiest idea on how to run and operate a shoe store. Your whole business life has been in the manufacturing area." Needless to say, he went ahead with the venture. I would miss him; he was a very willing and likable person and was not confrontational in any way. I knew that he had made a terrible mistake but could not talk him out of it. The deed was done.

My Italian was now conversational and I knew the ropes. The factories understood what I wanted and, in most instances, were very receptive. I hired an Italian technician to replace him and things seemed to be going well in the manufacturing area. It was over three years that we had been in Italy and I was starting to have a love/hate relationship with the country and the company. Actually, it wasn't a "hate" part of the relationship but an extremely frustrating one. Things were just difficult almost everywhere. Life was not so pleasant these days. The dollar was weak. There was a gasoline crisis in Italy. You could not travel on Sunday. My life was travel every day to the factories and gasoline was difficult to acquire with long queues everywhere. The "easy life" was gone.

The days were very long for the distances between factories were significant. It was becoming more and more difficult to achieve what you wanted to do. Maybe it was me, but I did not have the same vim and vigor as early on. No question, the country was in tougher shape and competition was fierce.

The kids were turning into Italians. Judy was not happy and I had strayed and made matters worse. I was just in a deep "funk".

The business was just OK but Italy was now more difficult in every way. Bandolino prices were rising and competition was fierce. Brazil was emerging. Zeichner had the ear of Arnold and Walter and wanted to break away Capezio's design and put on a person who had, in my estimation, no design ability. He knew all the right words but did not have the talent. Phil became involved for Arnold had no heart for this type of conflict. In retrospect, he just could not handle confrontation.

I went to New York to get this settled and we had a "knockdown, drag out" meeting. Phil, Zeichner, myself and Alan Jacobson, a stylist Norman wanted. He was working for U. S. Shoe in a division that made "dumb" women's comfort casuals, couldn't draw a straight line and lacked creativity. Zeichner wanted him because he had the same B.S. line that he was proposing, and wanted no part of me.

Well...Phil was being Solomon, at least he tried to be, and kept asking the questions re the business, etc. Finally, I spoke. I denounced Alan as being unfit for this job and laid down an ultimatum. "It's either him or me." And I walked out.

Well...I learned something that day. I used my leverage and won, but it was the beginning of the end at Marx & Newman. Zeichner lost out but what transpired was his zeal to now change the whole situation at Bandolino. He now enlisted everyone to pressure Arnold to make a change. I learned a lot during this period about politics, deceit and jealousy.

It was just a matter of months before the inevitable was near. It was somewhat of an interesting ending. Arnold did not have the guts to fire me. It was a scene right out of a melodrama. Arnold, stumbling around two sheets to the wind (it was after 5 o'clock) couldn't really tell me I was through. I can't remember if it was Howie Glick who told me that we had to make arrangements for a change. Phil got involved immediately. They ganged up on him to go along with the decision. I felt he did not have a choice. He did not want a war or a revolution. Phil came to New York and offered me another position that he had wanted to create for a while; Corporate Vice President of Product Development. It would be back in the States setting up the new post. I could be based in Boston or on the West Coast. It was my choice. The offer made everything much easier to swallow. I guess I was fired in the most peculiar way...let go and rehired to a prestigious corporate post. The whole thing was strange.

I had gone back after Howie told me and beat the living hell out of Arnold verbally for being such a coward. It was in front of the whole Marx & Newman staff and I then turned to Zeichner and said my piece. I regretted it years later and actually apologized to Arnold and made peace with Norman Zeichner.

Well...we had to make arrangements to go home. I have to say Marx & Newman did everything they possibly could to make the move back as easy as possible. We were able to take back the pieces we purchased for our apartment. I sold the automobile; I really didn't want to. Italy is in a class by itself. Somehow or another when we moved to Italy there weren't any official papers registered with the authorities which meant we could not get authorization to send our furniture back to the States. Mrs. Vannini called Salvino Del Bene, Marx & Newman's freight forwarder and he "found a way" to send the container. The kids finished the school year and departed. I stayed on to clean up the pending issues and finish the line. I had made the deal with Phil and was already making plans on how everything would work.

It was official now and the Cincinnati-based divisions knew of the new position. I started to have conversations with the division heads and line builders. It was not going to be a walk in the park working with them. It was natural for them to protect their independence and the question was just how much power I would have. I put a lot of thought on how I would go about working with each division. There would be a considerable amount of politics and at least now I was far more experienced in that game. The main thing was I had a job to come home to. The lease was up on our home and we could move back. The kids would be able to start school in September. The timing of everything was in our favor.

I had gone back to Italy early September to put to bed some last minute projects I felt they needed. I said goodbye to everyone. The factories were not happy with my departure. They did not understand the politics nor did they want to. Most design people had very little knowledge of manufacturing and were totally unaware of factory issues. They did not have that with me.

I started to have second thoughts about the new position. The problem in my mind was that I did not have any direct responsibility over the design teams of each division. They answered to their division head. I could only recommend, which meant, in most cases, the designer or line builder could reject my recommendations simply because they were mine and not theirs. I was concerned that I would be just a figurehead and needed a mandate from Phil to put together a better job description.

That was the situation when I left Italy and was returning to Boston on the Alitalia flight from Rome. I took my seat and sitting next to me was Ted Poland. Ted owned two factories in Maine and Bennett Importing Company. His reputation was legendary. He was a pioneer in Italy making sandals, in India buying huaraches and in Taiwan and China buying items of all kinds. The domestic factories produced low-cost flats and casuals for the chains. Ted's reputation preceded him. I had known him through the trade as an excellent product person with the ability to move quickly when he recognized a trend or an item.

He was no more than 5'6" tall, bald, well built with eyes that would penetrate stone. Ted dressed in the latest fashion and was as smart an individual you could ever meet. He grasped a new trend immediately and recalculated everything on that basis. He reminded me of Ralph Shapiro in many ways. He had that "tingle" in his eyes. Nothing could escape him.

As it was an 8½ hour trip to Boston, we had a lot of time to discuss the shoe world in depth. I told him about Bandolino and that I was leaving to return to the States for the product development position. He started to tell me about his business, mainly Bennett Importing, and his positions in Italy, India and Taiwan. It was amazing and I asked a lot of questions concerning the countries and product. I was excited at what I heard. I showed him some of my sketches and development that I had with me. He knew product and pulled out sketches that he thought were interesting. By the time we landed in Boston, I was President of Bennett Importing. The salary was settled, the BMW was mine and I would start in two weeks after I got settled.

There was a predicament. I had already taken the job at

U. S. Shoe and that was difficult. Rosh Hashanah was early that year and I caught Phil just before the evening of its start. I didn't know how to tell him but he understood and told me I would return and wished me well.

I was free from U. S. Shoe/Marx & Newman. I was back in my element; New England, private label, no politics, right to the point. I felt as if a load had been taken off my back.

The kids were not so happy. They loved Italy and had to reconnect with their friends. Ted had one year of high school left and took the move back much harder. I had to promise to send him back in the summer. Rachel was less of an issue. She was a fantastic athlete and fit in at Newton South High immediately. Judy was a trooper and I believe wanted to come home more than she said. I was looking forward to the change and the adventure that was about to begin. I didn't realize how important this segment of my life was about to become.

A New World

Chapter V

"I will prepare and someday my chance will come."
Abraham Lincoln

Bennett Importing was located in Lynn, MA. This was a shoe town in the 30's, 40's and 50's. At one time there were 100 shoe factories there and now I think there are one or two making slippers. Ted lived on the north shore of Boston and the office was convenient to his home. Newton was a half hour away.

He ran his domestic shoe business out of the same office and his two sales people worked out of there, servicing the major customers, J. C. Penney, Edison and the like. Bennett had a wing of the facility. I had a private office. The rest of the staff were seated in the open area. The building was really a warehouse with a portion fitted for an office.

We had a crackerjack gal, Davina, who was English and had been married to an American which did not work out. She was the glue that kept everything together, bright as well and not shy to speak up. She once told me she wished there was a service where she could order a fuck, just like a pizza. She was my right hand.

Bennett's position to the trade was its ability to have stock; product on the floor to deliver immediately. Poland had made his fortune in this manner. He had made a killing in Italian sandals. He would go to the Florence area and if he liked what he saw would buy 300,000-400,000 pairs. He would purchase out of season to really get the right price. The factories were just sandal plants and had three to four months of low production.

Poland bought during this period.

Poland had a great sense of styling. He was a student of the market. He knew what shoes should cost for he was a manufacturer. He was not afraid to buy if he believed in the product. Ted had gone to China very early, probably one of the first shoe persons. He saw the masses wearing what we call "the Kung Fu one strap", a black cotton fabric unconstructed padded sole ballerina. He recognized it as a volume article for our market. He bought a million pair at 30¢ each. It was a sensation.

I had to learn the ropes. The customers were new to me. Most of the clients I knew through Shapiro Bros. were a grade or two above Bennett. I had a good reputation and when I joined Bennett I received a tremendous vote of confidence from his customer group.

I spent the first two to three months getting to know the business and analyze what my contribution could be. Poland had bought stock. He had really laid in pairs on Taiwan product and some of them were not so great. The work was cut out for us to sell the stock. Needless to say, it was a risky business. Ted had the biggest set of balls I had ever seen. When he was right, it was fantastic. He could get prices that gave him incredible margins. They needed the shoes and we had them. Needless to say, when he was wrong it was not a pretty picture.

His customer base was vastly different than any one I had encountered. They had their hands out for favors of all kinds. Poland knew the game and I let him handle it.

The story goes that Ted and a salesperson went down to New York just before Christmas to pass out the gifts. He had bought ties for the buyers. They took the shuttle down and had a load of ties. Well, somehow or another, when they put them in the overhead, some got lost. Ted almost had a heart attack. It seems there were more than ties in those boxes.

Ted and I spoke the same language. He was mesmerized by my ability to design and produce styles so quickly. I was putting a whole group of sketches together to be sent over to Taiwan to get things started.

Bob Weiss, the sales manager, and I worked fairly well together. He felt he should have gotten the position. What he could not recognize was Ted wanted a creative guy at the head of the company and definitely wanted a product driven company. We made the tour of all the customers together. It was an interesting relationship for most of them only bought what we had in stock. There was a make-up business which we tried to expand. Ted had taught the customers to wait and see what he bought for stock. It all depended on how good the goods were good!

Finally, it was time to make my first trip to Taiwan and Bob Weiss was going to accompany me on the first trip to Taipei and beyond but at the last minute he got sick. Taiwan was not an easy trip. You flew Boston—Chicago—Anchorage—Japan. You missed the flight to Taipei so you slept at the Tokyo airport and got the morning flight arriving around 11:30 am. It took a day and a half. I did it ten times in a year.

Ted had an office in Taichung which was, at the time, over a three hour trip from Taipei. It was in the middle of the island and the shoe center. The office was run by Sunny Tsai with his right-hand man, Oliver Huang. Poland had bought the office from an old-time trader who retired. Sunny and Oliver stayed on. Sunny was a soft-spoken, few words kind of a guy. He was an excellent shoe man and knew the market. Oliver carried out his orders.

We got my bags and headed south. Before I left I sat down with Ted to discuss the programs we wanted to put together. "Ted, we will need to buy product in order to get everything developed. What is the budget? How much money can I spend? There has to be some parameters." "Kid," he called me 'kid', "there is no budget. You just buy the fucking shoes if you think they are right." I almost fell off the chair. He added, "I'll see you in India." It was a round the world trip; Taiwan, then to India and on to Italy.

The trip to Taichung was long and Sunny asked me if I would like to stop along the way to see one of our factories. It was about two hours south of Taipei. The factory made hand-sewn moccasins in synthetic and some in leather. I was not interested in the leather program because they were poor quality and overpriced. The synthetic moccasins were actually produced very well. The workmanship and construction were done extremely well. The rest of the product was a disaster. The last and pattern were wrong and ill-styled. The bottom construction was poorly designed and made.

I had brought a whole array of lasts and bottom constructions with me that I acquired and used in Italy. I pulled a last out of my bag and drew a pattern on the taped last and gave them an additional sketch. I went over the bottom construction and sole. We spent about two hours working on the two ideas. There were two brothers that owned the factory and did not speak English but they understood what I wanted and were very willing to work with us. I pulled out some P.U. (polyurethane) upper material that would work for these models that was in their stock room. Sunny wrote everything out for them. I told the brothers if the samples were right, we would consider buying this product...if the price was right.

We got in the car and proceeded to Taichung. I arrived at the Taichung Grand Hotel early evening after a light meal. The only thing "grand" about the hotel was its name. The bed was as if you were sleeping on bricks. I didn't know what was running around in the room. In the morning I went to breakfast. I ordered eggs and toast. Well, you could call them that. I could see this was the perfect place to lose weight.

Sunny picked me up and we drove to the office which was located in the heart of the city. Sitting in the lobby were the two brothers from the moccasin factory. They had made the samples, working all night. I believe they remade them twice for they were almost perfect. I couldn't believe it. And then I realized this is the place to get it done. No stories, just do it. If this was the work ethic of the Taiwanese, this is where I wanted to be. We proceeded to work with them and I bought 150,000 pairs at $2.30 a pair after a long drawn out negotiation before I left for India. There was no question this was the place. The opportunities here were in a class by itself. I was in my element. I could create and see it develop almost instantly before my eyes. This was shoe heaven and a creator's paradise.

Sunny never saw anyone draw and design as myself. Everyone that came here to work brought original shoes they had bought to copy. I not only sketched the shoes, I drew them on the last for the pattern makers to make the patterns. We had 5-6 factories that we worked with. All of them had sample rooms which we used. The problem was they made samples for other people. Everyone came to the sample room to see how they were progressing and saw what the other importer was doing. We could get knocked off before we saw our sample.

Sunny and I called Ted and told him we were going to build our own sample room in the office where we had total control. He OK'd it in a minute. We were the first company to build their own sample facility. It became the practice within a year for all concerned.

We were in business and started to develop interesting product in P.U. that simulated leather like no one else was able to do. We developed a finish on the P.U. (polyurethane) that gave it a burnished look as the Italian and Brazilian product. It was a real breakthrough. When I showed Ted the samples in India, he could not believe how great they looked.

I wanted to develop our whole line on this basis. I was in the office about ten to twelve days from 8:00 am to midnight, and had built a total collection. The sample room was being set up. I had met the manufacturers that were making for Bennett and gave them the party line for what plans we had and the future. Sunny was the perfect fit for me. He was a great product developer and made my life easy. He had a style sense which very few Chinese had. Besides that, he was a wonderful person. There was no question that I would be spending a lot of time here to get the job done. The core of manufacturers that made production for Bennett bought into the whole program when they saw my development and ability to create. They knew Poland would buy great product. They were onboard but there were huge problems to overcome. The component industry was not developed. Last-making was light years behind the rest of the world. They cast their lasts in metal instead of turning them on lathes in plastic for precision and quality. The components were made poorly and needed a whole new approach. In the last factory there were piles of sawdust surrounding the model maker. We were trying to make the wooden models and the humidity was 100%, sweat pouring down with the temperature in the 90's. Not only were we in pools of sweat but the wood model was now filled with humidity and would swell, changing the measurement drastically.

Sometimes the problems got to you. I remember standing in the so-called last factory area trying to make a fitting last. I just threw up my hands and said, "What the hell am I doing here!"

There were adventures. Poland was making crepe sole production in his domestic factories and Bennett was working on a whole set of new development with crepe-wrapped wedges and soles. Ted asked me if I would go to Malaysia from Taiwan and see if we could buy the crepe directly from the producers who had harvested the product and had a processing plant there. We would save approximately 25-30¢ per pair if it worked out. At the same time I was going to look at an Italian company that set up a factory in Malaysia, all in the same city.

It was probably one of the most interesting trips of my life. I arrived with the help of the crepe company and went to the hotel which was located in the jungle. The hotel was built on stilts so the wild animals and snakes could not get at you. The rooms were beautiful with every convenience. The entrance/

stairs to the hotel were drawn up every night.

They asked me if I wanted to take a tour of the plantation and I put on knee-high rubber boots and went to see the rubber trees tapped. It was amazing for it was very hard work and dangerous. I went to the processing plant and saw how the liquid rubber was made into crepe sheets. The majority of their production went to the auto industry, naturally tires. We were able to make an agreement and could buy the product direct and reduce the cost of the soles significantly. I saw the shoe factory. The product was just fair and the pricing was way out of line. I passed.

My thinking tended toward building a branded division. I felt we had an unbelievable opportunity to make great P.U. product that would retail at great price points with a significant gross margin to the retailer; to a whole new group of customers that Ted did not have. It was back to the branded game. I could see the product in every major department store at opening fashion price points. The product had to be, in my terms, semi-directional, tending to be more junior than basic. It was a cross between Bandolino and Capezio. I gave Ted a full presentation for I had made up a whole series of what the line would represent.

Ted loved the ideas and gave me the go-ahead to work out a total line. The beauty of the development was we could use it for branded and private label. I learned the principle early that if the branded line performed, the private label business that mimicked the brand would go through the roof. I took a whole set of prototypes with me to India where I would meet Ted.

I flew Taiwan—Hong Kong—Bombay...now Mumbai. All the flights leaving and arriving India came in around the same time, 2:00 am. Ted was there (he had come from the States) much to my surprise along with Malik, our agent, to greet me. India was an issue from the beginning. Immigration and customs were impossible. It took me over an hour to pass through. The ride in Malik's car to the hotel was an experience I will never forget. There had to be literally thousands sleeping on the sidewalks. It was that way almost all the way to the hotel.

We stayed at the Taj, the finest hotel in India. The contrast between the hotel and stepping out the door was almost impossible to explain; luxury to the abject depths of poverty. Malik met us for breakfast in the morning. He was a Hindu, sophisticated, tall, very bright and spoke English better than I. His family was originally from Pakistan when it was still India. When India became independent and was divided into Pakistan, Bangladesh and India, Malik's family came to India. I made the mistake of giving a beggar a coin when I went out of the hotel. I was surrounded by a throng of children screaming for the same. It was frightening.

Poland had done a significant business here and the Malik's had done an admirable job developing and producing the product. They had strength and financial power and Ted was more than willing to fund them. The story goes that when Ted first came three years earlier, he found them by accident, funded them, and made product that was a major win. He took the original Indian toe sandal, modified it and sold just over two million pairs over the three year period. He put the Malik's on the map and millions in his coffers.

India had labor and leather. Most people did not realize that India produced leather in huge quantities of calf, sheep and goat. The Muslims were the driving force in the leather industry, which was centered in Madras (now Chenai) and in the north of India in Kanpur. The Indian shoe industry was centered in different areas of the country. Bombay (Mumbai) made the majority of the sandals. Agra, where the Taj Mahal is located, made closed shoes. Madras made better footwear and, as I said, was the center of the leather industry. Kanpur and Calcutta made shoes and sandals and were the center of the heavy leather (calf) industry. It was not easy doing business there simply because the distances between shoe centers were very significant.

The infrastructure was a total disaster. India drives on the left as the British, but everyone drives in the middle of the road because the roads are terrible. So...it becomes a game of "dodge-ems".

Malik had his offices and factories in two locations, Bombay and Kanpur. The development and sandals were in Bombay. Malik had a brother who lived and ran the closed shoe and boot factory in Kanpur. We went to the Bombay factory and started working on a new program, huaraches. This was a flat sandal type with vegetable tanned leather, raw edges, and strapping that was a classic look in footwear for many years. It was the perfect article for India. It was woven strips which required hand labor as the principal labor cost...perfect for India. The product did not need to be machine lasted. The inner soles were slotted and the uppers were pulled through with a last on the inner sole just to adjust the straps. The soles then went on and they were ready for shipment with a cleaning and quality control check. They were slightly burnished to bring out the antiquing which was indigenous to the vegetable leather. In quantities we could buy them for $2.28.

The response was overwhelming. We flew the first hundred cases and they evaporated at retail. Within six months the demand was unbelievable. The problem was to send them by ocean took six to eight weeks. It was close to nine weeks to get the merchandise. Ted leased two 747's and we flew 88,000 pairs on each flight and delivered the product. We sold them, depending on the quantity and customer, $10.00 to $12.00 per pair. The sandals landed at $4.65 by air. We put in huge orders to be sent by sea, landing under $3.00. I lost track of how many we bought, but it was over a million pairs over a period of a year. Malik made a fortune. We owned the Indian market and were ready to develop the next thing.

On that first trip I went to Kanpur with Malik to visit the closed shoe factories. Ted stayed in Bombay. The city had eight million people and was a cesspool in every sense of the word. I had the "pleasure" of coming back more than twenty years later and I could swear it was the same or worse. The story was the factory owners did not want improvements. They wanted to keep the people and city locked into low cost manufacturing facilities. The poverty was beyond anything I had ever seen. It actually frightened me to see people living in this manner burning cow dung for fuel, defecating on the roadside, just appalling. The factory was making some closed shoes that were designed and made poorly. It needed a lot of work and different management.

We had to stay over for you took your life in your hands to drive at night and the last plane had already gone. There wasn't a hotel that we could stay in, they were unreal. Malik had made arrangements for us to stay at an ex-British club that was run by a local businessman. My room was small with a wash basin and what you could possibly call a shower. The bed was a whole story between the straw mattress and the bedbugs. I ended up sleeping in the rocking chair and having a banana and bottled Coca Cola for dinner.

The trip was an eye opener. India was a double-edge sword. It could kill you if you were a novice and destroy you if you did not know how to work with your agent and factory. I went back to Bombay and put together a program of samples with Malik's son who was very capable. Ted and I then went to Italy. It was, in a sense, like coming home. We landed in Rome and I drove to Florence. We stayed at the Excelsior and Ted's agent, Piero, picked us up the next morning. I believe I stayed in the shower for twenty minutes trying to scrub India off my body.

Ted's Italian business had dropped off dramatically. Italian sandal prices were over 30% more than when Ted was able to buy quantities. It was a different ballgame now and, for all intent and purposes, Ted was out of business in Italy.

I talked Ted into hiring an Italian technician on a part-time basis who had worked for me. He could put together a program that could generate some business and pay for himself. If we were to stay in Italy we needed someone of this caliber.

Piero was just an administrator.

It coincided with Linea Pelle, the leather and component show which drew worldwide participation. Poland, myself and Roberto worked the component show together and, as always, there were interesting items. We stopped at a unit sole supplier and thought the product line was terrific. We went down the aisle, Roberto says to me, "I took the sample of the unit." I said, "What?" Mr. Poland asked me to take it. "You take that unit and you return it right now!" Ted could be a rogue, a lovable one, but a rogue.

His stock position method could not be put into effect; he was priced out of the market for Italian shoes. Piero had been his agent from the beginning and had done a fantastic job. They had both made fortunes, but it was over. Ted kept looking for a deal with his old factories from Sagrominio. The closed shoes were just too expensive. We shopped Florence and bought a couple of shoes that would work for his domestic set-up. I made up a group of sketches for his domestic production. My emphasis now was on building a branded program on our products from Taiwan.

Ted had bought into the project and I was psyched. We were expanding our sales force, looking for another powerful private label sales person. We started to interview candidates. One of the guys that came in was supposed to be a real hitter. We talked for a while and he listed all the perks and benefits and salary that he expected. When he finished, I said, "Jake, that's a great list. Listen, when you find a job like that, will you call me, I'm interested!" We finally found one who was not a prince.

My job really turned into being totally involved with product development, manufacturing and merchandising the line. I left the selling to the three sales people. I really only sold one customer, Edison Bros., mainly because of my relationships. Sam Demoff was gone along with that whole way of doing business. But I still had the reputation and was able to do significant business.

In one year I made ten trips to Taiwan. I was there once a month, staying at least ten days. I went in the back of the bus, at least then the flights were not nearly full and two to three seats were generally available. Needless to say, it was grueling.

My old Marx & Newman technician re-appeared. He called me at home one night almost crying for he had bought this shoe store and the owner misrepresented the inventory, etc. He begged me to help him. I went to Connecticut to see the store and found a way for him to nullify the deal and get his money back...most of it. I proceeded to hire him on a freelance basis to go to Taiwan and work on the last-making and patterns. I had saved his ass with the store and got him a job.

Poland had this crazy thing about factories. Either he went overboard in their favor or just was unreasonable. We had an excellent espadrille source for the chains. In order to avoid the duty, fabric uppers, we had to weight the wedges to conform to the 10% duty instead of 37.5%. The factory had trouble weighting the wedges causing production problems. The espadrilles were $2.30 and we had sold them at great margins. We had purchased 50—60,000 pairs with backups. They were late on some of the initial orders, about 5—7,000 pairs. Poland sent a telex saying he wanted the entire production flown. Well, the cost based on weight and size would have cost over $5.00 per pair. The factory was up in arms. Poland insisted. Finally, Sunny and I called Poland at 2:00 am our time to plead the factory's case. There were many a night we worked that late. He agreed to 5,000 pairs flown. I later found out that the delivery to the customers had changed and there was no need to penalize the factory.

When we had to price the line, it was a marathon affair. We would call each factory in, one at a time, and go through the process. Dealing with the Chinese was a totally different situation than negotiating with the Italians. You could not bullshit a Taiwanese. It was impossible...these guys were super realists. The only way you could win is with orders or if they felt they couldn't live without the business. Pricing was always the last days of the trip and we would schedule the sessions into the night with the last factory around 2:00—3:00 am. I once negotiated over two hours over 15¢ with George Wong, our major factory Well Lead group. George would mimic Poland...100,000 pairs! Pulling teeth was easier. It was usually right from the negotiating table directly to the airport. Sunny would drive me and I would sleep. It was wild, but I loved it!

That summer Ted Finn was out of high school and actually working in the Bennett warehouse. He came to me one day during his lunch break and asked why some of the warehouse people were throwing some of the old stock shoes into the water. There had been a pipe that broke and flooded a small portion of the warehouse. It was a difficult conversation. I tried to get around it and decided to tell him the truth. Poland had a different set of values.

I had to go to Taiwan and I decided to take him with me. We had not spent a lot of time together and he was going off to college in the fall. I knew we needed the time together. It was a great trip. He was a flaming redhead with a fantastic Afro. Standing just about six feet, he certainly stood out in a crowd, especially in Taiwan. The Chinese never saw anyone coiffured in that manner. They wanted to touch his hair...he was a celebrity wherever he went. He understood what I was doing and how demanding the workload could be. I took him to Hong Kong for a weekend. It was only a ninety minute flight from Taipei and my first trip also. We stayed on Hong Kong Island at the Mandarin Hotel first class. We took in the whole island from the Peak to Stanley's Market. Both of us were tourists and it was a ball.

I do not know how Judy put up with me. The time in Taiwan was endless, ten days to two weeks a month. The problem was when I came home I was exhausted and it took me close to a week to recover. The flights were a killer for the non-stops of today did not exist. When I think back, I can't believe I was able to do it.

The workday in Taiwan was not long, it was almost ridiculous. Before the sample room was up and running, we used to work all day and go to the sample rooms after dinner and work out the issues, sometimes into the morning. It was not a problem for me. The hotel was a disaster and if I came back totally exhausted I didn't mind sleeping on the cement slab of a mattress with my little companions running around.

While all of this was going on, Phil started calling me, wanting me to return to the company. He was willing to put a real program together where I would have authority over the design departments in each division. He wanted me to set up a whole division for special projects. It was a totally different job than what he had offered me before. He was willing to reinstate my pension plan even though I had left the company. The salary was raised. I would have the option of setting up shop wherever I wanted.

Ted Poland and I never had a bad word between us. He admired my talent and I thought he had great vision, talent, strength, and was a risk-taker like I have never seen. But he also could be cruel and he used to beat up on the old time salesman, Frank. One day he was thrashing him in front of my office and

I just had it. I stepped out and yelled at Frank, "Don't let him talk to you that way. It's not right and tell him he's a bully." The whole office was quiet. Poland turned to me and gave me a look and walked away. He never did it again.

Davina was my right arm. She kept me in touch with everything that was going on in sales and the office. She did the telex every day, which was a job in itself. Poland had a habit of going over the telexes going out and, if he did not like something, he would change it or cut it out. He only changed one of my directions once and I went to his office and said that's not an issue but please tell me.

I was interviewed by Footwear News about our project in Taiwan. It was a full page article and Poland loved it. The article centered on our project to make better product in Taiwan and build a brand. We were the pioneers.

I was really fighting to put this branded program together. I went to Ted with a game plan. This was a major investment... salesmen, advertising, additional office staff. The concept for this type of program was totally different than Ted's existing business. The problem was this was not Marx & Newman or U. S. Shoe where you had a vast infrastructure to take the burden off you for all the incidental things so you could spend your time on line building and design.

I could see that the project interested him. At the same time, Ted had the type of personality that wanted instant gratification. He was not happy with long-range projects and investments that did not turn profitable quickly. I could see we were not on the same page. It was more than a year that we were together and I could see we were coming from different vantage points.

The trips to Taiwan and India were murder. If you cut them back you could not expect to achieve the same goals. I had developed a great rapport with the factories and Sunny. Something had to give. I was not being compensated enough for the work I was producing.

I decided the U. S. Shoe deal was right for me. I knew if I continued this pace my marriage would fail and I would lose contact with my children. Ted was not going to fund a branded project. I finally realized it was not in his DNA.

It was over a year that we were together. I felt terrible for I admired Ted immensely. I finally sat down with him and explained my situation. He was not happy. I gave him significant notice and was willing to go back to Taiwan and build next season's line so there would be a smooth transition for the incoming person. He agreed, but sent Bob Weiss with me to "oversee" that everything went smoothly. I thought it was a low blow but I just chalked it up to experience. All went well until we had to settle up the last few days. It cost me $25,000 and it hurt. I had done an excellent job for Bennett and was the major reason why the Taiwan operation became successful. I left giving him a head start for next season and he, more or less, gave me a fucking...there was no need for it, but that was the other half of Ted Poland, no quarter.

In retrospect, Poland gave me the opportunity to earn a Ph.D. I had majored in Taiwan and India and the thesis I was able to put together brought me great rewards. I had gained a Masters from Italy and the combination of the "two degrees" gave me a level of expertise few had in this industry. They paved the way for me to build a business for U. S. Shoe and eventually for myself. There's no question the opportunity Poland gave allowed me to broaden my horizon beyond anything I dreamed. I now had the experience level to move forward with confidence and a knowledge few people had in our shoe world.

Moving Forward

Chapter VI

"The most important thing is this; to sacrifice what you know for what you can become tomorrow."

Shannon L. Adler

I was back at U. S. Shoe. In a way, I never left. It was only fifteen months that I was gone. Phil gave me the world; a great salary, lots of stock options, an incentive to be worked out. I outlined the rest earlier. I decided to stay in Boston, both of our parents were old and needed our help, especially Judy's. So we set up the office in Boston.

U. S. Shoe owned Casual Corner and a store in our vicinity had a whole level they were not using. We started there. We refurbished the entire area and started to get the operation rolling. Phil took on a new President of the corporation, Stan Rutstein. He had come from Casual Corner and we seemed to hit it off from our very first meeting. He was a hands-on type and was not the political animal that seemed to be the norm at the company. Phil had picked the right guy. He was young and grew up in the garment business or, as we say, he was a "garmento"; no B.S., no drama, right to the point. Stan knew the Orient. Casual Corner's involvement was massive using agents and branded companies who resourced through Asia. When Stan heard of my experience level in Taiwan he was very open to the idea of setting up an office there for all of Asia. China was not open and Taiwan was the alternative.

As head of product development, I had all the design staffs reporting to me. Even though I had the authority to step in, I had to bite my tongue in many instances. The interplay with division heads and their designers was very political. You had to walk softly and carry a big stick. I had won over some of the divisions. The problem was that most of so-called designers were not designers. They were stylists or line builders. They had a good sense of style, studied the market and could take a piece of this and that and put it together. They had to see it; they could not create it.

The same issues always came up with the divisions that had this type of designer or product staff. They felt threatened when anyone with real creative talent came in to look at their line-ups. You just couldn't throw away their work. Compromise was the name of the game. You had to give them their due. It was not an easy chore to work with those who were protective of what they brought to the table. You would hear some rumblings along the way through Phil and Stan. I soon realized that you could not win them all and took a more philosophical approach to the whole process.

I hired Davina away from Bennett. She was unhappy there and we were able to pay her what she was worth. Poland had a German technician who worked for his domestic facilities whom I had known for quite some time and needed. He was a master pattern maker, last maker and quality control person. Herbert Hirsch and I set up an interview at my house. The time came and went and finally Herb showed up. His shirt and jacket were dirty, his car had broken down, and he finally got it going. He was completely flustered and was having a hard time getting his English out. I quickly started speaking German which startled him but put him at ease. Languages were easy for me. I had taken German in college and spoke Yiddish.

Herb had left Germany after finishing his apprenticeship and went to South Africa where he worked for ten years. He met his wife there and they immigrated to the U. S. He was sponsored originally by U. S. Shoe. Hans Bartnik was head of all technical personnel. His whole organization was manned by German technicians. Herb was only there a short time when he had other offers and left. He ended up working for Poland. We connected there for I had met him earlier in his career. He was a character; extremely funny, especially with his German accent. It was the start of a great working relationship and friendship to this day. We once figured out that we had worked overseas together an incredible amount of time.

Stan Rutstein was persistent about getting started in Asia. I knew it was the right move for the corporation. I also knew that it was the right move for me. I could see U. S. Shoe's domestic factory base eroding much quicker than they thought. It was an opportunity to stake out a major role in the company. The product development office and its duties were working, maybe not to the extent I would have liked, but it was unrealistic to think that each division was willing to totally give up their authority in the design area. They listened, they took suggestions, and they were respectful. But there was a limit to what they were willing to do. The answer was to be the manufacturer and developer for these divisions.

Phil was definitely on board with the Asian project. The seeds were planted and we started to put together a serious game plan. As head of product development, I was approached by Morse Shoe Co., a major discount retailer in the Northeast. They were looking for us to develop a children's casual brand for them. They had a major office in Taiwan that serviced their stores. They also developed a wholesale division, Morse International, a company selling to other retailers. They wanted us to work out this project and I got clearance from Stan to go ahead. One of the reasons they knocked on our door was I had a relationship with management. I had worked for Morse from age 15 through high school and college. During this time I knew many of the buyers and retail people who eventually became top management. I remember Poland saying to me, "Kid...always be nice to the assistant buyer."

We did the whole children's design project and the program was very successful. When it came time to make my exploratory trip to Taiwan, I went to their office to see their operation. At the same time, I tried to lure Sunny away from Bennett. He wanted to but would not go back on his promise to the original owner who sold to Poland. He asked Sunny to stay the course. He was that type of guy. Years later he told me his decision to stay was a mistake for he saw what we developed in Taiwan. However, I was able to take his second in command, Oliver Huang, who was also a good product guy. I had no regrets taking these people after the way Poland treated me in the money department. I admired Ted for all that he did. I couldn't believe that he would do that to me. It was a great lesson.

The real issue was getting someone to run the Taiwan office. The big disappointment was not being able to convince Sunny to jump ship. We needed someone that I could trust and had the ability, especially in the product development area, for that was the key. Administrators I could find. Shoe people with experience were tough, almost an impossibility.

My technician from Bandolino was a candidate. He was very organized and was willing to go to Taiwan with his family. I believed I could trust him. I knew his strengths and weaknesses, which to me was the reason for his selection. He needed programming and I felt that was the best way to go forward. It was Swiss/German mentality that worked best in the third world. They seemed to adjust and find a way to not only survive but to flourish.

While all of this building was going on, Phil came to me with a huge problem. He had a major dilemma with the Joyce division. Andy Robbins, the division President, had an affair with the line builder and everything fell apart with Andy's wife, etc. The division did not have a product person nor a president. Phil asked me to try to put it together and find the replacements. I had the Taiwan situation in play and now this. The building of the line was not an issue. I was able to put it together in ten days. The problem was political. The sales manager was the choice for the new presidency. He was just impossible, a real political product of the company. It was always necessary to count your fingers when you shook hands with him. I found the replacement for the line builder who came from the retail division. The line was received extremely well. Phil was ecstatic. I took my eye off the ball, which could not be helped, but I picked up a lot of points with Phil by getting him out of a tough situation.

My technician and I went on the first trip. Our purpose was to see where we would open an office, how we would handle the factories and put together a game plan. My first task was to decide where we would set up shop. The natural place was Taichung where Bennett had their facility and the immediate shoe world. There was only one major problem. Taichung was a wasteland. A westerner would have a difficult time making it there.

He had a wife and family. His kids were around eight and twelve years old and needed a school and an environment that would make them happy. We decided the office would be in Taipei. There was an American school and an American Club for expats. The whole surroundings were totally different than Taichung. There was an entire area that was populated by international families that worked and lived on the island. Housing was not an issue. Everything could be worked out.

We set up shop temporarily at the Grand Hotel built by Chiang Kai-shek and was the premier hotel in Taipei. Oliver Huang was now with us and became my right-hand man. Both Oliver and I were very familiar with Taichung but Taipei was a different story and we proceeded very carefully.

Taipei also had a considerable number of shoe factories and a vast number of small artisan types that made product for the domestic market. I started to feel a lot better about our choice of Taipei. Not only were the accommodations better, but Taipei's hotels were at least three stars or better. There were a lot of issues to address but first we had to find the office.

The three of us went over to see the Morse office and speak with their Western manager, Phil Karahalis. Morse had a big business in Taiwan. They had close to 800 stores and a wholesale business. Their buying power was formidable. Their facility was located very central to the hotels and within easy commuting distance to the residential area and highway. They were in the Olympic Commercial Building. It was easy to get there. All you had to say was "Cha Cha Bowling" which was directly across the street. It was a huge building and Morse was on the fourth floor, an unlucky number for the Chinese which meant a cheaper property to rent. They had half the floor. The other half was empty.

Phil Karahalis was very cordial and showed us his operation. He did not have his own sample room. All his samples were made in the factories. I asked him about the space across the hall and he was very non-committal. All he said was that it was vacant and I asked if the landlord was on the premises for we wanted to see the space. One hour later we were signing a lease. The space was perfect. It was about the same size as Morse facing southeast so we had the morning light. Karahalis was pissed. He wanted that space for he had expansion plans. We made arrangements to have the office completely redone. We worked on the plan and in less than two months we were ready to move in.

We bought a car, an old Cadillac which was owned by the government. It had dark windows and official flags mounted on the fenders. Jimmy, the driver, came with the deal. When the office was completed, I remember standing by the doorway and saying to myself, "God...it's big...will we ever fill it?" Within a year and a half we outgrew it. Part of the office was partitioned off for a small sample room. We did not know our needs.

Oliver, who came with me from Bennett, was indispensable in helping us get things moving. He had a good working knowledge of the factories and a good product sense. He was able to show us "the shortcuts" in getting the office functioning.

The next step was building a factory base. My whole theory was to develop better product, mostly leather, using the labor cost of Taiwan and to end up with very competitive price points. The ultimate goal was building product for the U. S.

divisions. They were going to need it down the road. The pricing in Italy and Spain was starting to be affected by Brazil. Taiwan would be emerging.

Taiwan was now ready for a leather project under the flag of U. S. Shoe. Unlike with Poland, we had the commitment from management and the resources, especially from Italy, to make it happen. We used them. All my IOU's were called in with the factories and component people to get us off the ground. Without the Italian connection I do not believe it would have happened. The learning curve that I lived through in Italy served as the basis for us getting off the ground properly. The money didn't hurt for U. S. Shoe had deep pockets. The first year we were a losing proposition, but not for long, making 30,000 pairs per day (six and a half days a week) after the first year.

The economic situation in Taiwan was superb. The island was loaded with business from shoes to apparel to housewares. The economy was booming. The shoe production was enormous, almost entirely discount-oriented. The manufacturers were programmed along these lines. We had to find the factories that had the vision and mentality to make better footwear. At the same time, we had to put ourselves on the map. We needed an item to get us started.

It's strange how things develop. I was working at the drawing board on a group of casuals that could be produced at great price points. When you sketch, sometimes the pencil takes over and you do themes you never planned. They just happen. The theme developed and out came a whole new category, it's what I called the "sandal sneaker" open toe, open back. I did a whole group of sketches. I colored them. They excited me and I picked up the phone and called Taiwan. "I'm sending you six sketches. I'll draw them to scale with measurements. They will go to you tomorrow. I want them done ASAP. We have the factory in Taichung that can make this product. Do not fuck it up! When they are done, I'm coming over." This was before faxes so they went by what we called SpeedPost.

They were done vulcanized as a sneaker. Eight days later Taiwan called and told me the trials were finished. We made the corrections and they would be ready when I would arrive. The factory was owned by a Taiwanese gentleman who was not only wealthy as a shoemaker but he owned land, a lot of it. I had an excellent relationship with him when I was with Poland. Oliver knew him and his son very well. I bring this out now for he was inundated with better priced propositions to make our product when it exploded at retail. He honored our orders.

We made the samples and the rest is history. I immediately applied for a patent on the construction. The first production was just by chance shipped to Nordstrom's two months later. I was sitting in Newton, MA about to have dinner with the family. Norman Saddis, the lead buyer, was on the line. I started to sweat. He told me he received the sneakers. All I could think of was bad quality, the packing was wrong. My thoughts were not positive. Norman, who was a friend, said, "You know those lousy sandal sneakers you shipped us...well you have a problem." I was waiting for the guillotine to fall. "It's a big problem...we sold out the first day!" We were on the map.

The factory geared up and we started making 5-6,000 pairs per day, seven days a week; just two Sundays off a month. The construction sold over 2 million pairs and our customer base exploded.

All these sales were done on a private label basis. We sold the shoes on a landed basis and made over a 42% markup. We needed this win for the Cincinnati based divisions were, without a question, not interested in Taiwan product. The success of this program was the start of a massive private label program to the better discounters. We were the talk of the industry.

When I made my deal with Phil I worked out an incentive program on all unbranded sales. No one, even myself, thought that anyone could generate that dollar volume. I actually sold 90% myself to five to six major users. It created an unbelievable amount of jealousy with the executive staff. Phil was happy for me.

Things changed quickly. Cobbie Cuddlers was developed as a competitor to the Mushrooms brand that was the forerunner of the comfort business. Europe and South America could not price the footwear. All the brands, including ours, were working on this program. The whole concept was based on urethane soles that had now come of age. We knew what had to be done. We had lived through the development in Italy once and were now ready to compete vs the U.S. domestic factories. We were able to deliver the right technology to the program, buying the right machines and mixture from Italy and Japan. Our organization was more adept, more creative, better priced in developing the program.

There was one major problem. We were now involved with a struggle between Taiwan-made and domestic production. It was war and they held all the advantages. They finally agreed to buy Taiwan product for they had no choice. The Red Cross division, who had the Cobbie Cuddler label, wanted all the patterns for production OK'd by the domestic product development group. I had to give in on that point and I knew it would create havoc.

Management knew that eventually they had to buy the Taiwan product. What management allowed to happen was almost disgraceful. The technical department for the domestic production wanted to protect their positions for they knew if Taiwan succeeded, they would lose out...probably their employment. They put into effect a set of standards that were far beyond those of the domestic production for Taiwan. They held our feet to the fire at every turn, over every issue, problem, and millimeter. Management was either blind to it or just turned their heads to not see the issues. We would have lost the war if we did not decide to change the rules and play by our own.

What transpired over the next few months was a story for the ages or the record books. We had worked with the line builders at Red Cross. I had developed a whole series of new and interesting constructions that were viable for this comfort line. The line builder came over and was excited with the collection and lined up an extensive program. The product line we developed was part of a whole grouping that was merged with the domestic development.

What emerged was fantastic sales on the Taiwan product and generally good sales on the domestic program. We had initial projections that were serious quantities. Everyone was pleased for we felt if this program was successful it would open up huge orders from the Red Cross division and the other brands of the company. We felt very comfortable making this type of product for it fit the ability of the factory and played to its strength.

When we developed the product line we took a different approach. This was a comfort line and, as far as we were concerned, there should be slightly more measurement in the last to secure the comfort factor. Mushrooms had made their mark by going overboard on softness and measurement which, in time, was a major screw-up in the making process for a variety of reasons.

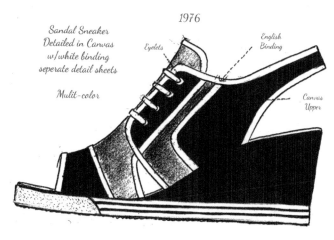

We proceeded with the pattern trials getting them ready to send to Cincinnati for confirmation. What happened next was quite unusual. The urethane soles came in from the maker. They were packed in urethane bags to protect them from damage. They had just been finished and immediately put into these bags. The odor from the finish drying was trapped in the bag. The soles were taken out of the bags and within minutes cemented on to the uppers. The whole process was accomplished quickly and then packed without time to stand on the conveyor as they would in production diminishing the fumes in the air. I was not there to see the trials but I had given explicit instructions they had to be perfect and shipped on time.

The trials arrived in Cincinnati and their product development team put them on their fit models. The shoes were fine on the foot. They had four sizes they tested and all the women thought they fit reasonably well. There were comments from the technicians. When they OK'd a pattern, they always had an "out" in case something went wrong. The comments would be written up as follows.

Sandal Sneaker
Detailed in Canvas
w/white boning
1976

The shoes fit reasonably well and had the following additional comments which went on about every detail that could possibly go wrong. They knew how to cover their asses. Then, one of the technicians picked up one of the trials and started to smell the soles. There was a scent coming from the sole. He and his group started smelling all the trials. They then started the fiasco. They sent the soles over to our chemical division that sold cements, etc. to the shoe trade. The results came back with a full explanation of what chemicals were involved in the sole. They read the list and saw there was a chemical called Cyclohexenone among the five to ten others. They looked it up in the chemical lexicon and it was classified as a poison.

It created a panic and then it spread. They were throwing

their guns in the snow and retreating. It was beyond reason. When I heard what happened, which didn't take five minutes from the discovery, I called my doctor friend at Harvard Medical School. I told him the story and he started to laugh. Cyclohexenone is classified as a poison if you drank a gallon or if you were locked in a room for a day and they kept pouring the fumes through the vent, you might have a stomach ache.

It turned into a witch hunt. Domestic product development was savoring the opportunity to put nails in our coffin. The Red Cross product development was afraid that Taiwan was going to put them out of business. They withstood the onslaught of Italy and Spain and survived. Taiwan was a different story. It attacked the heart of their production and was winning. They loathed our independence being based in Boston, free from all the bullshit and intrigue of the corporate offices. Lastly, it was jealousy directed at me for being the father of this Taiwan venture and my good fortune.

My report from Harvard Medical was not good enough for Cincinnati. They told me to stop production. They sent a team of two U. S. technicians in their chemical department over to Taiwan with hypodermic needles to test the soles. It had reached a level of lunacy beyond belief.

The Closed High Heel Sneaker
1976

We had already stitched over 40,000 pairs of uppers and a tremendous amount of soles completed. Meanwhile, back at the ranch, Cincinnati, we had a meeting on the whole situation. The brass were there; Phil, Stan, the Red Cross division president, Harry Robinson, the line builder, the domestic product people who "found" the issue and myself and Herbert. He and I were in Cincinnati for the meeting and to work with the quality control people. We were in the midst of showing them for the tenth time why this occurred and tried to be diplomatic about the whole situation. Suddenly, the head technician got up and pointed to his watch. It was 5:00 pm. "Well guys, that's it. Mama's got supper on the stove." They all left. Herbert and I looked at one another and the same words came out of our mouths, "There's no hope." We repeated it in German!

We presented our case. The Red Cross line builder picked up one of the sandals and started smelling the sole, I smell it...I smell it." The two chemical technicians finally gave their findings and agreed there was no reason to destroy the soles. They recommended not trapping the finished soles in plastic. We then showed them that when they sat on the conveyor for the required length of time you could detect no odor.

I never stopped production for it would have destroyed our reputation in Taiwan. The whole island knew about the problem. They wanted to see the outcome. It was a tremendous gamble but we had no choice. If we screwed up the production, either way we were dead. Cincinnati couldn't figure out how we delivered the production so quickly. It saved their ass. The end results were truly fitting.

The domestic factories were making part of the Cuddler program. They had a different philosophy on last-making. They preferred length rather than width. This worked reasonably well on closed footwear. They used the same principle on the comfort sandal package. It was a mistake. When their styles hit retail they had tremendous returns because of fit. Their sandals were not wide enough.

One of the styles we were producing, the "Twirler", carried the whole Cobbie Cuddler program and sold 800,000 pairs. Our technology and concepts were never challenged... until the next time! The war was not over even with such a decisive victory. We were now a factor with the divisions. Red Cross/Cobbie Cuddlers was now almost totally designed and made in Taiwan. The programs became the major part of the division's business. Our ability to produce polyurethane soles as well as Europe made us the key source. They couldn't do it domestically at anywhere near our pricing and quality.

The Taiwan experience was a true test of one's ability. There was nothing available. Everything had to be built. Everything had to be developed from scratch. There was a tremendous problem with mentality. They were penny wise and pound foolish. Terrible mistakes were made in the manufacturing process because someone tried to save three cents on an adhesive or a few pennies on a backing material. Every phase of the process had to be specified, developed and quality-controlled. Nothing could be left to chance. We were dealing with people who did not know how to make shoes. They didn't speak English. The problems were at times almost unsurmountable. Some of the manufacturers worked with you to conquer the problems while others kept trying to beat you for the extra dime. I had never worked in an environment such as this. It demanded total dedication from morning until midnight, seven days a week.

When you were not fighting to make the product right or designing it, you were at war with Cincinnati. There were wins and then there were losses and you started all over again. It was like having a set of building blocks. You put up more than half the structure and then it would fall because one block was defective. I had to use every ounce of energy to make the business work. I believe we only won because we covered every possible problem with a check system as a pilot goes through his check list.

Judy was livid. I was constantly working. The whole experience with the Red Cross division took on a personal note as well as a business issue. The line builder at Red Cross was a friend of mine. We had met in Maine where he worked for another company and lived the same back and forth schedule. We started to see one another on a regular basis with our wives. I was responsible for him being hired at the company. Phil took my recommendation and actually hired him over the phone.

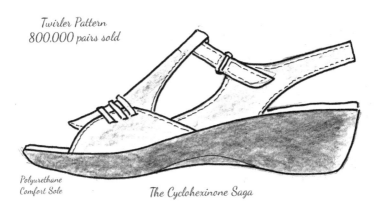

Twirler Pattern
800.000 pairs sold

Polyurethane
Comfort Sole

The Cyclohexinone Saga

We started to do business. It had the potential to be a fantastic account for product development. If it worked, the profits for the corporation would be over the top. Red Cross had the ability to buy literally millions of pairs. The line builder was in constant contact with me. He would call me endlessly whether it was in Taiwan or when I just arrived home after a six-week trip. Judy was off the wall. The Red Cross division was run by a mentality that was archaic. It was not only a "yesterday philosophy", the team, from its president down, only played defense. He did not understand and always ended up "second-guessing" every issue and the like. His quality control team did not want Taiwan in the picture.

They fought it in every way. They made the Cyclohexenone caper into what it became...almost turning corporate management against having a Taiwan presence.

They ended up with egg on their face. They were waiting for another opportunity to kill us. It would come because shoemaking and production are never trouble-free. I once told Phil later on that Red Cross quality control cost the corporation at least $5-7 million in air freight because they could not or would not OK the patterns in a reasonable length of time. There was no need for the situation.

The great success of the sandal sneaker made it much easier to find the factories that wanted to make better product. We interviewed a number of companies and came up with our group. There were two small factories that were Taiwanese and were only making product for the local market. They didn't even have English names.

There were Rocky and Frank. I came up with the name Rocky as the movie had just come out. He was a big, strong guy, especially for a Chinese. Rocky was much more aggressive than Frank and a better casual maker. Business was getting stronger and Rocky opened a second factory which we called Rocky 2 and then Rocky 3. I told Rocky I don't care how many movies they make, it stops at #3.

Frank was a happy go lucky guy, a dress shoemaker who did all the small lots and was able to do some handmade type constructions.

The first factory to come on board was Worldwide, situated in Taipei and owned by Chisun Chu. He was an extremely well-organized guy and worked the pattern trials himself to insure the production patterns were made properly. He made the Cobbie Cuddlers program and made as many as 8-10,000 pairs a day for us. It was a large factory but slowly it became a total U. S. Shoe factory.

There was C. Y Lee. C.Y. was probably the most creative Chinese I ever met. He was a master at making woven shoes and we used his expertise as much as possible. We made probably close to 750,000 to one million pairs over a two year period for Cobbie Cuddlers. They were all made with urethane soles. The product was second to none and put Cobbie Cuddlers over the top.

Tai Shoe was a specialty-type factory. It was owned by John Ho and his wife, Sophie. They were very Americanized and struggled early on making just fair product. Sophie came to my office and begged for another chance. I gave them a group I had just finished working on and they were off and running. They became a key factory developing a whole new construction concept.

Hai Fung evolved five to six months after we were on our way to building the business. Albert Wong had a small interest in Worldwide. He was the factory superintendent and ran the plant. He came to me and said he was going into business. Albert wanted a commitment on our part that we would support him. I told Albert that we would buy every pair he would make. Hai Fung made great product and as the business progressed we made as many as 5,000 pairs per day. I then said to Albert, "You hit your limit with us." Albert used our reputation and his ability to become the major resource for Payless, reaching quantities of 100,000 pairs per day. Albert and I became great friends and he never forgot my help. He repaid the favor years later.

We worked with the factories to upgrade their ability to make better footwear. What most people did not realize was that the best shoes are made with machines, not handmade. The machine is precise and doesn't get tired at 2:00 pm. The major problem in Taiwan was the humidity. We could not move forward in the whole process unless we were able to bring specific machinery to the production line. We needed heat setters and dryers that took the moisture out of the shoe as it moved down the conveyor. We took the key guys to Italy and had them buy the necessary machines to achieve a better quality level. It was an interesting trip trying to find Chinese restaurants in Tuscany!

We brought the Taiwanese manufacturers to Florence to buy equipment for the production lines and show them Italian factories. We were able to do this because of U. S. Shoe's presence in Italy and our personal relationships with the Bandolino factories. They brought their wives for this was the first time they had been to Italy or anywhere outside of Hong Kong. Chisun Chu's wife, Lola, was a real pistol and had a huge say in the business. In fact, she was the C.F.O. of WorldWide Shoe that made approximately 8-9000 pairs per day for U. S. Shoe Corp.

Lola found her way to Gucci with our help and "surveyed" the store. The clerk looked at her and automatically classified her as a non-buyer!" Lola stepped to the counter and asked to see three to four bags which the clerk reluctantly showed. When she pulled out her AMEX checks and purchased all four bags, the attitude in the store changed dramatically. The story doesn't end there, Lola decided to use one of the bags directly from the store. The bag had inked edges and it came off on Lola's mink jacket. Back to the store we went and had a "conversation" with the store manager who was more than willing to take care of the situation. Lola got her coat cleaned and an additional gift card for $500.00. Among the group, they must have spent over $50,000 between men's and women's clothing, bags and footwear in 1979 dollars.

This was the Wild West, anything was possible; whatever could happen, happened. The sandal sneaker became such a gigantic business we decided it needed additional sales help. We hired a high-powered guy who had worked for one of the better importers. Don Zeller was a pro. He was a good-looking, well-dressed, pretty smooth operator. His customer list was impressive and we felt we were lucky to get him. He didn't need to be programmed. All he needed was some knowledge of the product and a plane ticket. What I didn't know was that he was a nut-cake with delusions of grandeur. Don was out selling and doing a good job, at least I thought so. One day I get a call from Phil Barach. We talked about a number of projects, the business in general. He then brought up Don Zeller and I asked him why. He then proceeds to tell me that Don called him and said that he was the brains behind the operation and Norman should really be just involved in design under his authority. Phil started to laugh. He told me to straighten it out. I almost went through the roof and then calmed down. I realized this guy had some marbles loose upstairs. I called Don into the office and had a heart-to-heart with him. I thought everything was settled.

About two weeks later Phil calls me again and gives me the same story. He took the call for he thought Don was apologizing. Well, that was it. I called Don, got his samples and let him go. The fireworks were about to begin.

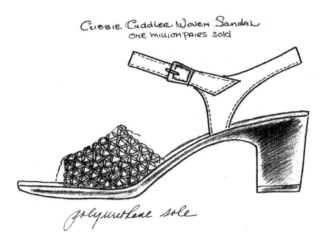

Cubbie Cuddler Woven Sandal
ONE million pairs sold

polyurethane sole

Don was an ex-Nordstrom buyer years earlier. He called Bruce Nordstrom and told him that we were overcharging them on the sneaker sandals and another program we were making for them. These were first/cost programs and we were entitled to commissions. Bruce called Phil and was not exactly cordial. I heard from Phil and called Bruce whom I knew. I told him I was coming to Seattle and explain the whole situation. I brought the cost sheets and went over the whole transaction. The problem was put to bed. The only good thing that came out of the situation was that I developed a very good relationship with Bruce Nordstrom. In fact, he came to Taiwan to see our operation on my invitation. I've enclosed a letter written by Phil acknowledging my contribution to the corporation. It was one of many. Phil wrote you a letter any time he heard good things about you.

Phil and Stan were both unhappy with the performance of Capezio which had stumbled around at Marx & Newman. They moved the division back to Cincinnati bringing in Errol Coleman as President. They wanted a moderate price point which meant sourcing in Taiwan. Errol and I were going to be the line builders/designers and went ahead on that basis. I knew Errol pretty well. He was a Bandolino salesperson in the Midwest and did a good job. He wanted to get into management and product development and got the opportunity. He was not a designer but had a good sense of style and merchandising. We worked well together.

Errol traveled with me to Europe twice a year and made the tour. We spent extra time in Italy working with the component people with whom I had developed relationships. The major issue was lasts. Taiwan just didn't have the technology to make plastic lasts which were needed to make better quality footwear. I had a relationship with Formificio Romangolo and used their model makers to make many of our needs. We paid them for the models and extreme sizes to check the fit. I finally got the Taiwanese last-maker to buy used equipment from Romangolo and set up a line. It was a major breakthrough.

I used to travel to Europe and look at the windows in four to five cities and generally would go to the last factory one stop before heading from Paris to Taipei. I had four cartons of lasts that were packed to travel. I was taking them with me because if they shipped them the duty would be 100% and take two months to get them. Well, the cartons came off the conveyor and started breaking. I was running around like a chicken with his head cut off trying to capture the lasts. Luckily there was a machine in the airport that put metal straps on the cartons. Life was a challenge at every turn.

The operation and the staff grew at a record pace. What I didn't appreciate was Phil sending me rejects that the divisions let go. I had an ongoing battle with him. He sent me his "prize" catch, a pattern maker who came from the Mushroom operation, our chief competitor. I could swear Mushrooms decided to let him go so that we would hire him and screw up our operation. He was a dandy.

The real weakness of the Taiwan shoe industry was its inability to solve the pre-production development which included making patterns either for samples or production. We started by bringing over American pattern makers which was a terrible mistake. I knew better but I was part of the corporation and had to play by part of the party line. Well, my Mushroom guy, Mark, was really a problem. When he came in the morning he would be down on the floor next to his desk for what he called his "thinking time". He would contemplate the day and then start working with a system for making patterns I had never seen. It took him a day to make one model and that wasn't going to sit well with me or Herbert who ran the pattern room.

What ended the story was rather a hilarious affair. The manufacturers were fighting over who would take us to dinner night after night. They were not dinners, they were banquets. Their interpretation of a good time was an endless array of "gambes"...toasting one another. Well, our Mushroom guy got into a drinking match with Rocky. The match went on throughout the meal and started to get "serious" with one after another. Well, the match was about to end as Mr. Mushroom (Mark) slipped totally under the table amid the laughter from us all. He was out like a light.....finally revived and was taken back to the hotel in Chisun's brand new Cadillac. As if we wrote the script, he chucked it all up in the back seat before they could stop the car. Needless to say, he was gone physically, mentally and on the plane home three days later.

We finally figured out how to develop the pattern department. We needed a considerable staff. We were developing literally thousands of ideas each year. First, we hired only European pattern makers who had apprenticed and were formally taught the craft. They worked on the last. We had bought form molding machines that would put a thin plastic sheet over the last, allowing the pattern maker to draw directly on the plastic. It could then be cut and flattened out to make patterns. It was a major breakthrough. This enabled us to eliminate the slow process of taping the lasts. It was much easier to draw on plastic.

We needed to find local people to work with our Europeans. Herb and I thought we could train young people who had artistic or mechanical skills. We went to the art schools and mechanical engineering schools and found the candidates. It worked to perfection and solved a major problem. All our mechanical drawings for unit soles, heels and certain shoe parts were now being done by local Taiwanese. We had all kinds of issues with the expats in the initial stages. Those that applied and came were either running away from debt, marriage, a drinking problem which unfortunately they took with them, or all of the above. The turnover became a problem. We finally started to hire expat quality control people working for other importers who had stood the test of time in Taiwan...Mistake #1.

THE UNITED STATES SHOE CORPORATION

CINCINNATI, OHIO 45212

PHILIP G. BARACH
Chairman and
Chief Executive Officer

April 14, 1980

Norman Finn
Director/Product Development

Dear Norman:

Both on a personal basis and on behalf of our Board of Directors, it is with a great deal of pleasure that I enclose the stock option award granted at our recent Board Meeting.

I need not tell you, this award represents a means of expressing our appreciation and gratitude for your contribution to the growth and progress of U. S. Shoe.

Norman, the job you have done will eventually be recorded in the history of the shoe industry as a fantastic job well done...to work with a country like Taiwan and to pioneer the multi-width fittings as well as the complicated shoemaking that was never known to that country.

In time it will contribute enormously to the strength of the corporation and I hope that in building the organization the way you have done...you will be able to find greater balance between your personal and professional life.

My personal appreciation and gratitude for your hard work, loyalty and professionalism.

Sincerely,

Phil Barach

PGB/bh
encl.

The quality control people working for the other importers were almost all Americans. They were never really trained as shoe technicians. They learned their trade working in the American domestic industry on the job. Formal training in the key aspects of pattern and last making and new production methods were not in their resume. We needed bodies to control the production when we started but we found out very quickly if the quality control technician did not have a working knowledge of pattern making; he was either handicapped or worthless.

The major deficiency in the Taiwan and Chinese industry then and even existing today is the lack of knowledge on how to make the pattern fit, look the part and work on the production line. All of these skills had to come from a knowledge of pattern making. We finally realized that hiring European senior technicians was the answer. They had apprenticed and were schooled in these areas and were able to, not only be a watchdog of the production, but actually correct the mistakes. Our Americans could only see the mistakes but did not have the know-how to fix them. It was hit or miss when in the pre-production process.

One morning during a Taiwan trip, the phone rings as I'm getting out of the shower. "Mr. Finn?" "Yes, whom am I speaking with?" "This is Mrs. Jackson, I am the wife of your new technician that I am going to kill." I had the towel wrapped around me and couldn't believe what I was hearing. "Mrs. Jackson, where are you and why are you so agitated?" "My husband is shacked up with some Chinese bitch and told me to go fuck off. I am here in Boston but I am going to take a flight to Taiwan and kill him." I don't know how I did it but I calmed her down and told her that I would talk to her husband this morning and assure her this situation will get cleared up. I made her promise not to take the flight here as she had planned the following morning. I was relieved and went to the office.

The quality control people were usually in the factories and not in the office on a regular basis. They came in some mornings with lead cases of production to try the shoes for fit, etc. Al Jackson happened to be in. I gave him the essence of my conversation with his wife, prefacing my remarks by saying I did not want to be involved in his personal life. "I do not want to know about this live-in. I just want the situation straightened out. I want you to come to somewhat of an agreement with your wife whatever that may be." He came to the office the next day and said the situation had been handled. There would be no re-occurrences. About two weeks went by and there was a morning call from Mrs. Jackson. She was not in Boston, she had just landed in Taipei and wanted a car to take her to her husband's apartment where she was going to kill him. She was not hysterical as she was last time, but cool as a cucumber. I called Jackson's house and caught him before he left for the day. He had heard from her moments earlier than I did. Well, I do not know whether he got rid of his live-in in time for her arrival but there were no fireworks or killings. The wife was in Taipei for two weeks. One morning Herb comes into my office and says you have to listen to this story. All the expat quality control people need an assistant mainly to translate their comments, etc. to the factory managers and line executives. They could not travel alone and the assistant also served as the driver. We had all the assistants buy automobiles which we financed and paid them per diem. It seems he picked up Mr. Jackson and had his itinerary for the factories. Al got in the car with his briefcase and gave instructions to the driver. "Today we are not going to the factories...take me to the airport." Al just left...no note, no warning, paying no bills. It was just a fucking disaster trying to pick up the pieces after him.

U. S. Shoe domestic manufacturing people came over, and some gave us serious issues. One of their pattern people arrived who actually worked for one of the divisions. We picked him up at the airport and brought him to the hotel. He had a few too many on the plane and was a happy guy when we finally got him into bed. Jack said he would be ready in the morning for breakfast. Well, breakfast came and went as well as lunch and we figured Jack was just jet-lagged and sleeping it off. When 2:00 pm came, we got scared and went to the hotel and opened his room. The bed had not been slept in; we really got worried. We found Jack with the gendarmes and they were not happy with Jack. He had proceeded to have an altercation at an American "girlie" club where he leveled three Chinese. We found a way to "compensate" the parties to be and closed the issue. Needless to say, Jack had a short stay.

It was a problem that was difficult to solve. In the early days we thought we needed the expertise of these expats. What eventually happened was interesting. The class and quality of these people became much better. As the factories in Italy and Spain closed, the technicians could not find work and were forced to take jobs away from their homeland. The tables had turned.

There were two major happenings that changed life for me as well as the company. I remember when the first fax machine arrived, a Ricoh rep brought it in for a test in Boston. When I saw my sketches being sent over the wire, my whole world changed. We could actually get the sketches to Taiwan in seconds. I was ecstatic. It meant I could work out of the States more often. The whole timetable for product development picked up at least a week. It also produced more work but the fax machine changed everything.

The other half of the equation was FedEx. The ability to send or receive packages in three to four days was unreal. It meant I could fax a sketch on Monday morning and have the sample on my desk on Friday if it was that important. Both of these advancements changed my world.

Phil and Stan Rutstein did not get along. As close as I was with Phil, I never really knew what happened. Phil kept the CEO and Presidency and decided to put in a president of the shoe complex. It was an $800 million division and needed a commander. He was off building the company with Casual Corner and Lenscrafters, which was becoming a monster. Lenscrafters was bought when it had three stores. As a corporate officer I reported directly to Phil. But I would also report to a new president of the shoe division which Phil was about to appoint. I believe he had the person in mind.

We had outgrown our fourth floor and had the sample room on part of the tenth floor. The tenth and eleventh became available and we moved up and built an internal stairway between the floors. When we started in Taiwan, we stayed at the Grand Hotel which we used as an office. We settled in there for quite some time. It was out of the way and expensive. There was only one other hotel in the city, The Hilton. Any shoe guy staying in Taipei ended up there. You had to fight the hookers off every night if you went in for a drink but it was the only decent game in town. We used to go out occasionally to a Tepanyaki joint that was palatable. Really, our only venturing out was with manufacturers who took us to dinner. We led a sheltered life, shuttling back and forth from hotel to office, etc.

We then moved to the Hilton Hotel which was more to our liking. All the shoe guys were there so it did offer a little diversity. There weren't many because most of the shoe business was done in Taichung so you only saw a limited amount of importers. Some of the brass from Pagoda Intl., a major importer out of Taiwan and the Far East, stayed in the hotel and we all became friendly. Harvey Levy was the CEO. He had a partner but called all the shots and was an excellent salesperson. We often spoke and occasionally had dinner. It broke the monotony of the same old, same old. Harvey did business like Johnny Flout, anything he had to do to get the order. We competed against Pagoda as well as the other importers. It was difficult going up against their type of salesmanship. The only way we could win was with interesting, new product. We could not compete with the "extras". That's how we won the game, always with innovation.

One night I was awakened around 3:00 am and heard tremendous noises, rumblings from the street. I must have been on the 15th floor. Half-awake I peeked out from the window shade and saw a whole row of tanks coming down the street. "Holy shit... we are at war with the mainland. How the hell are we going to get out of this mess?" About three minutes later I realized today was Double 10 Day, a national holiday there with a gigantic parade of the military and all its gear. I almost had a heart attack.

We had a significant amount of staff staying there and Steve Kaplan told me he had found a new hotel that had opened and wanted to try it. He moved out and went to the Ritz Hotel, which happened to be much closer to the office. I hadn't heard what he thought of the place and about three weeks later I saw him back at the Hilton. "What happened?" "Oh, the hotel is great but there's nobody there...so I'm back." We all went over to see the place and moved there the next day.

Phil decided to come to Taiwan; he had never been in the Far East. He had recovered fully and was his old self. We rolled out the red carpet for him. I arranged a major article about the company the following day of his arrival. There was a half-page picture of Phil in the China Daily and an article that covered the front page. Every morning the paper was slipped under the door of your room. The paper always arrived early. My phone rang at 6:00 am and it was Phil. "Why did you do this...there was no need for all this stuff for me...do you think I can get ten copies for my mother!" Phil could not believe our operation and what we had accomplished. He was sold on giving us more opportunities. But that was not his priority. He was in the midst of trying to buy Marshall's, Keds and expand Lenscrafters and Casual Corner. Unfortunately, he had a Board who were not risk-takers in any sense of the word. The major acquisitions did not go through. They were just lacking vision and were too conservative.

At the same time all was not well in the domestic factories. They had lost pairs to Brazil, Spain and Italy and us. They were trying to protect their positions and factory base. They used any means possible to find issues with our production and quality. How does it go? "Seek and you shall find." They had their rulers and tapes out measuring pattern trials and production. It wasn't war, it was nuclear and they had the upper hand because they confirmed the styles for production.

We were about to get a good kick where it hurts. Red Cross needed the production of the domestic plants and, although our product was better and more cost-effective, they pulled significant programs, even ones we designed and originated. Phil called and wanted to see me. He was aware I knew Lyle Burrows from Hahn's and wanted to tell me in person that he was making him president of the footwear division. I gave him my opinion for he asked for it. I was not a happy camper. He was a manipulator; that big smile that was actually laughable. He was very bright and a very hard worker. He had spent his whole life at retail and he now was running a company where the majority of the sales were wholesale. I knew there would be problems. Lyle liked the staff to agree. He liked to surround himself with "yes" people. Actually, he fit in well in Cincinnati for everyone except a few played the political game. The best example I could give is how the "Clycohexenone caper" went. He did not have the vision nor the experience level in manufacturing. He came in with a couple of strikes against him. Bob Stix, who ran manufacturing, did not like him. The Marx & Newman crew detested him and, naturally, I was not a fan. The retail shoe division knew his style and were not in his corner. He handled them entirely wrong by dumping wholesale mistakes in their lap. I believed he tried to put it together but just did not know how. My answer to George Shapiro years before seemed to come true. "He was trouble with a capital T."

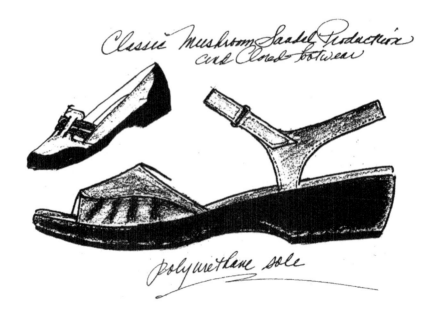

Classic Mushroom Sandal Production and Closed Footwear

polyurethane sole

With the slippage of Red Cross, I concentrated on Capezio and private label sales. Phil called me one Sunday morning, as usual, and asked me if I wanted to own Mushrooms, the brand that at one time was the main competitor to Cobbie Cuddlers. They had fallen, mainly because they were slipper people trying to make shoes they didn't know how to make. It was as simple an explanation as that. It really was a shame to see them fail. They had the right concept but they developed their polyurethane soles with the wrong durometer which meant they were too soft, so that the molding rate was dismal. They lost at least one of every three they molded; a recipe for a loss. There has to be a happy medium. Here sales insisted on the "soft soles" which caused all kinds of manufacturing issues and larger losses in the molding and making process. Management just didn't know how to find the middle ground which caused their own demise. Mushrooms had become a sensation almost overnight and their business soared to $50M in a very short time. Their downfall started when we, Brown Shoe Company and several others took aim at their niche and launched new brands to compete. We became the victor after two years.

Phil sent me to Columbus, Ohio to negotiate with Gordon Zack, who owned the business. They had a very successful slipper business and Mushrooms was pulling them down. I made the deal and was ecstatic for it was a brand that I could control.

Red Cross was up in arms; a new competitor in our own camp. What transpired was a compromise in their favor. Mushrooms would be run by our organization but it could only sell the discounters and volume retailers and not compete directly with Cobbie Cuddlers at the department store level. I agreed for there was a world out there to sell and we knew exactly where to go. The Mushrooms brand brought us back to full production and beyond.

Every major retailer bought the product...Sears, J C Penney, the major better discounters, etc. Footwear Unlimited became our branded outlet. They bought the shoes upfront and stocked them, selling to the small retailers. The name was magic and the product had quality, price and style. I loved doing business with Footwear. Denny Hadican and Mike Mooney were great to work with. Denny laid out the programs that I put on the table. We spoke the same language. Our overall private label business was growing at an incredible rate.

As head of product development, I had responsibility in Brazil and disbanded the original U. S. office which was a total flop. They tried to build their business as they worked in the domestic factories. I worked out a deal with a Dutch importer, Ruud Bresson to be our agent. I had to approach the situation in this manner so that our new Footwear President would be on board and I was not directly involved.

Alan Sorofman, a key person in our organization, coordinated with Ruud B. and the U. S. Shoe Divisions. It was not an easy chore working with the divisions. They did not have the courage of their convictions. They could never make up their minds. A decision to go ahead took an act of Congress on their part. The sad part was that creative, hard-working people were doing lots of business in Brazil. The market was wide open for U. S. Shoe and they found a way to screw it up mainly because they had little talent and vision. I could not get the divisions to be proactive and entrepreneurial, it just was not to be. All phases of the operation were in a defensive posture. Their ability to operate in Brazil was limited by their own methods. Whatever we were able to accomplish was only a small portion of what should have occurred. Alan knew how to handle them and developed a business with the Joyce Division as best he could.

Capezio's business went through the roof. Taiwan had great difficulty making closed footwear. Their exploding shoe industry was weighted heavily toward sandals, slippers, beachwear or opened up dress shoes. This occurred mainly because closed shoes need machinery which I have discussed earlier. Not only machinery but a lot more expertise starting with last and pattern development and shoemaking. We overcame it because Taiwan had great labor. We developed a new twist to the construction called "California construction". It enabled you to stitch the upper to a binding that could be used to put a padded insole inside and seal it. The construction needed excellent pattern making to make very precise patterns. When the upper was stitched, you then could put a last into the finished upper/sole and give it shape. It is called "forced lasted". You can then put the sole and heel on. You then solved the problem of making a closed shoe without major machinery. Why it was called "California", I'm not really sure but I think it came from an old time brand, California Cobblers.

This idea came to me when I was looking in the window of a London shop. Why can't we adopt this construction to a closed pump? It needed a new concept of last-making and incredibly good pattern development.

We developed the construction for Capezio and introduced it in a pattern called "Quadrille". We made them in soft suede with a leather binding. The construction enabled us to have a very flexible forepart with a rubber non-slip sole. It turned out to be one of the great patterns of our industry. We sold five million pairs between branded and private label sales. The industry probably sold at least twice that. Capezio had arrived from a dismal performing division to a $40M brand. The success of Capezio gave me a lot of satisfaction, remembering the situation at Marx & Newman and the decisions surrounding the outcome.

Lyle called me, "Phil had a heart attack but he will pull through." I called Bev Siple, his secretary, who would kill for Phil to get the story. She confirmed his condition and was in constant touch with the family and would call me if there was a change.

We needed dress shoe production in leather and Taiwan just was not the place to get it done. China was not open and Hong Kong became the major producer of kidskin dress shoes. We needed to build a base of operations there. I started going over there every Friday night and work with the manufacturers on Saturday and Sunday; coming back Sunday night. It was a ninety minute flight from Taipei. We started working with two factories to develop a line of dress product. I would either bring the plastic shells with the last for them to work on or give them the sketches. Their model people were trained properly. They had gone to England for shoe school.

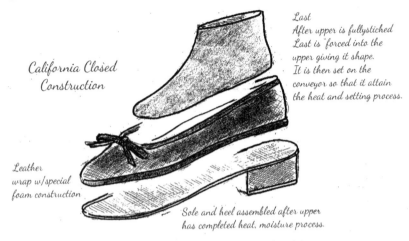

California Closed Construction

Last
After upper is fullystiched Last is forced into the upper giving it shape. It is then set on the conveyor so that it attain the heat and setting process.

Leather wrap w/special foam construction

Sole and heel assembled after upper has completed heat, moisture process.

Total pairage possibly close to 12 million pairs between branded and private label sales.

On one Friday on my way to Hong Kong, I stopped at one of our factories near the airport. As I was leaving, the office called all excited. "Norman, the U. S. just normalized relations with China...I'm concerned there could be trouble here in Taipei." "It's not a problem, I countered, "Sono Italiano."

The facilities to work the lines were non-existent. Hong Kong space was so expensive. The factories did not have decent show or work rooms. I used to take a suite at the Regent Hotel and have us work there. The hotel was magnificent with the greatest view of Hong Kong island. About eight to ten years ago I checked in and went up to my room to find a huge bouquet of flowers, champagne, candy, etc. I thought I was in the wrong room until I saw the card with my name on it. It read, "Welcome to the Regent for the 100th time!"

We were only semi-successful with our Hong Kong operation. Our major factory in Taiwan and then in China performed far better with more competitive pricing. Hong Kong was never a major factor in our business. The Hong Kong mentality was totally different than the Taiwanese. They were highly sophisticated and had experience going into China to work. What they lacked was expertise in shoemaking. They knew what to do and had the desire but could not pull it off on a regular basis. Their production was not smooth. One case would be perfect and the next a disaster. I did not want to depend on them for the heart of our programs and did not use my technical staff to run their production. We spent our efforts with our Taiwan resources.

When we became AmAsia, we opened a financial and administrative office there. It handled all the letter of credit transactions that were key to our business. The real definition of a letter of credit is an agreement between two entities who don't trust one another.

We were all up in the air over Phil. I found out later that Lyle assumed the CEO position which was never spelled out if Phil was incapable to lead. The decision was the Board's.

I went ahead with our programs and business. It was very difficult doing business with the divisions that were domestically based and it did not get better as we became more professional. They had long memories about what had transpired with Cyclohexenone and their antics trying to sabotage production in Taiwan.

The corporation licensed Calvin Klein. Lyle pushed for it and Phil and I were against it. He was difficult to work with and wanted a 10% royalty which was unheard of. Making a profit was going to be close to impossible. He pleaded and we went along with him. The Calvin line would be made in Italy. The Calvin Klein Sport would be done in Taiwan. Calvin had a design staff and we were given the responsibility of building the line. His designer, Guido H., sent us the sketches and details. When I opened up the package and looked at the program I was dumbfounded. The sketches were high-style, more for a fashion magazine than as a guide to make prototypes. I immediately called him and tried to explain the issues. If the sketches were not drawn to scale, the chances of him being pleased with the samples were slim. He became indignant and I read him the riot act. "If you want this line to be done properly, you better get your ass to Taipei. Otherwise, you will get what we perceive they should look like." He was pissed. He never came.

Quadrille California Construction

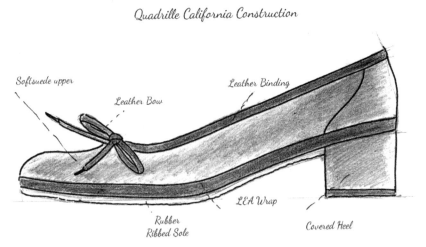

We made the samples. To me they looked pretty darn good and received a vote of confidence from Calvin Klein and their sales force. I felt our interpretation gave them style and functionality. I forgot about the whole situation. During the New York shoe show we set up the private label/Mushroom program in the Essex House, not the Presidential Suite as Ralph would have done. But yet again, we weren't selling stiletto heels in orange and green patent. I would divide my time between the U. S. Shoe show room and the hotel.

While at the U. S. Shoe office, I got a call from one of our guys that someone was waiting for me and when would I return. Actually, I was on my way. When I walked into the room, Vincent, one of our private label salesmen, told me he was waiting in the next room and started to smirk. Standing in front of me was what I believed was a man, possibly. He was dressed with a black matador jacket with arm holes and a yellow blouse with ruffled collar and cuffs. He had a black patent leather oversized bow tie and wore black velvet knickers. The outfit was topped off with white silk stockings with black pilgrim buckle shoes. I started to giggle for I thought someone had sent over a joke. It was Guido, who was unhappy with our interpretation. The conversation did not last long.

Our customer base for Mushrooms and private label was diversified but discount-oriented. We did a ton of business with Shoe Town, the originator of the better discount business. Lionel Levy, the owner, was a master negotiator and merchant. He bought almost all the closeouts from the U. S. factories and made a fortune. He was an extremely handsome man with silver hair, filled with energy and brilliant in making the deal. He was "connected" in every way both politically and philanthropically. We ended up vacationing with one another during the Christmas break in California. Lionel had a Rolls, a beautiful white Silver Cloud. I was coming out of the U. S. office during the show and Lionel pulled up with his driver and saw me. "Norman, where are you going? My driver will drop you." Sure enough, I was going over to the Sheraton where most of the companies were showing and we pulled up. Just as I was getting out of the car, two of my competitors were standing at the curb. I got out and said, "We had a great season!" His buyer, Alan Sesser was a practical joker and he looked it. Big horn-rimmed glasses, bald, short, almost looked like Woody Allen. He came to the Essex to look at the line. We had some of the samples laid out on the beds. I handled Shoe Town for it was a house account. "Alan, let me take you through the line." As I finished the sentence, he jumped on the bed. "Let me walk you through the line...great job!"

Lyle did not believe in the private label business we had developed. He constantly wanted to know who and what we were selling. He felt our sales were taking away orders for the brands which was not the case. The Mushrooms business we developed was a sore point with him. He wanted it cut back. I could see where this was heading and it was not to our liking. He definitely did not like Taiwan. His emphasis was on Brazil and insisted the divisions concentrate their efforts there. He was not wrong. Brazil was the natural next step from Italy, not Taiwan. Brazilian quality, styling and image were an easier sell at retail. What Lyle did not recognize was that there wasn't a team to make it happen there. You had to have the horses and he did not want to relinquish any of his power to allow product development to organize and make Brazil work. Jealousy and envy were the factors that created a dysfunctional office. What I did not understand was why he wanted to cut us back on product that had no relation to Brazil nor to what the divisions needed. It was very profitable margins for the corporation. You could argue that all shoes were in competition with one another. We were in a state of flux.

He deeply resented my personal relationship with Phil. I could see he was filled with envy and jealousy over our friendship. It was not a good situation. He thought I wanted his job which was the furthest thing from the truth. My strength and desire was to stay in the product area. I don't think he liked me because I was tall and he was short, it was as simple as that.

Phil was back in action, but with his interests in other areas besides shoes. I had Lyle hanging on my neck every day and second-guessing me. He became a major pain in the ass in every day operations. He wanted to be involved in issues that I gave to the staff to handle. It was micro-managing. I finally realized he was pissed that I had this great incentive deal and earning more than him, and war was inevitable.

U. S. Shoe was not using our potential. We had developed the finest product development facility in Asia and second only to the major Brazilian factory. The sample department consisted of 50-70 people, highly trained and able to react in record time. We had a Taiwanese woman running the administrative end and Herbert ran the technical area. Our western pattern making staff came from Russia, Germany, Italy and Slovakia and home-grown in Taiwan.

Gregory, the Russian, was the most interesting. He had been in the Russian Army in Siberia and was caught in a storm which resulted in frostbite, losing half his fingers. When he came in for the interview, I whispered to Herb, "How can he function?" Herb answered, "You'll see." We gave him two sketches to work on and they were done perfectly. When I congratulated him, he countered, "Just imagine what I could do if I had fingers!"

When Gregory was with us about a year in Taiwan he came to me and asked if he could take a week off for he wanted to vacation in the Philippines. He was due the time and more and off he went. About five days later he called in and asked if he could take an additional week. I hesitated and asked him why. "I found a wife and I'm getting married and need a honeymoon." End of story.

I found some interesting correspondence that will give you a good idea of what the situation and atmosphere was dealing with Cincinnati.

We seemed to be in two different camps with two separate interests, domestic vs international. It was more than that. It consisted of egos, jealousy and control. At times it was "no holds barred". For product development it was complicated always trying to breach the wall that divided us. We needed their involvement and orders. The programs really never happened as they should. In retrospect, the U. S. Shoe brands actually needed us more than we needed them for our private label business was booming. Their lives were actually in jeopardy staying with the same manufacturing base.

We were always at a disadvantage for we were in Boston or Taiwan. We could only fight back with memos. Putting it on paper was the only vehicle that gave us a voice. Our competition could not control this aspect of the corporate struggle. The memos gave us life.

Just a note of explanation, the Desma process is a molding system fusing the upper to an injected sole. The process is designed for volume production. The tooling is very expensive and only equates for mass production items such as athletic types. Cincinnati bought into the process for it meant a significant savings in labor and expertise when it was running properly. The quantities were always their issue and eventually was their demise.

Enclosed is a memo to Phil Barach which outlined my thoughts on a number of issues. I have eliminated names of those copied.

NORMAN FINN
DIRECTOR

PRODUCT DEVELOPMENT

July 25, 1986

Mr. Phil Barach
U.S. Shoe
One Eastwood Drive
Cincinnati, OH 45227

Dear Phil:

This isn't an, "I told you so" memo, but an analysis of where we are today vs. where we could have been. The important point here is not proving that anyone was right or wrong about the desma process, but where do we go from here by realizing what we missed. The major point is that by going with the desma process we inhibited the development of our positions in Brazil and Taiwan.

We allowed our competition, mainly Fisher in Brazil and Brown along with others in Taiwan, to take significant positions. By not making the "Cuddler" line in Brazil, we allowed Calico to gain a formidable position in the market place. They stepped in at price points below us when we could have been a real obstacle to their growth, and furthering our own position at the same time.

Further to this point, we would have had our own Brazilian office; avoiding all the problems of an agent. We could have had a significant presence. We did not follow our formula as we did with Marx-Newman, Europe, Spain, and Italy.

The saddest point is that this desma process lulled us to sleep and inhibited us from developing the organization needed to do business in the 80s and 90s. We did not develop the personnel to travel overseas; to live and work in these countries.

We would have been able to create this organization at the right pace and with thought. Now, we don't have a choice but to play "catch-up". We must have the agent or buy him out and expand without the proper personnel and timing.

I have talked about Brazil, but Taiwan has been effected also. The organization would have flourished with additional "Cuddler" pairs. The ability to make this kind of product line has always been the strength of Taiwan. If you remember, the biggest Cuddler was the "Twirler."

Mr. Phil Barach
July 25, 1986
Page 2

We took that away and the profit margins for the divisions. We now know
that our desma process is not competitive with either Brazil or Taiwan,
and as the competition mounts against us, the problem will become more
severe.

The 2½-3 million pair of uppers (or more) put on these machines today
would have been used to build our finished shoe positions in both countries.

No one is denying that during this 8-9 year period that domestic production
was not profitable-(only at times!). However, the profits vs. those which
could have been obtained in Brazil and Taiwan during the same time frame do not
even begin to equate. The difference is roughly $3-4.00 per pair! I
can't begin to imagine what the total dollar difference would be during
that 8-9 year period.

It is a sorry state of affairs when we who lead the way in Spain and Italy
became lost in Brazil and Taiwan.

I have never been a Monday morning quarterback, but I'll say it once more...
We are a marketing company, and that is the whole story.

We must regroup; we must make both of these countries as strong as Italy and
Spain in their time of glory. If we do not adopt this policy, we will be
left behind. It seems to me we have fallen more than a step backwards
already.

Regards,

Norman Fenn

rlb

In 1987 things were coming to a head. The war between
Lyle and I was coming to its height. We seemed to be on a
collision course, both of us not willing to give any quarter. It
opened a whole new outlook for what the future would bring.
I started thinking about a life without U. S. Shoe. My financial
situation was excellent. I had been granted significant options
over the years. U. S. Shoe stock for many years went nowhere
and suddenly the stock started to move. Most employees sold
early but I held on and was able to cash in on the high. The
tremendous bonuses and commission from unbranded sales
gave me financial security for almost a lifetime. I had been in on
the start of Nike. Phil had called me when we started in Taiwan
and asked me to check out the company. I saw firsthand what
was happening and we moved together. At one time I had a very
significant position in the stock.

What were my options? I could play the game here or find another job. I was a known quantity in the industry with a fine reputation. It was not a problem to find a challenging position. I had turned down Brown Shoe Company, running their Pagoda division and a stepping stone to top management at Brown Shoe Company. A new job was not an issue.

I started to review the state of the unknown, analyze the facts, the dreams and what the future could bring under a number of scenarios. I knew eventually I would lose the battle with Lyle. He was ruthless. He actually called a private label customer of mine and asked him to cancel orders and find another resource. The customer was a friend and called to tell me of his conversation. I was going to Cincinnati within the next few days and wanted to confront him. I walked into his office. "If you pull a stunt like that again...I'm going to throw you right through that window." Then I walked out. Lyle went to Phil and told him that he wanted no part of me and that Phil would have to supervise me. They were the same old reasons it wouldn't work. The situation with Red Cross/ Cobbie Cuddlers was already poisoned from the chemical affair. Their quality control people were just waiting to find something that would make them pull back the production. They had done it to me once and I was able to find alternative business which fueled the fires. Our success was not part of their plan.

It was bizarre, having people in your own company willing to sabotage the operation for their own personal issues. The Red Cross head technician came to Taiwan to OK the new pattern collection. He came with his golf clubs for a starter. It got worse. He refused to confirm a pattern because there was a 2 m/m slippage on an open toe pattern. I went through the roof and Herbert had to restrain me. Herbert tried to talk sense into him and finally he went ballistic and I had to restrain him. I took the technician by the back of the neck and threw him out of the office and sent him home.

I got a call from Phil who had heard from the president of the Red Cross division and Lyle. Phil laughed, "Did you have to throw him out?" "Phil, if I didn't throw him out, Herbert would have killed him." It just wasn't going to work.

Lyle did not believe in the Far East. He was still betting on Italy, Spain and the domestic production. As I said earlier, he was a big Brazilian fan. What he did not realize was that Brazil eventually would put the Italy and Spain and domestic factories more or less out of business with fashion footwear. Taiwan would be needed to make the types of basic footwear the domestic plants had made. He just didn't have the vision. I actually believe it was all clouded with jealousy. It was centered on my friendship with Phil. He wanted the same and it wasn't there. Between making more money than him and being taller, he just couldn't handle it. On top of that, he thought I wanted his job as president of the shoe division. It was the furthest thing from my mind. Lastly, I didn't have to live in Cincinnati. His wife hated it. He wanted me out one way or the other. His envy blinded him, for when he signed off letting me buy the Taiwan office, it set the company back five years or more and probably cost $50M.

Phil and I were more than friends. We were, in a sense, brothers. We saw each other in Boston when he came to visit his wife's family and kids who lived here. They lived around the corner and he was over the house consistently when in Newton.

I knew if I left the corporation Lyle would close the Taiwan operation. I had put my whole self into building this business. It had consumed a good portion of my life from 1976 to 1987. There was an office full of dedicated, talented people, both in the States and Taiwan who would lose their jobs. Factories would be in trouble for they had become, in most instances, exclusive. It was a terrible dilemma. I could not see all of this effort go up in smoke.

I started to think how I could take over this business. I

went to Phil and gave him the story of how I felt, what really was happening and that Lyle was not interested in Taiwan. Was it possible for me to buy the existing business including Mushrooms?

Phil realized that, one way or another, I was gone and he owed me for the work I had done in Italy and Taiwan. His emphasis was still on the other divisions and deals he was working on. Phil handled the whole situation behind the scenes. He let Lyle negotiate the deal with me. I know somehow he gave him his marching orders. We came up with a cost for the office and a royalty per pair on Mushroom sales. There was no deal if I did not get the Mushrooms label. Lyle wanted a pound of flesh, insisting on a high royalty. What he did not know was we had a very high overhead cost built into every price we quoted Cincinnati. We fought with him and let him win the argument over the royalty, knowing we really beat him.

China was about to open and we knew we could price the product anywhere from 75¢ to $1 less. That was the key. I made the decision because we bought a going business. Mushrooms and private label were the heart and soul, ready to break out. Our sales would trend higher simply because we no longer had the yoke of Red Cross over our necks. The customer base was about to expand at every level, branded and private label.

What could be a problem never materialized. I was concerned there might be a major defection of key people either to Cincinnati or seeking other employment. Would they come along to the new company? Nobody hesitated. They all came on board without an exception. The factories were all on board. As far as they were concerned, they did business with Norman Finn. U. S. Shoe was just a name and a by-product. I gave them the orders and the orders talk. I negotiated the prices, gave them the pairs, solved the problems and babysat when necessary. I proved my worth over the chemical issue.

I had enough cash to swing the deal. If necessary, I could find one of the factories to help finance the operation or take them in as a partner. Naturally, when it was U. S. Shoe, all I needed to do was just ask for almost unlimited funds. We needed a credit line. The advantage was we had most of our business on a letter of credit basis.

Ted Finn was now a finished product. He had done his internship in Taiwan and worked in Italy. He now was with Macy's running their private label European business. Leslie, his wife, who had two Master degrees, an M.A. and an M.B.A., was a banker in New York. Actually Leslie came on board first. She had the experience level. Under U. S. Shoe, the financial end of the business was handled by Cincinnati. They were responsible for shipping, some administration and personnel through their international division. We had to set everything up ourselves. The factories did everything they could to help.

Leslie was indispensable in putting the financial plan together. She not only understood the financial aspects, but was blessed with "street smarts" and made decisions based on good business needs, not just financial. My strengths were product, design and manufacturing. I had vision but I was very weak in administration and finance. I realized if I was going into business I needed the talents of both of them. Actually, I made the decision that if they were not interested in being my partners, the deal would not happen. I worked out an arrangement re the partnership and had one of the best financial people in the country set up the companies here and overseas. The decision was made to give Ted and Leslie equal shares. I felt it was the right thing to do in order to create the right atmosphere in the business and our personal lives. Leslie would not be a second-class citizen.

I was smart enough to realize my weaknesses. We were a family and involved in different areas of the business. It was always a work in progress. When Ted and Leslie joined us I gathered all the key executives together. "They are coming on board. This business is only for those who can pull their own weight. If they do not, they are out...no exceptions."

The deal was finally done. It was not the best deal for I used a friend who was a lawyer and learned a great lesson that day. Get the best, it's always the cheapest! I wanted "out" so badly that I did not negotiate the best deal I could have, mainly the Mushroom royalty.

I originally wanted the company to be called Finn International but Mr. "X" objected. He was my technician for many years and I gave him a 20% stake as the manager of the Taiwan office. He had been with me since 1971 and he was family, at that time. We decided on AmAsia Intl. and registered the business as such. Our name in Chinese stayed the same as before; it translates as wonderful, great company, which it was. AmAsia became a reality on October 24, 1987. I was in Cincinnati to clean up some odds and ends. Phil was there and I left him a letter for I didn't expect to see him. It was a long letter thanking him for everything. I ended it with the following. "Phil, no matter what happens in this life or the next...you will always be my CEO." As the years went by, Phil always used to remind me what I wrote; the words hit home for him and for me.

My Dream

Chapter VII

"When a great moment knocks on the door of your life, it is often no louder than the beating of your heart, and it is very easy to miss it."

Boris Pasternak

It was hard to believe that it really was happening. It had taken our team twelve years to put it together. The bottom line was U. S. Shoe sold a great asset for ego and jealousy, a sad commentary but a great one for me.

I went to Taiwan directly after the takeover. My first customer was a Canadian, actually a Joyce division of U. S. Shoe licensee. Hugh Woods was just a wonderful person; jovial, clever, a shoe dog and a great eye for the item. We started to do business. He was Mr. Clark's in Canada and was a major factor in hooking me up with Lance Clark. Hugh's parting words as he left the office were, "Norman, do you have "interesting" photos of the U. S. Shoe brass. There isn't any other reason why they should have sold you this office!" I was hysterical.

I was very fortunate to have found the perfect person to run the administrative side of product development. Nancy Chang had been married to Clark Chang's son. Clark was the premier maker in Taiwan. Nancy ran his sample rom, detailed the product and worked with customers. I was a dear friend of Clark. I actually did some work with him when I could afford his prices. When Nancy divorced, she had a hard time getting a position for she wanted to work.

The Taiwanese factories did not want to offend Clark and stayed away. Nancy called me and I immediately put her to work. Her expertise freed me up to be in the States selling. I had no problem sending her a sketch and knowing it would be detailed and made correctly. She was more than my right hand. Her English was perfect. She had that "touch" for later on in life she made fantastic jewelry. Clark never said a word and we remained good friends. Nancy traveled with me and Alan throughout Europe. She made the notes and organized the components that we purchased. Her comments on what we saw were extremely helpful.

I concentrated on our Mushrooms business. Denny Hadican who was once with a key account of ours, Footwear Unlimited, was now on board. He was my Mushrooms sales manager and we put together a salesforce.

Our business grew, not only with Sears, Montgomery Ward and J. C. Penney. We started to explode the business with Mervyn's, a west coast discounter. We developed a key relationship there and began major programs with dress footwear. Taiwan was not a dress shoe resource. The factories were not makers of plain pumps, especially those made in kidskin. These articles were made in Hong Kong and China. I went there to find the factories.

What transpired next was almost a death blow. The Taiwan dollar, which was roughly 42NT to the U. S. dollar, became incredibly strong. It was heading to 26 and choking us to death. If this trend continued, it would have put us out of business. All our orders and contracts were based on 42. Our only salvation was to get to China as soon as possible.

Our factory base reacted. Chisun Chu (WorldWide) operated in Xiamen and Albert (Ever Rite) in Guan Zhou. Chisun chose Xiamen because it was exactly across the straits to Taiwan. He hoped there would be a direct transport link between the two. Albert was amazing and developed a facility on the waterfront in Guanzhou. It was a huge complex and it started production quickly. Albert had taken on a "partner", somewhat of a silent partner. He was the commander of the southern region of the Chinese Army. We did not have any power issues for China was notorious for losing a day here or there every week. We moved the finished product in Army trucks. There were no political issues with the local government. Both factories produced almost our entire needs, except for specialty items. The Taiwanese found the way to not only get it done, they also knew how to administer it. They knew how to handle the local government. They found the ways to get around the red tape and ridiculous customs requirements. They made it happen. What most people did not realize was that it was the Taiwanese who built the great industries in China. They came with the expertise, funds and the will to make it happen. It would not have happened without them.

There was a mammoth task ahead of us and it was a situation where every day counted. The dollar was strangling us, as I said, and the only salvation was production in China which was moving forward. Only the Taiwanese could have moved an industry to China. It took not only a major effort on their part, but on ours. We invested heavily in time, ability and cash to make the necessary adaptations to our business.

We had to set up a whole new system to handle the logistics of doing it across the Taiwan straits. The commitment on the part of our quality control and production personnel was beyond the call of duty. They had to understand the Chinese mentality. They dedicated themselves seven days a week, twelve to fourteen hours a day, to make it happen. We paid them well but it was pride, dedication to the company and to me that made it happen. They knew my commitment to them. They knew I was committed to building a new company under the AmAsia banner for all of us. I am indebted to them for pulling us through the SARS epidemic by staying the course and assuming greater responsibility.

U.S. Shoe divests Taipai assets to AmAsia

AmAsia will take over the former U.S. Shoe facility in Taipei and continue to maintain its domestic headquarters at 90 Main St., Reading, Mass.

In addition, Finn said, his new company will open a warehouse on the West Coast, linked by computer with the Reading office. The company will stock key shoes and will hire a sales force of six to seven people. Finn said he already has hired Denny Hedican, former sales coordinator at Footwear Unlimited, as vice president of sales.

"We're going to take a position on key items so they will be in our warehouse in the states for immediate delivery," Finn said.

"There also will be a significant difference in the way our line is presented. Footwear Unlimited offered a narrowed line. They wanted a tight package. We think we will be doing 35 percent of our business in the part of the line they didn't carry. This will represent a real opportunity for retailers to have the whole line."

Mushrooms sales up

Finn said Mushrooms sales are up 65 percent so far this year and running at an annual pace in excess of $32 million. "That is on a letter-of-credit basis, which is like $50 million of regular business," he added. "And that is only Mushrooms, and does not include the unbranded business. Mushrooms business at retail has been phenomenal. At some stores, sell rates are 40 percent ahead of last year."

Finn, who created U.S. Shoe's state-of-the-art product development center in Taiwan and introduced many aspects of better footwear manufacturing to the country, initiated U.S. Shoe's Cobby Cuddlers line and also oversaw the production of shoes for a number of the company's other divisions, including Joyce, Red Cross, Liz Claiborne, Bandolino, Capezio and Pappagallo.

Finn said he will continue to design the Mushrooms line and also will be doing more private-label footwear.

Advertising expansion

"We were limited in private label because we did not want to compete with ourselves," he said. "But now we are free to do it, and we already have been approached by a number of people to be their agent in the Orient."

Charley Boersig, retired director of advertising for U.S. Shoe, is acting as an advertising consultant to Finn.

"In the past, Mushrooms spent a major amount of its advertising dollars on spot market television, primarily in the South and Southwest," Boersig said. "We plan to continue that, but also to go national and add print advertising in women's magazines."

Finn said he plans to hire a sales force prior to the New York show. He said the new Mushrooms line will be shown Nov. 29 through Dec. 3 at the Ritz Carlton Hotel.

Our two smaller factories, Frank and Rocky, had a different story. They did not want to go to China. They were ethnic Taiwanese and wanted to stay in Taiwan, whereas Chisun and Albert came from the mainland in their youth. Both were very appreciative of our relationship. Rocky, who had grown his business to three factories, was very realistic. "Norman...both Frank and I have been extremely fortunate and have been very successful making shoes for you. We have bought significant real estate and are not dependent on the shoe industry. We feel sad that we will not be able to go to China because we are not cut out to do business there. We will continue to make for the Taiwan local market. It is not in our best interest." This conversation was in Chinese translated by Nancy whom they respected. They told me they had family in California and were going to spend considerable time there, hoping to learn English. We finished working with them over the next few months. It was not their world. Years later, at a shoe show in Las Vegas, Rocky appeared. He now spoke reasonable English and we were glad to see one another. I asked him about his family, etc. Then he hugged me, "Norman, everything is fine but I miss working with you. We are great friends forever." It choked me up and I never forgot it.

It was in late April and May 1988 when problems started to arise with Mr. "X". He had turned into a "Grand Signore". His expenses went through the roof. Leslie started to show me what was going on. He was not working. I didn't find him in the office when he should have been there. What precipitated these events were his involvement in other activities. He had lost control of the situation. We formulated a plan to take over the running of the office. The legal and financial elements were put into place. Arrangements were made for Ted and Leslie to temporarily head up the office. Ted had worked in Taiwan and knew the operation. We would have to buy back the stock that I had given him. The whole situation and negotiation was not "a walk in the park". In fact it was extremely difficult considering the long relationship.

I needed to finish this situation with him as soon as possible. We had struck a deal and I wanted it signed and put to bed. His shares had to be re-purchased. My funds were tied up and I needed the cash to finalize. I went to Albert Wong and he did not hesitate. In fact, he asked if I needed more. He was so appreciative that I had given him the opportunity of getting started. I paid Albert back the following week when the funds were available. I don't know if the other manufacturers would have done so. I guess I will never know.

It was a traumatic period, probably the most that I experienced. I guess I would classify it as some of the darkest hours.

Unfortunately, the pressure was on everyone. The move to China drove me even harder with less time at home. I was extremely worried over everything. Ted and Leslie were in Taiwan running the office and I was trying to bolster them up. I traveled back and forth constantly.

My major project was to replace him with someone we could count on and trust. We were fortunate enough to have found Amy Lo. She was a shoe veteran working for agencies and Clark Chang, my friend and manufacturer. It was a great windfall, we had come up with the right leader with tons of experience. Ted and Leslie could now come home and we could get on with the original plan.

It's hard to remember all the timing but Judy did not feel well and, over a course of a few months, got worse. There was an abscess over her kidney and no one knew it was there. It was killing her. She was in the hospital and I was beside myself. I thought the cancer was back, the dark days, the pain and anguish. I cried by myself. It was so unfair for her to go through this again. But, we got lucky. They punctured the abscess by accident and she recovered. She was so close to death and then it was over. Judy had the knack of coming in contact with physicians who did not believe what she told them. Time after time, when she complained about pain and unusual circumstance they passed over it. Her remarks went unanswered and eventually turned into reality. I remember leaning over her and kissing her, thanking God she was going to be OK. Ted and Leslie were there. It was all a blur in a sense. I was in another world. I didn't believe it was over but it was. But, was it going to happen again and again? I didn't care. She was safe and I held her in my arms.

There was always a crisis in our business. We lived from one to another. I can't remember one from the other at this point in time. We were expanding our horizons. Our business was growing and our star in the industry was rising. The world was changing and we had to change with it.

We had a significant pump business with Kobacker, a major discounter with 600+ stores and it was growing. We had the product to perfection for their price range. We had the resources to make a discount product far better than our competitors. This was the private label "cut-throat" business and the stakes were high. Everything was predicated on price, quality had little voice in the final decisions. It only mattered down the line if there was a claim. We lost the business for twenty cents. I implored them to buy our product to no avail based on the quality level. The bottom line was that six months later, after they received the first product from their new resource, they came back after suffering major quality issues. The private label philosophy was difficult to understand where you would roll the dice over ten to twenty cents.

The day of the company existing without brands was over. Without that umbrella, you were prey to any discount retailer for a 10¢ piece or less. The brand gave you authenticity in the market, not only for a legitimate landed business (branded product at retail) but gave you the edge for private label sales. As the branded business went, so went the private label business but at a great rate when the brand was actually performing.

I would never have gone into business without

acquiring the Mushrooms brand; the bottom line is you do not have a business without a brand. Companies were "sheep" and followed the branded leaders. We needed another brand besides our Mushrooms business. We would then be able to grow AmAsia.

We had gone through a series of talks with people who were interested in buying the company. It was extremely frustrating to go to great ends to make a deal and fail for a number of reasons that were beyond our control. We negotiated with Brown Shoe Company because of my dear friend, Joe Cramer, whom I had known since my days at Shapiro Bros.

Joe, although retired, was one of the great shoe men of his day and was the major advisor to the CEO of Brown. He wanted us on board to make Brown entrepreneurial. Joe actually wanted me to be the next leader of the company. It didn't happen because Brown was too political and their CEO did not understand the fashion business. He was the classic example of a CEO that did not understand product. I had learned my lesson at U. S. Shoe. We had fifteen different shoe divisions. Every time we appointed a divisional president that did not understand fashion and product, the business either never produced or failed. It was a tremendous drain on my and everyone's time; trying to fix what should never have been broken.

Joe was instrumental in setting up a meeting with the Bruno Magli family who wanted me to style their line. Bruno Magli was one of the great women's fashion brands and was sold worldwide. When Joe brought up the proposition I declined. I was running a business that demanded my time. They were aligned with a German-American company and I made the deal only based on us getting the Miss Magli license for North America. I did not realize the family was literally at war with one another after Bruno's death. I remember very vividly one Magli addressing me to tell another Magli what he wanted to transpire. I was the go-between in a family feud, all in Italian! Ted and Leslie were up in arms over a dilution of my time. I wanted the brand. When it didn't work, I abandoned the position. The inability of the family to live together was something I just couldn't fathom. I was in a similar position and knew that it would not be easy for all of us to live without issues. It would take work to keep us all on the same page.

I was searching for the brand or alliance that could take us to the next level and beyond. We became aware that the Caressa brand was for sale. Caressa was owned by AEA, a venture capital group which was a massive company, about $6 billion. AEA was made up of retired CEO's of Fortune-500 companies. Some of their stockholders were in government, such as Henry Kissinger. You were on the "hook" for $5M on any venture they wished to do. Why they bought Caressa, I will never know.

The story of Caressa under the new management was troubled in every area. It was not in the greatest shape when they took it over but it was more than salvageable with AEA funding. At one time in the mid-70s, Caressa and its stable of brands, Allure, Caressa, SRO and Protégé were the #1 brands at retail. Caressa was the 'Nine West" of its day, possibly even to a greater scale. They proceeded to run into major problems in most areas and wanted Caressa and SRO to be Italian. It was very Spanish and dress-oriented. It was not their business model. Their whole shoe education was basic classic footwear which was exactly what the Caressa brands were not. They did not have the creativity and style mentality to put the team together and put it on the right track. The business was done by committee and had a parade of designers, one after another, to fix it to no avail. The stories I heard about the way they did business were incredible. They could not make decisions when they needed to compete in the marketplace.

Actually we started to do business earlier with this group in China and had bad experiences a year or two before we started negotiating to buy the business. It ended up costing us $100,000 and they did not pay their portion of the costs. I don't remember the whole story, but it left a bad taste in everyone's mouth. We had severe run-ins with their people over customer issues because we tried to help them. Their unbranded salesman, after we helped him, turned on us and actually went to our key customer running us down. I demanded an apology. They tried to smooth it over.

When we started the negotiations with AEA, I didn't have any idea of what they wanted and why they really wanted to sell. I found out quickly in a meeting that Caressa top management did not attend. The company had lost a ton of money, $70M to be exact. AEA had poured in unlimited funds and Caressa was faltering badly. They thought new management was going to be "the force and face" for the brand. It was just the opposite. When they finished telling me what went on, I was amazed. AEA did not want to continue. They wanted out and they were willing to take a severe beating on the price for complete and total confidentiality. The embarrassment of losing was the most important point they wished to avoid and the agreement spelled it out in no uncertain terms.

Ted and Leslie were at first opposed to buying Caressa. They felt it was too big a deal for us and that we would be better off to keep going in the direction we were headed. I slowly won them over and we went ahead. We negotiated an interesting deal. We bought the assets of the company and not the liabilities. We agreed to a royalty, a dollar amount per pair with minimums. We ended up with the receivables, etc. It was a tough negotiation. We started to get deeply involved before we actually bought the business. The season was upon us. Caressa management decided to take control of the styling and personally worked on the spring line we would show in New York in August. They showed me the collection and it was so bad that I could not believe it. I rushed to add four to five looks to salvage the season. What had come to my realization was Caressa management did not fit as product people nor as marketing or sales personnel. They were strictly P.R. We discovered a number of situations which were beyond explanation.

They imported kidskin from Italy when Spain had the best kidskin in the world. They endorsed bringing the lasts and heels from Italy when Spain's were more than sufficient, much cheaper and more convenient. It just didn't figure. They had brought Italian technicians to Spain to help Caressa. They only made things worse. It was a continual fight between Spanish and Italian personalities and mentality. Actually it would have been more difficult to make Caressa product in Italy than Spain. The whole concept was wrong.

The more information we put together, the more we realized their management could not be part of the deal. Caressa, from its inception, had been a Florida-based company. They kept the administrative offices there and had a huge showroom next to Bergdorf-Goodman. I believe the rent was $60,000 per month. I always had this idea of a New York office; it was too big during the week and too small for a shoe show. Hotels were better and cheaper.

The deal was developing. It had rhythm. We got along extremely well with the AEA people and they gave us the opportunity to start formulating things for the takeover before everything was worked out. We went to the showrooms before the New York show in June and introduced ourselves to all the staff and salesforce. The industry was already buzzing with these developments. We gathered all the personnel from all the divisions together and I introduced myself and the company. We met separately with management. I gave them our history and outlined what I thought would be an overall plan to bring all of us together.

I had a very difficult task and that was to face top management and tell them that they were not part of the deal. Where would they fit? The long and the short of it was they didn't fit anywhere and over a period of the next few weeks we parted and would run the business within our own organization.

It's a sad commentary to a situation which could not have had a happy ending. People have unrealistic expectations and goals regarding business ability or creative talent. How do you tell someone that he does not have it? It's a no-win situation. That was the crux of the story when we finally put the Caressa deal to bed.

We still had to be in Spain for the time being and we had to keep the continuity. It involved setting up a totally different system. We put together an agency agreement with Eddie D. who was put in command by the owners before AEA. Born in Gibraltar and with an English wife, he had complete command of both Spanish and English. He was not a shoe person, but an administrator with lots of bad habits which we soon discovered.

We owned Caressa at the Vegas Show, which was in August of 1992. We were on our way. One of the major problems was to show our customers that our China production, quality and know-how was the equal of Spain.

We had the tools and ability to build product and the best factory in China. We were able to take our Spanish product and reproduce it in China at much better pricing. Actually, the China product was better-made in premium leathers. It was not easy to win over some of the retailers. The stigma of China still was in the air. We were still able to turn the tide toward Chinese production by producing great quality with incredible delivery. What eventually happened was, instead of insisting on Spanish production, they were now singing the praises of our China production.

We had a situation with Gary S. who sold private label for Caressa. I never liked his superior attitude but I was willing to go along with him if he continued to produce. When we discussed his details, he became very aggressive, demanding a numbers of perks, etc. I was willing to go along until he said that maybe he would be better off if he went into business for himself. "Gary, you are absolutely right. You are in your own business right now...all by yourself."

We needed a warehouse situation for Caressa and our other brands. The best location was on the west coast since most of the production was coming from China. Denny had a good friend who had played professional soccer with him. He had retired and was looking for a situation.

Mark was the perfect choice. He was tough and knew how to handle the staff. The warehouse became a key factor in our business with huge in-stock programs for all the brands. We had as many as 400-600,000 pairs on the shelves depending on the time of the year. Caressa could generate in-stock sales every Monday morning, 15-20,000 pairs of fill-ins. When the Nordstrom comfort program came on line, the warehouse tripled in size.

Mark lived in San Jose and the warehouse was in Hayward, California, a few miles up the road. We had additional programs for Mushrooms and SRO. The pump programs were the mainstay of our business. The running of the warehouse and the ability to move quickly was Mark's domain and he did it well. Our key Mushrooms customer was Mervyn's, which was headquartered a half mile away from the warehouse. I was at Mervyn's often and spent time every day to visit Mark. Mark was a blessing.

There were situations where the warehouse served as more than just a storage facility. Taiwan was just humidity, rain and more humidity, especially at certain times of the year. If the production cases were not packed properly, mold became a serious issue. We had these situations a number of times, generally not a serious issue involving a total shipment. What we would do is set up tables in the parking lot of the warehouse and lay out the product covered with mold. The California sun would be the vehicle that cleansed the footwear for sun and dry heat turns the mold to powder. All you had to do is wipe them down. When this was accomplished and the goods repackaged, the product was perfect.

We had developed a manufacturer in Taiwan who had the mentality to make better footwear. He was an original Taiwanese, which was a bit unusual as he had the mentality and desire to become more than a local manufacturer. He became our person to make Caressa product when we moved to China.

It took me a week of non-stop pleading and promising to finally get him to make the move to the mainland. We took him to Europe, showed him Italian factories and told him to buy this machine and that to build the right kind of production line. We showed him how to make patterns and our people worked with him daily to make better shoes. He became our main factory, Taiwan and then China, producing the bulk of our dress product. His quality level was second to none and his ability to produce was in a class by himself. We gave him guidance along the way but he seized the moment and did everything he could to produce a quality product. The problem was that he was the most difficult person I ever dealt with. At times he was totally unreasonable on programs and pricing. He was our ticket to making the changeover from Spain to China a non-issue. Without his willingness to make the product at the highest level of quality, the move to China would have taken much longer and with many issues. In that sense, he was the perfect partner; in another, a disaster.

We had a tremendous job rebuilding the Caressa brand. As I said earlier, if I had known how tough it was going to be, I probably would not have bought the company. We had to re-organize everything. The administration for Caressa was in Florida and we moved everything to Boston. Only one key person was willing to come. Britt Daw had worked for the original company and knew where all the bodies were buried. She was an important part of the re-organization. It was not going to be an easy job. We were trying to juggle the development and merchandise the two entities. We had moved to a larger facility before Caressa and it was really too small. The business was now on two continents and it made life more difficult.

Spain, under Eddie, was problematic because he just didn't have the respect of the staff or the factory nor did he have the technical expertise. It took me a couple of trips to realize that he just couldn't get the job done. We were doing business with actually two factories with most of the business going to Pandora. José Ignacio and his family had worked for Caressa from inception of the brand. We eventually parted with Eddie.....it wasn't pleasant. He had his hand in the cookie jar.....actually his whole arm. Actually, it came down to one event. I received a call from the staff reiterating what Eddie had told them.....that he was going on vacation and could not pay them until he returned. I picked up the phone and fired him.

I was working with a bright young product person, Carlos Sirera. We hit it off from the beginning and I made Carlos head of our office. Carlos had a great fashion sense and was capable of making major decisions on the prototypes without my presence. Along with Carlos, we had Pepe who, in my estimation, was one of the best technical pattern makers I ever worked with. Both of them ended up in our China operation.

The work load was tremendous. I was working a minimum of twelve to fourteen hours a day, seven days a week, in order to get the lines done. When I returned to the States, I was at my desk drawing every night. It was necessary to keep up with the line development time schedule. I was designing Caressa, Allure, SRO, Mushrooms and private label programs. I had some help but it was minimal.

What made life extremely difficult on the styling trips was the inability to have a conversation with anyone. Thea Rooke, the English woman, was not a conversationalist in any sense of the word. I just didn't have anything in common with her. I could not even play "shoe ping-pong" with her. She was a designer with no sense of merchandising. I had to program her every day, every project, in every way. She was an excellent designer when you gave her specific instructions, themes or constructions to work on. I needed to find an additional person to work with.

The nights in Taiwan were filled with work and it was a godsend in a way. I was almost alone in Taipei. The shoe friends that I had either moved south to Taichung or opened offices in Hong Kong. Herb and the other western staff had their friends and hangouts in China. There weren't many people to talk with after dark.

There were only two parts of Taiwan away from business that I enjoyed. One was the Jewish holidays when I attended the synagogue in Taipei. The other was the Taipei Museum which held the riches of China. When Chiang Kai-shek left China, he took magnificence with him. The major art of China was now in a Taipei museum. The entire collection was rotated every three months.

It was a very interesting congregation and Rabbi. They came from all over the world to Taiwan to either work or study Chinese. The congregation was made up of business people from the U. S., Europe, Australia and Israel. There was a large contingent of Israelis in Taiwan for the armament business. The Rabbi was one of the most interesting persons I've ever met. He was born in Germany and escaped the Nazis as a kid. He was raised in the U.K. and the States where he became a Rabbi. For some unknown reason, he left the Rabbinate and ended up in Taiwan where he was a trader and a major commercial representative of the Republic of China throughout Eastern Europe and Central America.

He was the Rabbi for Taipei and spoke twelve languages. I always went to his study groups on the weekend whenever I could. His memory rivalled the encyclopedia. It was one of the bright spots of being in Taiwan. I was raised an Orthodox Jew and the services were, in a sense, music to my ears. I did not mind being in Taiwan if the holidays fell at that time.

The job at hand was Caressa first and it was tough work for all concerned to get it right in every area. We all had to live through the learning curve and it taxed our abilities, ingenuity and staying power. I had a good working relationship with the key sales people. Peter Brunnell was the President of Caressa and a very decent executive. He was a good administrator but, more importantly, liked by the trade. Tony Casey, known to everyone, including his wife, as Casey, was the head of Allure, the better line totally made in Spain. I really didn't know Casey that well; he seemed to carry the ball. I just wasn't sure what was going on in that division.

SRO and Protégé were put in mothballs for the moment. They were to surface very quickly in the AmAsia private label division made in China. We seemed to be on the right track but Caressa had a lot of rebuilding to do.

The AmAsia division was a different story. We were flourishing and the private label business was trending up. Our Mushroom business was on fire. Caressa opened up a whole new segment for private label. It was the classic situation. The private label customers wanted to buy similar styling as the Caressa brands.

Denny Hadican had worked for Footwear Unlimited, which was a major customer, and we had developed a relationship that went beyond the business. He was underpaid at Footwear and the opportunity with us was far better. He had come with me from U. S. Shoe and joined us in the new venture. Denny was a great salesman but his forte was not administration.

He lived in St. Louis, which was very central, and had that knack of developing relationships with the customers. He understood product and was perfectly cast in basic comfort product covering Mushrooms and private label sales.

Denny pushed me to hire Bill Knowles to run the SRO division. Bill had that knack of bothering you enough that you gave him the order to get rid of him. His great attribute was his work ethic. He had an excellent relationship with many buyers, principally Nordstrom's, and he was constantly in contact with them.

Denny was a great soccer player in college (All American) and he had that competitive spirit. We worked extremely well together in every aspect and thought alike on key issues. He was a risk-taker and I could talk to him. He sought my advice on everything and vice versa. He was like a brother, a kid brother.

The situation between Denny and Ted was not working. I cannot blame Ted in this instance. He had his administrative agendas and Denny could not continue to ad-lib and fly solo as he had done in the past. The business was too advanced with too many balls in the air. Denny was offered a major position in St. Louis with Brown Shoe Company and gave his notice. What bothered me most of all, besides losing a key person, was the personal relationship. No one likes to see a dedicated person leave and it really took some steam out of me. But we re-grouped and the end results turned positive.

We hired Guy Lynch, a bright, young salesman who lived in California and was perfect to handle our key customer, Mervyn's. Guy lived five miles away from their headquarters. I had developed the Mushrooms business with Mervyn's in the early years at U. S. Shoe and grew the account into a monster with the Mushrooms brand. We won an award for selling 60,000 pairs in one week. I believe the record still stands.

Maureen Kyer, a bright, hard-nosed lady, was the buyer

who gave us the opportunity to become a major supplier. We not only developed Mushrooms, but a whole series of dress footwear that made us a $10-12M account. She was in our corner and, as she was promoted, our business grew.

Maureen and Denny were oil and water! It made the transition from Denny to Guy a lot easier. Guy was able to service the account and developed a good relationship with the account.

We made Guy our key private label and Mushrooms salesperson. I spent a lot of time training him and leading him by the hand to our major customers. He was bright and well-organized, the exact opposite of Denny. Guy was more than a pleasant surprise. He brought a new, fresh outlook to the company and it was received extremely well.

We had considerable changes during this period and it put a tremendous amount of stress on me and the company. Peter Brunnell, the President of Caressa, tendered his resignation. I was horrified. I felt we just couldn't lose him. I had a tremendous amount of faith in Peter. He had been offered and accepted the presidency of my old stomping grounds, Bandolino. Ted, Leslie and I came up with an offer that would have given him a huge salary and potential to have stock in the company. I thank God that he did not accept it.

He left and we promoted Casey as President of Caressa. It was the best move we made. I didn't know Casey that well but in a very short time I realized we had lucked out and he was "our man". Casey had what Peter lacked, product ability. He was extremely bright, hardworking and creative. Peter knew only how to function in a structured environment and could not cope with an office in his house and travel. He was used to a corporate environment in New York with all the trimmings. He just couldn't handle this new lifestyle. Casey clued me in months later. Peter and Casey were friends and confided in one another. As I said, I was in shock but Casey was the man. He, unlike Peter, liked this new unstructured style. We did not have the corporate office in New York. Casey worked out of his house in Weston, Connecticut and went into the city or to Boston when needed. He had worked that way before and it was second nature to him. We would show at hotels and eventually ended up at the Rihga Royal (now The London) in two beautiful suites. We brought ten to twelve companies there and, in fact, had our own mini shoe show.

I did not like losing people and I had lost three key people in the space of five to six months. Some were replaced, Denny with Guy Lynch, Peter with Casey, but Alan Sorofman, my right-hand in product, was gone.

Alan had worked with me in the early days in Taiwan. He had been with me since the beginning at U. S. Shoe. He was 6'4" and made George Clooney look bad; long hair and a mustache, he had that rugged handsome look of the Marlboro man... Alan could have been their model. He was a shoe man through and through, about as accomplished as one could get. His weakness was staying power and "the grass is always greener on the other side" syndrome. We clashed often over direction of the lines and content. It was good in a way. Alan loved casual footwear and this was not Caressa's strength. He got easily frustrated by the salesforce. This was not unusual in our industry or any fashion company.

When I interviewed him for the initial position he was straight to the point. Alan had been working for the corporation in Cincinnati. "I heard you were a real tough S.O.B." I countered, "You are partially right...it only happens when you're not talented or a phony."

Alan had a marvelous disposition and sense of humor. He told me he was married three times because he loved the ceremony! It was a delight to travel and be with him. We raised hell after hours. We truly liked one another and sought each other's company. When he left, life was very tough. I hired Thea Rooke, whom I talked about earlier. Thea was not Alan in any sense of the word but she did her job as a journeyman designer. Alan came back to the company after a brief stop in Greece. I told him if he ever left again not to clean out his desk, for he would be back!

My world became very narrow and very lonely after twelve to fourteen hour days. Judy did not enjoy traveling to the Orient. She was insecure about her health and remembered the trip quite some time ago that was difficult. When she was well I would take her on my European trips. They were usually ten day affairs and then she would go home and I would head out for the Far East. I was alone. In a way it didn't matter because I was so tired out with the long days that I was exhausted and fell asleep almost immediately. My sleep apnea was under control with the machine but then I began to get these coughing jags and regurgitation of my food. It became steadily worse and I was just a basket case. I was totally miserable and ended up seeing an ear/nose/throat specialist who diagnosed Zenker's diverticulum, which was an obstruction in my throat. To make a long story short, the first operation did not work. I thought I was going to lose my mind. I was sleep-deprived, coughing my insides out and, as a result, completely exhausted but working just as hard. Thankfully, the second operation was a success.

Judy was there for me every minute. She did everything possible to make me comfortable during this ordeal. In fact, if it wasn't for her urging, I would have put it off as long as possible. This whole process covered six to eight months. I have to say I never felt worse in all my life.

I've always felt that when I was going on a product development trip it was a mission. It always centered on a fashion education and translating the information into a successful new collection. We (for I always tried to go with someone) wanted to be totally aware of the fashion picture from every aspect. To me it was important to go with someone so you could bounce ideas off them, also so they would see things you missed. To capture the feeling and the knowledge of the total market was the real goal. Today you can surf the internet and see almost anything in the world of fashion. It is a great tool but does not suffice for seeing it in person in context with what is going on in real time. I have learned more watching customers pick up merchandise or trying on their selections than any other situation. I am a touchy-feely person and being unable to not only see but handle the merchandise is impossible. The advantage of actually seeing the entire collection is something that cannot be duplicated by looking at a screen. It really does not portray the real picture.

When you shop certain stores, you develop relationships with retail management or sales people who are able to give you valuable information on the sales and a different perspective. I find this process seems to work if you find the management that has a grasp of the market and a good analysis of what they are selling. There are key people throughout this country and in countries where you shop that fall into this category.

I have seen certain companies buy hundreds of pairs on their style trips to copy or use pieces of the style. I do not pretend to pass judgment on this system for some brands come up with great collections using this method. We all have our own systems to construct our lines.

We generally buy the originals for last or construction which includes new heel shapes or actual unit constructions. Last and construction development is difficult and time consuming. Any item that would guide or shorten the development cycle is, in my estimation, key. This system was almost essential when you were developing product in the third world. It varies dramatically based on where the development would take place and at what price level for the product. Product developed for semi-lux and lux market would be developed on a more creative basis.

We are really talking about Italian better product where we would be creating almost the entire product concept from inception. As I said, the other methods, which more than likely would be used at moderate to discount price points, would come from the third world. There are a number of similarities no matter what grade of product you are developing. At times the level of creativity to achieve product at certain price points demands a higher degree of ability than producing lux product.

I have worked at all levels and price points. They all have their issues and limitations. They all demand a certain level of creativity in their own way. If you are a true designer, there are projects that bring out your talents more than others. However, if you're truly talented, there is nothing you can't accomplish by applying yourself to the challenge. As in every phase of life, especially the business portion, the gallery prefers to put you into categories where you are only able to work. I have fought this concept my whole working life and do not believe people are one dimensional. If there is true talent, this concept of categories of creativity does not exist. I shall always believe this.

Caressa was not moving at a pace that I wished. It did not carve out a place for itself as it had in the past because the dress shoe category was totally different. Women had changed their lifestyle. They did not shop or go to business in high heel pumps. We had to remake Caressa into a lifestyle brand and not just a dress shoe label.

We were on two continents now in full force. Our production and quality control team was in gear and the product coming off the China production lines seemed to measure up to the standards we wished. We still had our administrative offices and sample room in Taiwan. We had started the changeover of the sample room to China. Some of our key sample people came over. The single men mostly came. The problem was with the couples. The level of sophistication and sheer ability in the sample process was extremely difficult to reproduce in China. We needed all our experience level to make it happen. Running two sample rooms was expensive and difficult to operate. The need to get it done was paramount.

It was extremely difficult to work in this manner. We weren't far enough along to make all the samples and prototypes in one place or another. We had to make the changeover sometime. It took us an additional six months and we determined it was time. We had moved the production in 1987 and it had now been two years and we still had a Taiwan presence. We had two people who handled components for the industries supporting shoemaking were slow in coming. The rest of the staff was in Taipei. We still had a full administrative staff that coordinated the orders and schedules with the factories. Since all the factories were Taiwanese-owned, they had offices in Taipei or Taichung so the communication between the two was the same as it had been since we started.

We had enticed two women in administration to come to China. We used them as the nucleus to build a staff around them. It was time to close the office. Taiwan was becoming very expensive. The employees, all women, who ran the administrative side of the company were all married and, even if they wanted to, they could not leave their families. It was, in a sense, tragic as most of us had been together since 1976 as part of U. S. Shoe and it was now thirteen years later. I had been to their weddings and seen their children grow. We all went to dinner and talked about old times, the good ones mostly. Each of them got a month's salary for each year they were employed. I wish I could have afforded to give them more. I have never been back since.

My mother passed away in 1991 at the age of 97. She was failing and I came back from Taiwan and saw her just before she died. I have written a few words previously about her. She was a handsome woman in her youth and had come from Russia with her sister, Jenny. I had their passports written in French as it was the international language. How they got to Worcester was sort of a mystery but there had to be family there. My grandfather came first with his son, Arthur, "Alta" in Yiddish. The sisters followed and then my grandmother came with another daughter.

My father was crazy about my mother and couldn't do enough for her. They were a loving couple. It didn't happen often then. Marriages were generally a matter of convenience. It was a hard world. Julia and I had our hard times when I fought her will and married Judy. But she finally came around and when she did, she was all on board. When Judy was not treated as a full Jew, my mother came down on those with a vengeance. Years later, Julia used to come and stay at our house in Newton and, when she did, she would change the kitchen over to her specifications. She never dropped anything, it jumped out of her hand!

She loved my son, not only because he was Ted Finn, but he came to see her on a regular basis. She lived alone and went shopping by herself until she was 95. When Julia had the stroke, shutting down her left side, she didn't want to "hang around" as she put it. She had full command of her faculties until the very end.

I still can't figure out how she did it; six children, no husband, keeping us together and functioning. She was the iron lady and used every ounce of strength to help her children. When Ted and Leslie got married, she got all of us together and gave each of us $5,000. How she managed to do that I will never know. Yes, we all gave her money, but it was amazing. Julia wrote the book on how to make it on a budget. She would shop each market to get the prices before she made the purchase. There was no way to "con" her, she was the best negotiator. Enclosed is the eulogy I read at graveside.

Eulogy for Julia Finn

My mother was truly a lady of valor. To me....she was both mother and father. Julia only understood and demanded excellence and it shone in every facet of her life.

As a child, I remember her so vividly...."schlepping" the bundles up Columbia Street or talking to Tante Jennie.....her sister and confidante.

She never tired, never wavered in her endless workday. She taught me the meaning of staying power and sheer will to achieve your goals. It was engraved in my psyche.

I'll never forget my pajamas heating on the big black kitchen stove and that wonderful caress before falling off to sleep.

She loved all of us with such a great love and poured her whole self into all our needs. My mother only lived for her family....literally and figuratively. We consumed her life.

How do you say goodbye to such a courageous figure? How can we ever truly understand what drove this wonderful person to make our lives safe and secure? She used every ounce of cunning and strength to keep her family together.

Her great love was gone so early....so quickly....so cruelly without warning. How did she ever sustain the hurt? How did she keep us together? Only a woman of such valor, character and fortitude could have won the day.

I cried when I saw her so distraught at my father's grave. It was her only sign of not being super-human.

Their souls are finally together after all these years of being apart. I cannot believe otherwise.

I know she is with us today....pushing, prodding, and commanding all of us to be better Jews, better parents and better human beings. She was always in charge whether it was rearranging your kitchen or giving you sound advice.

It was her time and she chose to go alone....without burdening her family....in the peace and quiet of a summer afternoon. I shall always remember that day.

We had developed a number of labels before we bought Caressa, one of which was our best, CrossTown. We had tried to build it into a legitimate brand but it was a difficult task without a major investment. Now that we had Caressa I thought we could bring the two names together under Caressa/ Crosstown construction. I liked the name and sat down to design and develop a construction that would bring Caressa into this whole lifestyle image. What I came up with was a complete new molding process that would allow two densities to be put into the sole. Along with this attribute of hard and soft, we developed a non-skid surface. The final result was the new construction under the Caressa name. What made the new sole construction so desirable was, not only its unique flexibility and comfort, but it was not expensive to produce.

We were able to patent the process and protect our research and creativity. We put this construction into all our new pump collections and it was a sensation. We re-designed the interior of the pump to work with this new sole to give it the utmost comfort. We were the darlings of the department store world and our business grew by 25% overnight. The construction translated itself into the majority of types we could make. We had come from falling behind to being the leader.

the "CrossTown pump"

Lord & Taylor was the first to buy it and sell it extremely well. It was not an accident as some of their other sources faltered and we had the opening to put the Caressa Crosstown construction on the map. The shoes were incredibly comfortable and priced right at $59.00 retail. Our business with Lord & Taylor was on fire and the CEO called us in to see who we were. We gave him a presentation with the new product and got rave reviews. He tried to pin me down re the company's volume. I replied between 50 and 150 million. He smiled.

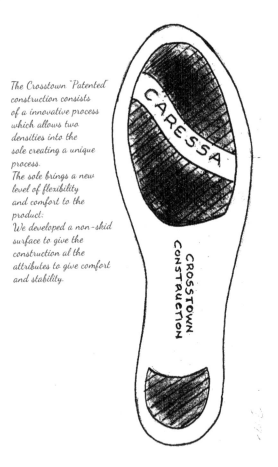

The Crosstown "Patented" construction consists of a innovative process which allows two densities into the sole creating a unique process.
The sole brings a new level of flexibility and comfort to the product.
We developed a non-skid surface to give the construction al the attributes to give comfort and stability.

We were on our way. As I said, we were the fair-haired boys of the industry. We expanded Crosstown to include different heel heights of pumps and new types of tailored and casual footwear. We defended our patent and won judgments maintaining our exclusivity.

Ted was more than growing into the job and I made him President and COO of the company. He was an excellent administrator and great with the logistics of production. We had components coming from around the globe and the ability to put the schedules together was key. He was gaining credibility with the trade and our staff. It is difficult to live in the shadow of your Dad. I do not know how you teach someone credibility, you have to earn it from your peers and customers. I believe he did so by running a 100 million dollar business from the administrative and manufacturing sides.

We came from two different points of view. To me, the glass was always half full, but that's me, the eternal optimist. Over the years, I have to say the balance of two different positions actually served us well. His conservatism many times kept me in line.

Our horizon had expanded. We were trying to get started in Thailand. We had found a great factory owned and run by a wonderful person, Narong Chokwatana. If you were looking for a partner, you could not find a better one. He had a Chinese working for him who kept coming to the office and pleading with me to go to Thailand and see the operation.

We tried unsuccessfully to put programs together. Everything we tried in the early days under Crosstown, before we owned Caressa, was a failure. Somehow or another, we couldn't get it done. It bothered me tremendously because I wanted so much to succeed with Narong and his company. He was a major supplier to Nike, Reebok, Adidas, and with all his success in this area, he wanted a dress shoe or, as they say today, a Brown Shoe business. We set up a line and brought a technician to Thailand to run the production line. It didn't work. Somehow or another, one obstacle after another got in our way. It was a disappointment and failure that still bothers me to this day. I went back years later when we had Caressa to try again. We were both willing, but it did not happen. China had come of age and Thailand just could not compete against the know-how of the Taiwanese and the cheaper labor.

Leslie finally became pregnant. They had been married quite some time (1987) and before one knew it, Taylor was born. I was there in Thailand when Taylor arrived on April 4th. They were wonderful to me. I changed my reservations and flew home through Europe to be there the next day. They brought me to the airport and gave me the most wonderful teddy bear (it was huge) to bring home. I'll never forget it. It was more than a business relationship.

When I was with Shapiro Bros., part of the Hahn organization was Mort Lerner of Lerner's Shoes. U. S. Shoe, who owned Hahn's, had bought Mort's business, Lerner's Shoes, and turned it over to the Hahn organization, Rack Room, headquartered in Charlotte. Eventually U. S. Shoe sold off the Hahn complex and Mort bought the business back. He sold out to Deichmann Shoe Co., a German company located in Essen, which had a major position in the discount shoe business in Europe with close to 4,000 stores. They were the "Payless" of Europe and tough competitors.

AmAsia's business with Mort was fantastic with the Mushroom brand and we were the #2 resource in the stores. This led us to reach out and call on the Deichmann group. Mr. Deichmann was an ex-clergyman and extremely philanthropic to Israel. He felt he owed the Jewish people for all that happened under the Nazi's. He also believed that the Savior would not come unless there was an Israel.

We started doing business with our Mushroom-type product under their label. We worked through Heino, the son, who was general merchandise manager, and the buyers answered to him. We became a major resource and we were in Germany on a regular basis.

When the elder Mr. Deichmann came to the States, we entertained him at our home, giving him a tour of the city, and also at our summer home by the sea. They were extremely difficult to do business with. The pricing they demanded was almost to the point of being unreasonable. They wanted you to work on 3% which was impossible since the actual office expenses were 3%. We started to have an impasse over the pricing. We were doing all the styling and development and they did not want to pay for it. We still held on at Rack Room, but Deichmann's business went away.

The first/cost business is cut-throat and unless you have a brand to protect you, you're always facing a pricing problem. Deichmann went directly to our factory and placed the orders. Albert came to us and asked what he should do. I could not tell him not to take them. So, where does an elephant sleep? Anywhere he wants!

Eventually Deichmann threw the Mushroom brand out of Rack Room and went completely unbranded. What I found out later was Deichmann ran all his first/cost business through Switzerland or Liechtenstein and avoided duties and taxes. We could not compete on that basis when the brand was not in play.

There were a number of experiences I will never forget. Always looking for better pricing and good producers, I went up to see Clark Chang's son, Spencer. He opened a factory in Shanghai, at that time almost completely made by hand. Shanghai had a history of a shoe industry and experienced workers. The factory was producing a very well-made product and one of my friends was buying most of the production. Spencer took me out of the city to see a number of factories. It was late November and the cold had arrived. It was a damp, penetrating cold. I knew this type of climate from my days in Florence, but this was far worse. It seemed that China did not have any form of heating from Shanghai south, only to the north. So, we were in the "no heat zone".

We were in the middle of nowhere to see this factory and, after visiting the plant, were going to have lunch there. It was freezing and even though I was dressed for the weather, I was still freezing. When we sat down to eat, I did not take my gloves off. I manipulated the chop sticks the best I could. Living in New England, I had experienced cold weather and was used to it. However, I have never been that cold in my life. Needless to say, we did not work with this factory.

We had limited quality control and to send people into the hinterlands just didn't equate. My Italian friend from Marx & Newman, Simoneto Mori, opened a factory in the north of China. He was totally financed by the zone's administration but he was in the middle of nowhere. The delivery time worked out to be a minimum of four to five weeks longer than factories in the south. Although he could produce great product, it just didn't work for the fashion business and he failed.

MORE SIZES, MORE WIDTHS, MORE STYLES.

5 ½ 6 ½ 7 ½ 8 ½ 9 ½ 10 11 12

TRACTION

FIT

FLEXIBILITY

SHOCK ABSORPTION

CROSSTOWN

Different Strokes

Chapter VIII

"Expect everything so that nothing comes unexpected."
Norton Juster – The Phantom Toll Booth

Our overall business was good. All the divisions were carrying themselves. We had established ourselves branded and private label as a major player. I received a call from Lance Clark, who was the major stockholder of Clarks of England. We had met years earlier when I was with U. S. Shoe and we had a mutual friend, Hugh Woods, whom I became friendly with from Taiwan. Lance had a problem. His term on the Clark Board was up and he wanted to replace himself with someone who was a "shoe man". The existing Board was made up of family members and financial people, no one had any industry experience. Lance was the perfect example of someone who marches to the beat of a different drummer. Tall, broad shoulders, dressed in British tweed and very artistic, he was schooled in shoemaking and just was never able to put his programs together. He knew what to do but could not get it done. He came to me and asked me to join the Board. "Lance...I have a significant business to run. This is a demanding position. You meet every month in London. I need a good reason to give you my time." "We will make it worth your while. Clark has zero presence in Asia and you can take them there and manufacture their needs." I passed the family interviews and became a Board member.

Just as Lance said, the Board members were bright but lacked shoe experience whether it be manufacturing, wholesale or retail, except for one instance. One Board member had retail stores. They had hired a new CEO who was a finance person and had to learn the ins and outs, not only of the business, but also the industry. I first met the CEO in Boston. He had come to visit Clarks NA, which was the star performer in the company. It was part of the "interview". I believe we ended up interviewing each other. Tim Parker was brought in to do what the family was not prepared to do, close the factories in the U.K. and Ireland. The world had changed and the plants were not competitive in the world markets. They didn't want to do it themselves and hired a Hessian. They were buying product in Italy and Eastern Europe through importers. It was not the total answer.

It's always interesting to analyze the reasoning of families in relation to their business holdings. The Clark's at that time were in business for over one hundred twenty-five years, most of that time producing the product in the north of England and the U.K. As I said, they were deathly afraid of their reputations. In came Tim and he was the "bad guy". The family was still able to wear "white hats".

They tried ventures that were leading to nowhere. They asked me to look at the direct injection program for children's product. Clark's had a "lock" on the children's business in the U.K. One of their major programs was buying finished uppers in India and bringing them in to the factory for injection and finishing. The injection process enabled the factory to make finished product easier, cleaner and less expensive. The drawbacks were its limited flexibility and the cost of the molds. The machines were capable of running almost continually and, if the product was designed properly, it could simulate more expensive constructions. You needed volume and the children's business had the pairs. The process was excellent for children's product because it gave them wear-ability. The same product could have been made in China for approximately $2.00 cheaper and with less issues.

They needed to move quickly and my expertise played an important contribution in making it happen. Tim did his job and made the hard choices but he had not addressed the problem of relocating the production and developing product. At dinner I suggested he go out and hire the best product development person he could find. He needed the same combination that made "The Gap" great, a two-man team, Don Fisher and Mickey Drexler. To me, that was the answer. It was never done.

We became a key resource, not only as a maker but bringing style and design to the division. Their style team would come to Boston and see our product mix and select what they needed. We developed their ideas and designs. Between the two processes, we built a significant package of footwear for their retail in the U.K.

ASTER
HOOPLA
HAUTE
GAME
MARPLE
PORTO
PACO
HEART
HAYDN
HUM
ROMANCE
SQUEEZE
MONTRO
MEDEA
META
MOBILE
MOSCOW
MANY
MAINE
TITA
Caressa
Fall 1995
SPELL
GANTRY
PINO
MARACA
MEADE
GATSBY
VROOM
VICAR
GLEN
VALET
GAZE
GLITZ
PLATO
HEATH

The Board was made up of family members. Roger Pedder was a brother-in-law and Chairman. He was extremely capable and, although he was a pompous ass, he did an excellent job. There was an outsider who was strictly a financial person and said little except when it came to review the numbers. There were two additional family members. Tim, the CEO, was the only full-time employee on the Board. He had great influence for he had done the dirty work and the business seemed to be turning upward. One of the Clark's lived in Baltimore and had retail shoe stores that sold the Clark's products as well as comfort footwear from other brands. He was bright and understood retail but had zero knowledge on how a wholesale and manufacturing business should run. The woman had no knowledge of the shoe industry in any area. She was intelligent, didn't say much, and listened.

We had three non-executive members on the Board with no voting power who brought issues, problems and ideas to the meetings. Peter Bolliger was head of retail and a true shoe man. He had come up through the ranks of the industry and understood retail and manufacturing. He had a good sense of fashion and I classified him as a real shoe person. Robin was the CFO and was extremely capable.

The Board meetings were monthly. I would take the day flight from Boston to London arriving at 7:30 pm. A car would pick me up and take me to Street in Somerset to the Clarks headquarters. It was a good 2½ hour ride without traffic. The meeting started early and finished around 2 o'clock. I would rush to Heathrow to get the 6:30 pm British Airways flight back to Boston. Many times it would be an additional day for I would work with the buyers developing the program.

We took Clark's to Asia. The major program was in Vietnam. We had a long time relationship from the early years in Taiwan with Tom, who was the major partner in "StrongBunch". We had a very good relationship with him for we were a major customer in the factory from the early days in Taiwan. He had a factory in China that we were using and had opened a facility in Vietnam. The Taiwanese were the ones who really pioneered Vietnam.

We put emphasis on Vietnam for it did not have countervailing duties as China into the U.K. and EEC. Tom was a pleasure to work with and we built the business into a major program, making as many as 5-6,000 pairs daily. It became the mainstay of the Clark's business. We also developed their "Kay" label which was more classic styling with a comfort factor. We were running on all cylinders.

They say nothing lasts forever. Clark's wanted and needed to open their own office in China. We realized this level of business couldn't continue. Tim wanted to explore buying us and actually came to China to see our operation. I believe it would have happened if he stayed. He received an offer, as we say, he "couldn't refuse" and left before any deal could be finalized.

Peter Bolliger was tapped to be the CEO and he brought in a woman who ran the children's division as his replacement. The deal was put on hold. He felt he could build his own office. The director of product was not one of our fans and he had the inside track. What bothered me to no end was "stealing" one of our key people. The problem was simple. "Where does an elephant sleep? Anywhere he wants!" Even though I was on the Board, they were able to get away with taking the employee. I had to bite my tongue. Clark's business was more than paying the bills.

Clark's NA, led by Bob Infantino, outshined the Clark's operations in the UK. In a sense, it was the "tail that wagged the dog". I used the same analogy with Wohl Shoe and Brown. Bob knew his business, his niche in the market. He had come over from Rockport years earlier. The company was in shambles run by an Englishman from their offices. They sent a Brit to run an American business. It just doesn't work that way. Bob took over and did an unbelievably good job. He gave presentations to the Board from time to time. We became great friends and worked together on certain projects. I was very influential in his receiving his deserved compensation and bonuses.

My days on the Board were numbered as my term was ending. It was six years and they held a "retirement" dinner which was quite moving. Lance and I have remained great friends along with Galahad, his oldest son. I trained Galahad in Taiwan. He worked in the pattern room and actually reached a point where he could cut a pattern and stitch the upper. We are all very close today. I was disappointed that my replacement on the board had no experience in footwear or the fashion business. I know it was a mistake and set a pattern of bringing additional executives into the company with very limited experience in vital areas. There were cracks in the dike.

There were scoundrels you met along the way. I became a partner in a Hong Kong venture with a small factory making dress shoes. There were two brothers and myself. Gabriel, the spokesman, put the deal together. I had known him for quite some time and he seemed to be a fairly upstanding individual. His brother was the inside man and ran the factory.

Gabriel had a relationship with a major Chinese trading company and was able to get finished uppers from China and have them brought to Hong Kong where they became finished shoes. The concept was right but it just didn't work. Gabriel absconded with the money, mine and his brother's and ran off to Canada, never to be seen again. He also is not very welcome in China for he happened to screw the Chinese out of serious money. He was a likable rogue but when he left his brother behind "holding the bag", it was not a very happy ending. My participation was limited but it was a great lesson; it was my second partnership and both ended badly. Gabriel disappeared in the wilds of Canada and no one has heard from him in many years.

I had additional minor incidents. I became part of an investment group dealing in oil and gas and invested substantially in the project. My manufacturers knew about the deal and wanted to join in. I finally relented and let them invest. It didn't work and we all took a serious hit; they, more than me, for I did not go in with both hands. I warned them but they wanted part of the action. They had tied their wagon onto mine as far as the shoe business was concerned and had made fortunes. They thought the same would happen, a rude awakening.

My European friend, Ruud Bresson, had huge financial problems and I tried to get him straight by forgoing my commissions on European sales for a period of six to eight months. Ruud, whom I spoke of before, just did not know how to live as a regular human being. It cost me, but willingly, for he was a genuine person and friend. The only perk came from using his marvelous sailing vessel—a *Swan*—which we used in Sardinia and the Caribbean. It was worth every penny!

Most of the people I lent money to never paid me back and actually I never really expected they ever would. What bothered me was they tried to hide and that made me angry. I guess it was human nature but it hurt. All in all, I look back at these incidents and blame myself for not looking into some of these ventures more carefully. We had done well and the money was not an issue and I just went ahead in a sense "blindly", probably a little too greedy.

Against my better judgment, I also tried to solve India with an agent, Maury Plavin. Maury had worked for me a short time when I was with Shapiro Bros. I still don't know why to this day I went along with the deal. I had experienced great success there with Poland. I thought I could somehow find the right situation again. The Malik's were low cost makers and did not fit into our price ranges. Agra was the place where better footwear was made. Maury just couldn't get it done and I was dumb enough to think he could.

India, by right, should have made more leather shoes than any country in the world. It has unlimited supplies of leather, calf and sheep, and the cheapest and greatest hands in the world. They spoke English and the business community was very bright. The workers, although incredibly poor, have wonderful dexterity. I believe I was just too early in the game. All the ventures failed. I once got off the plane from Frankfurt to Delhi and proceeded to drive to Agra. The drive turned into a seven hour trip with death on every turn. I have never experienced such a ride into hell as I did that night. As I said, the flights arrive in India midnight or later so it was even more frightening than one could ever imagine.

The strange situation about India is that as a leather supplier to the world, the country works. China depends on Indian leather and it works on a grand scale. I tried to put a situation together with one of our main tanners. He not only made beautiful kidskin and some calf, but he was a leather apparel maker for Armani, etc. He cut and stitched a major amount of uppers for some of the best shoe companies in Europe, Gabor and Bally. He put together a plant to make the finished product. I got him a technician, actually Gregory the Russian, and it still didn't work. I don't want to dwell on these points but I realized how stressful and frustrating certain parts of my life had become because of these ventures. I was taking my eye off the ball and I could see the effects. I was losing focus with too many of these projects that were too involved and not cut out for our organization.

Hard Lessons

CHAPTER IX

"I know now we never get over great losses; we absorb them and
they carve us into different, often wiser, creatures. No matter how
smart we may think we are, no matter how committed we are to our
goals, we can lose our way."
Gail Caldwell – Let's take the Long Way Home: A Memoir of
Friendship

We encountered a period of unusual circumstances that
were challenging. I have tried to look at them as objectively as
possible, always coming away with the same conclusions. I am
angry with myself in one sense. I should have seen some of this
coming. Hindsight is foresight.

We started a major program with Nordstrom's and
developed a comfort pump program that was a major win for all
concerned. It was a private label program where we stocked the
product in a wide variety of sizes and colors. We shipped them
directly from our warehouse to theirs and, in some instances,
directly to the stores. I had developed this construction and sold
it to them on an exclusive basis. I shook hands with management
and put $5M in stock on the floor. There were two patterns which
were two pumps, high and low heel.

The program would have not occurred without the creative
abilities of two people, one of them being myself for putting the
product together and the other, Harry Home, the Nordstrom
product person who understood the concept immediately and
pushed to get it done. This was not the average Nordstrom buyer.

Harry was a brilliant shoe person who not only knew product but had the personality to sell it to management. I do not believe the program would have ever seen the light of day without him.

The pumps were called Sidewalk and Sensation and they were one of the great programs of the industry. The program went on for five years, updating colors and size structure. We sold over six million pairs. The Nordstrom Comfort Construction was the envy of everyone in the industry. We designed a new patented dual density comfort system that was built around a unique polyurethane sole and a super soft interior. It gave the product a whole new concept in comfort.

Our ability to service them was unparalleled. The factory turned product around in two to three weeks because we always had the basic colors in leather in our warehouse. We had, at all times, 150,000 pairs in stock for them. The program was so successful that May Co. and Federated wanted the same. We honored our commitment to Nordstrom and kept it exclusive. We felt, as good as the program was, it should have been even more diversified with additional looks. We could not convince the buyers to expand into additional patterns mainly because Harry was gone from the company. It was a natural, but management at that time was run by accountants rather than shoe people which was not the original Nordstrom culture. It was the reoccurring situation in the fashion business, the inability to move forward because either lack of product sense or "frozen at the wheel" syndrome.

The construction was unbeatable. Two situations were occurring at the same time. The factory we had developed over the years and made the Nordstrom program decided they wanted to develop their own brand and go into business. They hired an excellent Italian designer and a very experienced salesforce. They "expected" us to continue using them as our resource and, at the same time, compete against us. We could not go along with a situation as this and were prepared to switch the production to our other major factory that made the same quality level.

Nordstrom wanted to buy the fashion product from the new entity. The program was supposed to be exclusive for Nordstrom. In order to get the factory to make the constructions they needed volume. They had to find basic pairs to give them. They gave them our program. They honored the stock we had on the floor for them but at a reduced price. Their argument was they wanted the product made in the same factory. I showed them the product from our other factory that was identical. They took the program away from us with no real notice. You would think a long-standing relationship deserved a three to six month time frame. Our construction actually was proprietary for we had a patent. We did not want to end up in a legal battle over the patent. We had equipment, etc. with their logos on it. There was a payment made to clear up the equipment charges.

My dear friend, Phil Barach, who was a member of our Board, was livid. He knew the Nordstrom's on a personal basis and insisted on going to Seattle with me to say our piece to no avail. I predicted to their faces that they would not "live" long-term with this factory because of the egoism and paranoid personality of the owner; all that I said came true quickly. It destroyed my faith in humankind and my sense of fair play.

At the same time, our salesman who handled Nordstrom went to work for this factory secretly. He actually was collecting two salaries for some time before giving us notice. I later found out from Leslie that he would buy me ties and shirts every time he would come to the office using a company credit card. I would not have minded, but his taste was awful!

These courses of events were hard to believe. Our portfolio of diversified brands and private label accounts and programs enabled us to weather the storm and move forward. All of this happened at the same time as business in general was off. The rise of athletics and faux-sport product was the major influence. What bothered me most was I lost all my faith in expecting people of character to handle themselves in a just manner. They buckled and let a possible win change their values. I will never understand their decisions and will never forgive their selfishness.

We had a "claim" against this factory. They had delivered a group which was not up to standard. It was a major shipment that was sub-standard and we would have to take a significant loss selling them off as "seconds" quality to our usual jobbers. All of this was going on when they were trying to compete with us by building their own brand and hiring away our sales people. They did not recognize any part of the claim. We sent them production that showed the issues. They rejected their existence. We had invoices from them that needed to be paid and we held up payment until this was settled. They sent two truckloads of workers to our office to picket the surroundings and actually went into the offices and threatened our Director. I went to China over this issue and tried to reason with the factory. They would not recognize any wrongdoing even though I showed them significant evidence.

It got worse. They sent the workers en masse again and I was literally held hostage in the offices. We sent for the police to lift the siege. I was personally threatened and warned that I would receive bodily harm. Alan Sorofman was with me and drove to the border as soon as possible with the help of the police.

We finally settled with the factory. It was a nasty negotiation. Months later when I was in Dusseldorf for the Fair, I was looking at an exhibit and suddenly I was attacked and beaten on my back. The owner of the factory in question hit me. I turned, grabbed him, and somehow or another refrained from beating the living daylights out of him. I didn't want to end up in a German jail or court. What makes this story so unreal is that we put this man in business, taught him how to make the product and took him to Europe for machinery and an education. We talked him into going to China where he became incredibly successful because of being the resource for Caressa.

When I re-think the story and, unfortunately, have to write about it, I get sick just thinking about it. You lose faith in your fellow man all along the way.

We were in line to win major programs for sourcing in Europe and the States. Some of these opportunities came to fruition. They did not offset the loss of the Nordstrom program but lessened the blow.

It was not just business for I was under the impression our association with Nordstrom was more than just a business relationship. I guess I was naïve and unrealistic and I discussed it with Phil. I came to the conclusion "the meek shall not inherit the earth." As hard as I took it, Phil felt worse. He thought his relationship with Nordstrom would win the day for me. He was visibly in mourning over the whole situation.

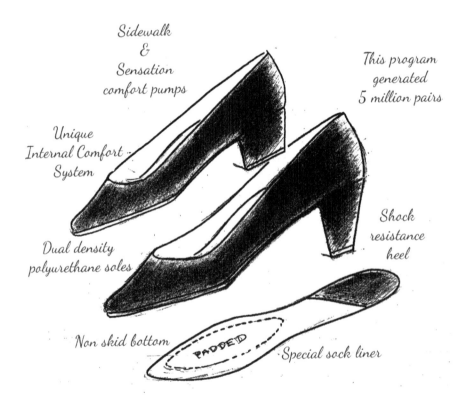

Sidewalk & Sensation comfort pumps

This program generated 5 million pairs

Unique Internal Comfort System

Dual density polyurethane soles

Shock resistance heel

Non skid bottom

PADDED

Special sock liner

We were not moving forward with any great ideas or programs. What had happened was rather predictable as I look back. We were playing defense. Our CrossTown pump business was starting to show signs of needed change. Our inventory levels at the warehouse and at retail did not warrant such a move. It would have cost a fortune to bite the bullet and make the necessary changes. Initially we had taken the right steps and put new product into the stores and wiped out the competition with new product in the right size ranges at great pricing.

Our business was running flat. I believe I had allowed the pump mentality to control our overall business. We had offers for the business over the last few years. I think some of them were real. Either the price was too low or we had priced it too high. I believe we should have made a deal with two opportunities but we passed. Looking back, it was a mistake.

We were then approached by Bennett Importing, the old company that I worked for. Poland had sold his interests to a group of his sales people led by two key sales executives. I do not exactly know how it developed but Poland sold out all his interests. They now owned the business which was geared to sell to discounters or mass merchants. Their business partner was a Chinese who developed a great factory base that translated to a whole series of wins for Bennett. It put them temporarily on the map in the discount area.

Somehow or another they got together with Steven Rubin, who owned Pentland Industries and had acquired a major stake in their company, and licensed Franco Sarto to the company. It was the classic Steven Rubin move, investing in a company that was having issues but had potential. The Franco Sarto brand had been a secondary brand when it was taken over by Bennett. They moved the product to Brazil working with a very astute agent. The brand became a hit with great product designed by Franco and developed into a powerful source with all the department and specialty stores. It also generated an excellent private label business. The business was trending sideways until the brand took over. They had found their niche with Sarto and exploited it to the hilt.

They approached us for the acquisition at the same time they started working with us. They did not have a China resource and we more or less became their agent. Their Chinese partner was gone and they needed "boots on the ground". They were not "shoe people" in the true sense of the word. They weren't retailers or manufacturing oriented, but salesmen in executive positions. Their business was important to us for it brought an additional major private label account. Doing business with another wholesaler is never an easy relationship. There is always a margin issue and a desire on both parties to maintain their independence. It was not easy living in these conditions.

I received a call saying that Steven Rubin was in New York and wanted to see me. He owned a good share of Bennett and was the licensee for Franco Sarto. I had known Steven for many years when I was with U. S. Shoe. He came to our Taiwan office wanting us to be his agent for the U.K. and other countries for a new brand that he acquired for $77,000 called Reebok. I could not take his business for we just signed Hi-Tec, a Dutch-based company, to be their exclusive agent in the Far East. The rest was history. It's strange how things happen.

Steven wanted to buy our business. We were a major resource for Bennett and they were paying us hefty commissions. He wanted our brands and our product development capabilities and know-how. I liked Steven for he was a straight shooter and had a fine reputation. We had a very productive meeting and put on the table a number of options. Steven wanted someone and an organization to fine tune the whole production and product development of Pentland. It all sounded interesting. Bennett had given him significant information. Bennett would not be buying it. I would not have sold to Bennett at any price. The deal would be between Pentland Group and AmAsia Intl. He asked me to forward all the information to him as soon as possible.

We set up a date in London in two weeks. We discussed old times and how the business could be developed with Pentland's divisions. It seemed to be a good approach if we could agree on a price.

He had a method of doing business. He liked to buy companies at the right price that were not in trouble but were either treading water or had started to trend down. He felt he would find one that could be a big winner with his resources. It was a strategy that seemed to work for him.

When I had come back from New York and told Ted about what had transpired, he said, "Dad, do you think we should sell?" "Ted, I have to think about it...YES!" We were at a point where, in order to compete with the major brands, it needed a major infusion of capital and additional personnel. A major advertising campaign for Caressa and a wider in-stock program would be needed. I was at a stage of my life where I did not want to take $3-5M out of my pocket to bet on the future. It reminded me of when I sat with George Shapiro and heard his story. History repeats itself.

Ted and I went to London with our financial person and saw the operation. Pentland's prize was Speedo, which was the #1 brand in the swim market. The business was worldwide and Steve ran it by licensing the brand in most countries. He had a design staff and the manufacturing facilities and received the royalties.

There were shoe brands involved, LaCoste being the jewel in the crown. He had built a marvelous facility/campus together. Our meetings went well. He had gone over our financials and had come up with a price. He knew we wanted to sell and when I countered with a price, he accepted. The whole deal took a little over two weeks.

We became a division of Pentland, answering to their American subsidiary run by Sonny Shar, a long-time confidante and employee. Sonny handled all his investments in the States which included real estate, a fast-food chain and the shoe business. He checked Bennett's books, another shoe company in the cold weather boot business and us. Sonny was pleasant, seemed reasonable, still spoke with a South African accent after 25 years in the U. S. He was a no-nonsense type, "just the facts gentlemen...just the facts". You got along with him as long as you were profitable, a fair bargain.

Steven bought us, not so much for the brands, but for our product development expertise and office. We had a proprietary position in this area. He funded us to build a new facility that would house all Pentland's needs in China. We found a building near our old facility and put together our programs and let them work on their part. There were four floors. We needed the first floor for warehousing of materials and an additional floor for administration and product development. The facility, for all our needs, was more than sufficient. They had plenty of space for administration and growth. I envisioned the operation in China as our division being the provider for all their product development. I believe it also was Steven's, but it didn't work out that way.

Steven took a trip to China and was impressed with the facility and basically was in full agreement with how I envisioned we would work. His idea was brilliant. The new entity would be the product development center for all the English and U.S. brands. We would create a place for the divisions to work and develop the product. The pricing would be direct and not through agents with savings in the range of 30% minimum and total control.

I should have known better. There is a saying in Italian, "Tutto il mundo un paese" which translates "All the world is the same." No division wants to give up their independence in any way, especially if it is to Americans.

We could not get to first base with any of the U.K. based divisions. They had their local resources who serviced them, wined and dined them and were kinfolk. We were the outsiders even though we showed them more than a number of instances that we could price the product 30% to 50% cheaper, no exaggerations. Steven had long ago left these duties to his son, Andy, who did not want to rock the boat. At least that was our impression. It got to the point where it was almost impossible to get an appointment with the divisions in the U.K. What I thought was going to be an integral part of the business turned out to be a tug-of-war with London that we could not win. What should have been a mutual project that delivered what both organizations needed became a one-way street, or should I say, no street at all.

Our two year agreement was coming to an end and we were now free to go about our business and develop a new plan of action with our European customers and sources.

Life is filled with learning experiences and you must sometimes step back and see where they have actually taken you. The question always arises: Did you do the right thing?

Moving On

Chapter X

"For an occurrence to be an adventure, it is necessary for one to recount it."

Jean-Paul Sartre

I had known Bill Snowden in the early years in Taiwan and again in China. He had worked for Nordstrom's as a children's shoe buyer and importer. He went into business for himself and founded Topline. No one worked harder than Bill. He built a very significant business with key discount accounts as Payless, Pic n Pay and discounters in the south. Bill focused on young footwear and had an excellent style eye. He was part of that era where the players in Taiwan and early days in China were part of what I call "the wild West". He spent not weeks but months in Asia building his business. All his energy was centered on making the business successful. I know the story well.

When I was finished with Pentland, Bill called me that week wanting me to come to work as a consultant, actually on a full-time basis. He admired my talent and my vision building my business and being the first to develop a sample facility. Bill followed my lead and built a very fine product development facility as well. He wanted me to run product development for the Report division which was a semi-young branded line with a customer base built around Nordstrom's, Macy's and the like. Bill hired two young design people who were talented but needed direction. The gal was Korean, very sharp and oriented more to detailing and handling the administrative side of the line building. She reminded me of Nancy who worked with me. The young man was a talented designer who needed direction. He knew very little of retail and merchandising. Bill spelled out what he wanted. They needed discipline and a plan. He had been running the two and giving them direction. The problem was he did it part-time. He had the retention span of about sixty seconds.

Topline was based in Seattle and I would go out for a week at a time, generally at least once a month. The facility was top notch. The product area was second to none. Bill was a firm believer in spending what it takes to develop the line. His private label development force was exceptional. They traveled the world buying original shoes to copy and develop versions thereof. The operation was run by a Brazilian, Claudio, who had been with Bill from the outset. He was very talented and knew his business.

My first day Bill picked me up at the hotel in his Ferrari, the second day in his Lamborghini, and the third in his Mercedes. He was a rogue, a very likable rogue. Bill weighed no more than 135 pounds, about 5'8" and always wearing Dolce and Gabana. He had an interesting face with high cheekbones and a receding hairline. His schedule was totally unpredictable and half the time nobody knew where he was.

The two design people were used to dealing with Bill who treated the gal, especially, as a prima donna. I could see this was going to be an ongoing problem. She had a direct pipeline to Bill which she used on a regular basis.

Looking back, I wanted to get into fixing Report's problems and probably came across too strong. This was not my business and there was a learning curve I had to conform to. There were basic problems. Report's product lacked a quality look. All the great product work they had done was nullified by the choice of materials. I immediately called upon the resources I knew to solve the issues.

I used my resource in Bangladesh that solved the problem. Amin was a different kind of a tanner. He had spent twelve years in Italy learning how to make the product. He spoke Italian like a native. In fact, we conversed in Italian more than English. The leather was phenomenal. Bangladesh had great skins. Amin knew how to develop a product that was Italian, not Asian. I actually became his agent and lined up factories to use his material.

My trip to Bangladesh was quite interesting. Actually the poverty in India was more widespread and intensive which was surprising. Amin met me at the airport after passing through customs and immigration with the hordes of mankind. Westerners paid their visa bills, I believe it was $50 to $75 to enter the country. The hotel was fine; a Sheraton with reasonable accommodations. The tannery was, more or less, what I expected. It was relatively clean and seemed to function quite well. The leather coming off the production line was sensational. Bangladesh had the best raw material, gazebo calf, midsize skins, smooth with few imperfections. The climate and conditions were perfect; high humidity kept the skins of the animals soft and pliable. They did not have scars because there wasn't any wire. Amin's ability to make great leather was evident in the product.

I was only there for two and a half days. Amin had set up a date with his bank to have me give them a "talk" on the opportunities in our markets. It served Amin well and he was most appreciative. Amin took me to the shopping area where you could see the handiwork of the country. I bought a number of items, one of which was a king-size bedspread, pillow cases and case that was totally embroidered with a story done in black and white. It took three months and two people to work on it. It was magnificent, it cost less than $200.

I needed new resources and inexpensive leathers that would work and have the right fashion looks. I enlisted my old friends from India, the Malik's, to make my flat sandal collection.

They gave me a great leather source, their own, which became an important part of the program. Kareema not only became a major resource for Topline but a resource for a number of companies. Abdullah was the son of the owner and extremely capable.

Kareema became a major resource of our unbranded programs. The ability to have prices 15—30% below the market gave us a great advantage. It enabled us to compete favorably in the marketplace.

Topline was run on a daily basis by Bryan Collins who handled sales. Rich Philby ran the operational and financial ends. We all got along extremely well. I took Bryan and his wife to India to see the opportunities. We saw Mumbai, Malik's operation, and New Delhi and Agra. Agra was the heart of the Indian shoe industry. I had developed a relationship with a factory that, in my estimation, should have been a major resource for not only Topline, but the U. S. market. The owner was bright, willing to listen and understood the need for product development. He had invested in the latest machinery and two European technicians who spent three months at a time at the factory. He hired designers to do his collections. His pre-production equipment was state of the art. I was absolutely "sold" on the man and the factory. I brought Bryan there so he could see firsthand what I was so excited about. The problem was he wasn't Bill. Years before, Bill had tried India and it was a disaster. I tried to get him to come but it was useless. I actually got a test order from Clark's. You cannot believe what I had to do to get the test. The boots were very successful. Management saw them at retail and were more than pleased. Why did it not go forward? Everything was right with the product and the pricing was $2—4 less per pair under China. The test was in the States through Clark's NA. The answer was simple, how could the U.K. admit that Clark's NA had developed a product line that made them look as if they had "missed the boat"? Both groups put the project on hold. I really never understood why.

Resource departments had their own sources and wanted to stay with them for a number of reasons, some of which did not equate.

I felt this was important to go over at this point. India had found its place with European brands and importers. It did not do the same in the U. S. or Canada. Part of it was distance. The lead times with Europe were less and the key factor was little or no duty to the EEC, a major factor.

Bryan saw the Taj Mahal and I enjoyed it again. We went back to Delhi and flew home from there. The leathers that I inserted into the line were extremely well received. The overall quality of the line was significantly improved. However, I had made a judgment call that was wrong centering the collection in a little less junior and we stumbled. Bill was not pleased and stepped in to rectify the mistake. It was his business and money on the line and I understood. I would have done the same.

There were so many areas that needed to be overhauled. I spent time in the China office trying to straighten out the issues. They needed to replace some of the technicians. They were not performing. The whole pre-production process needed to be revamped. The sample room needed a major change in direction and procedure. I hired a Spanish pattern maker of mine to solve the pre-production pattern process. He was an immediate help and simplified the process, especially the last-making and confirmation. Pepe brought a whole different approach to the technical issues. The problem is when one does not wish to change.

I called a meeting in Seattle to discuss a total re-organization of the sample process. We had everyone there who had a responsibility in the process along with the brass. I had everything charted on the blackboard to show how it works. I had proposed a radically new system. In Seattle we had four to five excellent artists that drew up the ideas for the collections. They came from art schools or worked in mechanical drawing. The stylists for private labels worked in this manner generally off original shoes. They would have the artists draw up the sketches, asking them to make new looks based on the construction of the original shoe. These sketches were detailed and sent over to China to be made. The first order of the process was to have the Chinese pattern makers take the drawing and translate it into a pattern by drawing it on the plastic form over the last and making the pieces for the samples.

My idea was to train the artists in Seattle to draw on the last, cutting out a whole process. It would eliminate more than a step; the artist who had more of a "feel" for the designer would do a far better job. It would take less than a month to train the artists. Productivity would improve and there would be less corrections rather than allowing Chinese pattern makers, who hadn't a real sense of style, to make the decision on how the initial model would be made. Translating sketches by designers who knew nothing of the market only caused correction after correction.

The major problem in the sample-making as it existed was that all the work that went into the process was useless once we wanted to make the pattern for production. They were not making the paper patterns correctly. The necessary additional measurements were not done accurately, a process that would have taken minutes. Instead, they haphazardly put them into the pattern. I believe the major fashion brands doing business in China should adopt this system of development. The benefits are enormous saving time and creating a better product.

When the uppers were stitched, they needed to be lasted. When the laster/sample maker did this by hand, he was able to juggle the pattern and compensate for the mistakes. The pattern was useless for production. If we were to go forward with production, we had to start from scratch and redo it completely. The whole process would be better off if we proceeded as I outlined. The patterns would be at least three fourths of the way there if used for production.

Bill thought it was a great idea but would slow down the whole process. I argued that it would speed everything up. We had a real problem with last making. They did not use a standard. The last shape was usually copied from the toe shape of the original shoe. The sample room didn't use standard back parts or OK'd lasts and put the new toe shapes on the copied original shoe. Again, everything had to be redone. This process was costly from every viewpoint.

I set up a system for the confirmation process. What I wanted to do was standardize everything. My concept was based on what was happening in China. Prices were rising. The factories were all located around Guangzhou when we started and now, in order to achieve price points, you had to travel a very significant distance. Topline had to open an office in the north. My idea was to make the confirmation process easier. I wanted to OK all the patterns right in our office by using the same lasting machines in each of our factories. We could then make the patterns and approve them right in our office. Everyone would have the same elements to deal with. Standardization was and still is the key.

Everyone loved the idea. It never happened. I know the reason, no one wanted to take the time or give the effort to put it together. It was the same story with the sample project. It took time to make it right. What nobody was willing to admit was the end result would be better shoes with less effort and cost. I bring this up now for the distances in China are even greater. Just the time it took for the technicians to get to the factories was reason enough to adopt the system.

I had been with Topline for three years and had worked in every area of the business. They felt they had grown their organization to a level where they didn't need an expensive consultant. I agreed. I would have liked to fully implement some of the programs that I just outlined but that was not to be. We achieved only some partially. Shortly after, Bill sold the business and sailed his new yacht off in the sunset.

Probably on a personal level I re-learned how to work for someone else. It was not so easy. Bill could be a Jekyll & Hyde, but the kind I understood. It was an experience. The other win was finding the best travel agent that handled Topline. She handles all the travel for me and Horizon Footwear.

Before selling the business to Pentland, we had talked with a long-time friend, Gianni Zilioto. He was the major principle in "Everybody", a well-known brand in Europe. Gianni had been to our offices in China and we actually priced some product for him. He was duly impressed with our operation and we were at ease with one another for we all spoke Italian which was a major win since Gianni did not speak English. Gianni's reputation as a designer was unparalleled in the European market. Short in stature with an amazing amount of energy, he was always dressed in the latest fashion. The friendship between us was real and we both recognized each other's talents.

Everybody, or the parent company, BZ Moda, is located in Stra which sits five to six miles from Venice in the area they call the Riva Brenta. It is an interesting place for the Venetian princes dug a canal from Venice to Stra so they could escape the heat and malaria.

They built magnificent palazzos on the banks.

The Everybody brand had a proprietary position in northern Europe. Their strength was in the German market where they sold every major better outlet and boutique. The brand was distributed in the Netherlands, Germany, Belgium, Scandinavia and France. The product was placed in forty countries, mainly through the International Fairs, namely Dusseldorf and Milan. The concept of the collection was built on a unique tannage of ultra-soft glove leather that was almost impossible to duplicate. The special finishing process gave it life and dimension like no other. The combination of Gianni's original design concepts in conjunction with this glove material gave the product a look and feel that set it apart.

A great classification from our branded lines

We had the experience level in China and worked with them to set up the production. Their facilities in Slovakia were not competitive. They had to come to China. We worked out a contractual agreement that gave us the right to produce Everybody with our development and production for North America and the UK. Pentland was not interested at all in this venture. The discussions did not materialize with London because our contractual agreement with Pentland ran out. We were free to go about an agreement. We felt the niche market for Everybody was better for individual retailers and boutiques. We would avoid the discounters, including Macy's. We did seek legitimate stores as Nordstrom and the internet organizations.

The business was set up as Ted's business. I would be involved in the product development process. I had my fill of administration, customer issues and local shoe shows. I still enjoyed the styling process and wanted to continue along those lines. Ted set up a salesforce covering the country and Canada. Start-ups are not easy and we seemed to have a reasonable beginning. We found some great reps and the collection was superb.

Everybody had some American customers. They never had a salesperson in the U.S. or an organization. There was and still is a group of savvy, independent retailers that came to Milan to buy Italian product and were good customers. They formed the nucleus of our clients. We now used these satisfied retailers to spread the word. Our type of business had to be built on word of mouth. The audience was much wider for now we were able to offer the customers terms and service in their area.

Ted had the experience level and the right personality to work with this client base. He was soft-spoken.....not overbearing and more than willing to work out any issues. My only real involvement was working on the collection and presenting the product line at the sales meeting. Some of the meetings tested your ability to restrain yourself. Salesmen had the bad habit of coming to the meeting unprepared. They did not do their "homework" studying the market.

Ted built the business one customer at a time and put on 20% increases in a down market in consecutive years. It was a real partnership, producing the production together and developing the collections four to six times a year. Our contribution not only covered design but every aspect of the operation.

Thoughts Unfold

CHAPTER XI

"The soul becomes dyed with the color of its thoughts."
Marcus Aurelius, Meditations

I have lived through some very difficult situations in my years in this business. What I am about to write about is probably one of the most disappointing scenarios in my experiences. It destroys my faith in my fellow-man. I have always been the eternal optimist. It has shaken my beliefs.

I was approached by a salesman who had a fine reputation in the industry. He asked if I would work as his agent and designer on a new line he had started. Normally I wouldn't even consider such a request. He captured my interest as I really liked him. He was "wicked smart", a great eye, and the greatest sense of humor. He had all the experience, talent and aptitude to get the job done. What sealed the deal was his ability to find an anchor customer to give him the pairs to launch. I said "yes" and developed a collection for him to show. He understood how the process worked and was an asset in putting the collection together. We worked as a team, traveled to Europe and talked every day on developing the collection. It was a pleasure to work with him on this program.

The first collection was fairly well-received and sold in the same manner. The second collection, which was developed by us, seemed to be well-designed and placed reasonably well. The third collection was problematic. The production was rated, in my estimation, as a C+ and he had to come up with markdown money. It turned out to be in his interpretation a much bigger problem. He brought me production pairs to discuss with the factory and there was some evidence there was a reason for a partial claim. But it was left open to see how the situation played out, it was his choice. We wanted the issue settled. We had financed the entire project and were on the hook for a serious sum of money. It was no laughing matter.

We went ahead with the spring collection as always. He came up to Boston a day before the show and I went over the whole spring program. He loved the sandals. He took the collection with him for the show which was starting tomorrow. I had gone down to New York for our showing and tried contacting him late in the day to see if he had any reaction. I could not get him on his cell phone that day or the next. I sent him an email that the missing samples had arrived. He replied that he was sending a service to pick them up. I knew something was dramatically wrong.

That day I received a letter from his attorney stating that he was suing us for $1M for the bad production, etc. We were only acting as his agent and our agreement stated this and would represent him in any legal issues with the factories. We had protected ourselves by tying him personally to the agreement, not just his company. It was hard to believe. The end result was hearing that he went to China to work with a new resource and the factories, which he owed the money to, persuaded him to pay. All of this could have been avoided. It still bothers me that a situation of this kind was allowed to occur.

I did not wish him ill will; he panicked and didn't think it out. We were prepared to help him in every way, negotiating with the factories over the claim. It is hard at times to understand why people do certain things and make illogical responses that turn around and somehow rise up and "bite" you. Some lessons are expensive learning experiences.

Shoe production is moving around the world. There are alternatives that exist today on where shoe production can flourish and be more efficient in many ways. The question is what type of footwear you are producing and what suits your particular need. My knowledge is limited to women's fashion product so my comments are in this area.

CHINA - We brought better shoemaking there, first through our Taiwanese factories that moved to the mainland in 1987. Our Caressa brand was the first legitimate leather branded product to be made in China. Today there are many manufacturing facilities for women's footwear on the mainland. They fall into distinct categories.

To understand the scope of the industry one only has to go to Guanzhou Shoe Market which is the center of the retail/wholesale distributors. The leather, component, synthetic suppliers are all located there. More than 30,000 visitors per day attend the complex, seven days a week.

The industry has been moving inland to take advantage of less expensive labor, real estate and the cost of competing with the electronic industry, etc. The major brands, whether European or American, control the better makers and are now feeling the price pressure of rising labor and other costs. What used to be a shoe zone around Guanzhou and Dongguan has now been moved to the further reaches of the countryside and beyond to create better price points.

There already has been serious movement in the industry further inland. I believe shoe prices will rise significantly for they have been suppressed for years. Making shoes is a difficult process and pricing is catching up to reality.

Technology will be the next story for the manufacturers. The major factories will adopt the latest in equipment and robotics to stem the price rises. I cannot believe this will not happen. The big change really falls in the political area.

The industry was developed by the Taiwanese. Today it is the local Chinese that have taken over the market. They compete on a different level since they are taxed at a different rate than Taiwanese-owned factories. It will not be long before the industry will be totally home-grown plants. This will be an even more difficult situation for the importers and brands.

We have experienced in our manufacturing that it is far more difficult to deal with Chinese-owned plants. They are less sophisticated, less experienced and less willing to follow the instructions of any western technical staff. There are exceptions but few and far between.

What does all this mean? It's an additional learning curve for all concerned and there will be casualties for those who are not willing to bend and cooperate. This is already happening every day. There will be a "shake out" and those that are left will become the core makers. I cannot see China not being a major player in this industry. It has too many plusses on its side to lose their proprietary position. Yes, they have problems, but far less than their competitors. This is not only true of the shoe industry but other related business models that were developed by the Taiwanese.

INDIA - For all intent and purposes, they should be the leading resource and producers of leather footwear worldwide. Most people don't realize the vast quantities of raw material that are available on the Indian sub-continent. I include Bangladesh and Pakistan.

They are the major leather suppliers to China and send to Italy substantial quantities of skins to be finished. They have all the pieces to reach the #1 position; labor, material, and education. They have access to a middle management group that speaks the King's English and have the education to go along with it. The labor pool is endless.

Up until now the government has been a major obstacle in developing the industry. With tariffs between Indian states, bringing in machinery, custom duties and regulations have been the major causes to hinder the development. The infrastructure is another obstacle. Nothing in this world can duplicate their transportation systems. Their roads and rail system are all at least seventy-five years behind the times. Part of the issue is the personality and mores of India. They need to find a way to link the shoe centers through a modern infrastructure of roadways.

There is a turn-around in the early stages. They have been able to harness mass production only on a small scale. It should happen, the question is when?

SOUTHEAST ASIA, LAOS, CAMBODIA - These small countries have a role, but it is not major and will continue to grow but at a slower pace. They do not have indigenous materials and the component industry is in its infancy on getting parts from China.

VIETNAM - Today they are the only true competitors to China. There has been a major trend of Taiwanese-owned entities moving from China to Vietnam. It is not only labor cost, the Taiwanese are uneasy with their position in China. Vietnam has created a niche market for vulcanized footwear and has done an excellent job developing fashion and contemporary footwear. The Taiwanese dominate the market as they did in the early years in China.

U.S.A. - I believe there is a very bright future for the American industry. It is definitely tied to the athletic business. Until now the athletic import shoe industry has been centered in Asia with the bulk of production in China, followed by Vietnam.

Today the whole concept of development and styling has changed. Leather was the original material, this has changed dramatically. The major materials used in athletic product are fabrications and synthetics. With the emphasis on the materials, it has spawned a whole new way to manufacture the product. The process is now heat sear, laser, and electronic bonding, the need for stitching is minimal to non-existent. Since the upper represents at least 70% of the labor, these new processes will generate a whole new approach to where the product will be made. The use of robotics and 3-D printers and the ability to have very significant quantities of each model will allow the industry to gear up to produce with maximum efficiency at minimal cost.

With rising costs in China and throughout Asia, I believe you will see the rebirth of an industry here. What happened in the auto industry will re-occur in footwear. The Chinese manufacturers, driven by the key brands; Nike, New Balance, etc. will set up plants here in the States. They will awaken an industry that has almost vanished from the American scene.

I am extremely confident that this new impetus will become reality in the next five years. I do not see the same happening for what we call the "brown shoe" or fashion shoe business which has a totally different approach in the making process.

BURMA - Eventually it will be important for it has leather and labor like India. The question is when will it happen? The political situation will dictate the timetable.

EASTERN EUROPE - The Italian manufacturers use these countries to make the product. All the components as of now are coming from Italy and they are able to produce the bottom end of the better shoe market. They are in competition with China and can only exist if the Chinese currency is strong. Their life expectancy is still up in the air.

AFRICA - It will happen, but slowly starting with low cost discount items and generic goods that are simple and huge quantities. How will it grow? That remains to be seen. Ethiopia is the principal model. It has the backing of both the government and Chinese investors. Let's see how it develops.

ITALY - There will always be an "Italia". The need for couture product will always be there. The market for Italian product under $200 is practically non-existent.

They are still the fashion leaders, and the industry finds a way to keep their product in the limelight. Creativity is rewarded, for there is a segment of the market that desires Italian product at any price.

CHAPTER XII

"Try not to be a man of success...rather a man of value."
Albert Einstein

I've written about Phil Barach in portions of the book but only in broad generalities. He had such an influence on my life that it is hard to describe almost any aspect where he was not involved. He was the reason I went to Italy and later gave me the opportunity to run product development and the Far East. During that period we bonded and became friends, but that was only the beginning. Phil set the stage to allow me to buy the offices in Taiwan and go into business. He could have killed the deal anytime but he let it happen. I do not believe anyone else in his position would have gone along with the deal.

The relationship with Phil grew as I went into business. We kept in touch on a regular basis and he started to take me into his confidence. The U.S. Shoe Board was killing him. They were very conservative and did not have the vision to see what Phil wanted to build. Lenscrafters was going through the roof. The total company was doing $2.6 billion with room to grow.

Phil was 59 years old when he vacated the CEO spot and handed it over to Ban Hudson, who had been CEO of Lenscrafters. It was his choice. Phil had a three-year contract as Chairman and it was an extremely hard time for him. He did not share the new vision of the CEO and was constantly agitated over the footwear and apparel part of the business. I learned many years ago that you had to have a person with vision and a style sense to run a fashion company. We became closer, talking two to three times a day. His parting with the corporation was not pleasant. Phil did not go along with many of the programs the Board and Hudson put forth and actually stood up at a stockholder's meeting and gave his piece. Luxotica eventually bought U. S. Shoe in a hostile takeover for $1.4 billion. They sold off the shoe division to Nine West and Casual Corner to a group of Italian investors. They wanted the market in the U. S. and Lenscrafters gave it to them.

I never understood the situation at U.S. Shoe. When Phil retired they did nothing for him. He had taken the company from $100 million to $2.6 billion and they didn't even have a luncheon in his honor. Even the staff didn't have the "where-with-all" to do something. Well...I did. We had a surprise party in New York where we invited his non-shoe friends as well as a whole group of shoe executives. He was totally surprised and was appreciative of the gesture his whole life. We opened two scholarships in his name and gave him the honors he so much deserved. Phil was the only other member of our Board and I constantly reminded him that he was still my CEO.

It was a tough period for him and I was extremely supportive. In a way, it was payback for him on my part for all that he had done for me. When things were rough and Judy and I were having our problems, Phil literally saved my marriage putting us back together. He constantly spoke to Judy on my behalf. It was that "rebound philosophy" of his, never stop lobbying for your position. He wrote recommendations for our kids for school and work. He even wrote to my mother. He was always there. We talked almost every day and saw each other when he was in the area. I knew months before he died that he had cancer and spoke with him the day before he passed away. We contacted most of the people who knew him and put together a memorial service for friends and family that was a fitting tribute to such a special person. I miss him every day. I've had friends but none like Phil. He was such a force in my life and there is a hole, which I believe will never be filled.

There are many people who in their own way helped me along. There were the key people; Ralph Shapiro, Dick Herman, Phil Barach, Carl Berger, George Shapiro, naturally my wife and children. But there were others along the road who had compassion and wanted to help some young man make it. I had the opportunity in many of these instances to return the favor to some of these wonderful people. I am eternally grateful for having been given the opportunity to do so.

My brother-in-law was a father figure to me in my teens and helped me in many ways. I more or less lived with them during those years, babysitting my nieces and nephew. Abe Solomon died early in his fifties, never knowing that he would have two grandsons. Bram Hubbell turned out to be a great kid and stayed with us so he could work and earn his tuition for graduate school. One day he came to me and told me he was returning home because he couldn't earn enough and would figure out a new course of action. I sat him down and wrote him a check for the needed funds. "Bram...I am giving you this money because your grandfather helped me when I needed it. And it will be your responsibility to help someone else when you're in a position to do so. That's the way it works."

There was constant stress in running AmAsia and working for Pentland, probably more so with them, but it had reached a new level.

My sister, Lillian, died suddenly and I was left with a 43 year old nephew named Ted who was autistic. It was a difficult situation for he lived in Worcester approximately 45 miles away. I was the only family member who could take care of him. Ted did work and was fairly self-sufficient. His real handicap was a mother who had not allowed him to do anything for himself. We arranged for help during the week and were with him every weekend. We gave him the opportunity to be more self-sufficient and he did remarkably well. With weekly supervision, Ted seemed to like his new life with more freedom. He was a classical music enthusiast and built his whole life around playing the flute and clarinet and listening to recordings. Ted suddenly had problems with his leg and it was cancerous. The initial operation seemed to work for six months. However, it had spread and within six months he was gone. It was six years since my sister died and Ted had become a different person. His quality of life had been raised significantly. That was the tragedy. He had come so far, and it ended so soon. The family was heart-broken.

I haven't written a great deal about my Dad because I really don't know anything about him firsthand. He died when I was six weeks old and left my Mom with six children. So, I haven't any memories, just stories told to me by my family. Theodore Finn was a personable man who had an automobile repair business in Worcester, Massachusetts. He was an extremely able technician, not only with automobiles but anything mechanical. He had tinkered with working a variety of inventions and actually an airplane just before his death. He always had his shortwave radio with him after dinner, listening to the events in Europe. Ted died while driving from Leominster, Massachusetts back to Worcester, supposedly from a heart attack and went off the road. There was some question regarding his death for he was gassed during the war and suffered attacks and it seems there was a genetic flaw in his family tree where the male members all had heart defects and issues. He was setting up a Chevrolet agency in Leominster when this occurred.

My mother did not know the first thing about their finances. She was given poor advice from her brother who only wanted to distance himself fearing he would have to help support us. When he saw my mother on the Jewish shopping street, he would cross the street and try to disappear. I believe I saw him only three to four times in my early years. All was lost and the end result was being "dirt poor". There wasn't any significant insurance and only a Soldier's Relief Pension for this was before Social Security. I have often thought about how different my life would have been if my Dad had lived his normal years. Would I have taken the same path or would I have opted for another much different road? The possibilities are endless as is the speculation. What if he had developed the "Chevy" agency? Would I now be the owner of a number of agencies?

Teddy Finn was a visionary of a sort, realizing the potential of the automobile in 1935. I've often fantasized on where fate would have taken me. They say I inherited his vision and work ethic. I know my Mom taught me to stay the course and gave no quarter. She did not have that option in her situation.

My grandfather painted murals in the churches of Russia and lived his dream of coming to America. That's where the artistic ability comes from. Rachel and I received that gene. My son, Ted, received the mechanical one from his grandfather. My brother has given me the most insight into my Dad for he was almost twelve years old when he died. Ben remembers the big dark green Marmon with mohair upholstery that was my Dad's pride and joy. I have a large photo of Ted Finn in his army uniform as he fought in World War I. He was a handsome man around 5'9". I turned out to be the tallest in the family as my mother was almost his height.

I was always reminded of my Dad when I said "Kaddish" for him on the anniversary of his death every year since I can remember. In my early years I was petrified when men from the "shul" stood over me waiting to pounce on any possible mistake while chanting the prayers. I have tried to analyze my feelings toward my Dad. It's been a difficult time trying to come to grips with the idea of where my Dad was in my life. Maybe it was a defense mechanism? Maybe I was angry that he was not here to help me, to love me, to see who I was. It's something that I have never been able to sort out. I guess I really never will.

My mother was both father and mother and I find it hard to differentiate if there was a need for two. Julia was such a powerful figure in my life that I never really felt I was missing a Dad. She was always there. He is there somehow in the total mix. I believe he has influenced my life by continually making me realize that I needed to do it on my own for he was not there. I wonder what he would have thought of me.

I really haven't talked about my siblings. My sisters and brother have been very dear to me. Actually I didn't get to know them until I was older for they were older and left the house for their own lives. It's a story for another book.

Having grown up without a father, I did not have the experiences one has with their Dad. I tried to give both my children what I did not have, love from a male figure, a loving Dad. Here are letters from both my children that I cherish.

MARCH 1, 1994

DEAR DAD,

HAPPY BIRTHDAY!
I HOPE YOUR SKI TRIP WAS GREAT AND YOU GOT SOME MAJOR VERTICAL & POWDER CONDITIONS. I'M SURE IT WAS BEAUTIFUL THERE.

I'D LIKE TO TAKE THIS OPPORTUNITY TO THANK YOU FOR ALL YOU'VE DONE FOR ME. I COULD NEVER TRULLY THANK YOU FOR THE OPPORTUNITY YOU HAVE GIVEN ME AS AN ARTIST. TO BE ABLE TO CONCENTRATE SOLELY ON PAINTING IS SOMETHING MOST ARTISTS NEVER EXPERIENCE. I HAVE TRIED TO USE THIS ADVANTAGE TO THE FULLEST. YOUR EXAMPLE OF PASSION & ULTRA-HIGH INTEGRITY IN YOUR OWN WORK HAS BEEN A FINE EXAMPLE. I HAVE LEARNED SO MUCH & AM VERY GRATEFUL.

I ALSO REALIZE THAT IT IS AN INCREDIBLE FINANCIAL BURDEN ON YOU. ████ THIS IS SOMETHING I'VE ALWAYS BEEN UNEASY ABOUT. I FEEL THAT IT IS PAST DUE THAT I TRY & ASSUME THESE RESPONSIBILITIES. I HAD A CRAZY IDEA A FEW YEARS BACK THAT I'D BE DOING THAT BY NOW WITH MY PAINTING BUT THAT WAS OVERLY IDEALISTIC THINKING.

I'M TRYING TO FIGURE OUT AN EMPLOYMENT SOLUTION THAT ENABLES ME TO EXIST IN 2 LOCATIONS BUT THIS HAS BEEN DIFF-ICULT. I PLAN ON FINDING A JOB HERE IN LAKE PLACID FOR THE SUMMER/SPRING TO HELP OUT. AFTER THAT I'M NOT SURE YET, BUT AM WORKING ON A FEW IDEAS. I'M PRETTY HAPPY WITH MY OWN WORK RIGHT NOW, I FEEL ▨▨▨ ▨▨ ▨▨▨▨▨▨ INTO MY OWN IN A VERY FOCUSED WAY.

I JUST WANTED TO LET YOU KNOW THAT I'VE BEEN THINK-ING OF LATELY & THAT I'M WORKING ON A SOLUTION.

YOU ARE A GREAT DAD, DAD. I'M A VERY LUCKY PERSON.

HAPPY BIRTHDAY.

I LOVE YOU.

Forward   Forward as Attachment   Reply   Reply All   Message List

Unread   Delete

Subject: FD

From: "Ted Finn" <tedjfinn@gmail.com>

Date: Sun, June 21, 2015 9:11 am

To: "Norman Finn" <nfinn@horizonftwr.com>

Cc: "Ted Finn" <Tedjfinn@gmail.com>

Priority: Normal

Options: View Full Header | View Printable Version | Download this as a file | View Message Details

Dear Dad,

Had a very nice visit with Rosalie & Michele they both send their love to you and Mom. Please pass along regards.

Best wishes for a happy fathers day. I am very proud of all that you have accomplished. In spite of difficult environment working together these past years has been quite enjoyable and as always educational. Your support, assistance, and unconditional love over these years deeply appreciated and respected. I know most times I am not prone to big displays of emotion but that by no means represents how I feel and where my heart is on matters. So just so you know you have my love and respect.

I know now is a time of new challenges with taking on more responsibilities at home and also looking after your own health. You have always stressed and lived your life teaching and acting on the value of family and I want to thank you for teaching those values to me. Also the gift of taking us to Italy and taking us skiing both near and far are experiences that shaped our lives in so many fundamental and positive ways. These are just a few of the many wonderful things you have done for us and just wanted to let you know how important this is and how thankful I am. Thanks for being a great Father :-).
Love

Ted

Move to: INBOX   Move   Delete & Prev | Unread & Prev | Unread & Next
Delete & Next

Mel Brooks wrote a song, "Hope for the Best, Expect the Worst". I believe hope is important but I never lived my life on hope alone. Oh yes, it was there, but I depended on my talent, drive and intelligence (at times) to achieve my goals. I heard the song on his TV special and got a good laugh. I then started to think about the title. My words and theme were quite different than Mel's.

Hope for the best. Opportunity only comes to those who are strong.
The ability to stay the course short or long.

Hope for the best. It's important to find that road
For life is always a test of one's code.

Hope for the best. Life does not reward those lost
For success comes at a cost.

Let's hope for the best.....but make sure it's not dependent
On life's lottery or purse
Or expect the worst.

It's been quite a while since I've been an employee of U.S. Shoe. It was October of '87 when I said goodbye to Phil and the corporation. There has been a lot of water under the bridge. My time there was filled with a whole array of emotions. Hostility, fierce politics, jealousy, egos, wins and some good times and friends, made up my seventeen years.

Writing this book has brought back most of those memories. Some of them even now are hard to believe they happened. But, most of it I chalk up to learning to live in an imperfect world with very imperfect people, myself among them.

A few months ago I had the occasion to speak to an ex-U. S. Shoe employee living in Cincinnati. He was part of a group trying to set up a reunion of the company. They were making a list of people to invite. He then told me they were not going to invite Lyle, the ex-president of the shoe division. I didn't say anything, just smiled. These were the same people who worked directly for him and sang his praises. They were "yes" people and almost never had the courage to stand up to him when he was wrong or just to debate. Just thought of it! You know, I never got an invitation either, oh my!

I realize they didn't want to lose their jobs or get put in the "doghouse", but it went far beyond that when it was not necessary. No one had more reason to throw stones at him than I. But when I heard what they planned to do, I was appalled. He was an employee who, in his own way, did his best and should have been given the same invitation as everyone else. I finally saw the true character of this group. They were all on the same page. It only confirmed my opinion of the team. They were never there for him and when he was down, they kicked him, hard and often.

I am not in the business of running down U. S. Shoe. On the contrary, it gave me the opportunity to have incredible opportunities for myself and family. It put me in business and made my future very bright. I probably would have never left under different circumstances. Events brought me good fortune. I owe a debt to Phil and to the company for allowing it to happen. I shall ever be grateful.

When Phil died I called Lyle to tell him. He was distraught and said he couldn't come to the funeral because he had cancer. I did not know what to say. My heart went out to him.

In Retrospect

Chapter XIII

"It's so difficult, isn't it, to see what's going on when you're in the absolute middle of something? It's only with hindsight we can see things for what they are."

S. J. Watson...Before I go to Sleep

Herb Hirsch, my head technician, and I have discussed many times our history in Taiwan and the early days in China. We estimated that between us we spent close to eight years through constant trips between 1975 and 2004. It's hard to believe that we traveled there over a period of thirty years. The trips were anywhere from ten days to over a month during this period.

At that time Taiwan was a personal wasteland. There was no reason to be there if you weren't making shoes. Outside of the office and developing the business, a westerner had little choice for entertainment. It was the "knock-off" book store or "Jimmy, the tailor" for shirts and lousy suits made to order as the main source of entertainment. The rest was trouble.

The book store sold little quotation signs that would sit on your desk. I bought two.

The first, Rule #1 – The boss is always right. Rule #2 – If the boss is wrong, see Rule 1!

The second, when you have them by the balls, their hearts and minds will follow. They are still sitting on my desk and are rules I tried to live by at times.

Between 1975 and the early eighties, we worked

unending hours where we developed everything ourselves. The last and component industries were built by our sweat and expertise besides working with the factories. I've talked about the sample room where we visited them after midnight and the seven-day work weeks. We were mainly consumed in this manner. What we would take for granted today did not exist. We really were the pioneers totally on new ground.

1. No one outside of the hotel spoke English, if you ventured out, you better have a hotel card.

2. There was only Chinese television or movie theatres.

3. Entertainment was mingling in the hotel restaurant or lobby. I can't tell you how many times I walked down to the lobby hoping to find someone I knew or could talk with.

4. The major form of entertainment was the factories taking us to dinner.

5. There was an expat community and club designed for families, not us singles, and really not accessible from the hotel.

6. What was available were the "girlie" bars in the vicinity. Some of us could not pass them up.

Work was the motivator, clearly every day you worked toward achieving your agenda if it was a day earlier you could go home. Actually, that was a fallacy, you had to set a date to return for the workload never ceased nor did the issues.

So, what occurred was fairly predictable. The desire for companionship was ever present. Loneliness was the element nobody expected when they signed up for this duty, for it was duty. My daughter, Rachel, had a great saying when she struggled in New York City. "You have to be a soldier every day." It was so true at that time in Taiwan.

Loneliness became an acid that ate away at you. We thought we could lick it with the punishing work schedule and some occasional "harmless" activities. When the work became weeks and turned into months, we looked for companionship and sex. I was there on one trip almost two months. We strayed and often.

There was a continuous stream of department and specialty store buyers that came over on a regular basis more than willing to share their loneliness with you. Both parties had needs and we spent fun evenings together. There were relationships that developed for they came on a regular basis. We all knew what it was, it served everyone's needs.

There were Asian women who were just the most beautiful and could not do enough for you. They all had an agenda, at least most of them. Life was not easy and if you wanted to be with them, it would cost you one way or another. It was very tempting to say the least, you know the saying, "Western house, Chinese food, Asian wife". It made life palatable but loneliness was always there, you could not escape. The landscape was so foreign, the language, the mentality, the personalities were so different than westerners. It was a constant learning curve to understand the culture in every area.

I spoke to Judy every day, sometimes twice. I always felt guilty. We were having a 7.2 quake and I was on the swaying twelfth floor of the Ritz Hotel calling Judy to tell her I was OK. I thought it was over. She had to contend with all the issues; children, running the house, etc. We paid dues big time. We always talk about it. The problems were endless, the trips became longer and more frequent. Sometimes I was home for ten days and then returned. Without constant scrutiny of the operation, failure was a certainty.

I don't know if it made sense. I was involved in a monumental project trying to do something never done before. Maybe that's what drove me. A warm body next to me did not hurt and sex was the consolation when you can't have love. There were some serious affairs. It wasn't difficult to think they were meaningful. You woke up and either party backed out for the ultimate demands could or would not be met.

What was crucial was getting the job done and these "diversions" after hours allowed you to maintain your sanity and continue. At times I carried it to the extreme but I was living in two distinct worlds and had to exist in both the best way I knew.

I would come home with gifts, mostly jewelry, watches, electronics. I was seeking "absolution". Somewhere in my psyche I rationalized the lifestyle. The "confession", so to speak, does not condone my actions or believe circumstances gave credence to my behavior. It happened and it was part of the total picture. We lived this "unreal" life and this was a part of it.

What happened was a situation that I regret to this day. I became involved here and it almost triggered a divorce. Luckily, I woke up at the eleventh hour and was able to rebuild my life with Judy. The rest is too personal and difficult for me to relate. I just can't put into words the rest of the story for it is ongoing and heartbreaking. I believe there is some retribution for your actions. Unfortunately, sometimes others have to also pay for your mistakes. That's what makes it difficult, seeing this happen.

Jerry Miller wrote his story and impressions of the shoe world in his book, "The Wandering Shoe". He started in footwear working in the family's shoe factory where the prestigious I. Miller line was produced. He created his own line, Margot Jerrold, with his wife, who at the time was a very talented designer. They were very successful. He turned his attention to retailing in the 60's and leased the shoe department at Bendel's. He represented the great brands of Italy; Pancaldi, Walter Steiger, Pollini and the like. He operated manufacturing operations in Greece, Spain, Italy and the Philippines. He launched the Shoe Biz line which was widely acclaimed. Jerry died in the south of France where he lived in 2003.

"He was truly an outstanding and unique person who contributed so much to our industry", Bruce Nordstrom quoted to Footwear News. Jerry was an "experience" in every way. He always told it like it was and took no prisoners along the way. You either loved him or loathed him. There was no middle ground. He had a cutting edge tongue and knew how to use it. His life was traumatic, both mentally and physically. He lived in turmoil with himself and the world. I had the opportunity to spend time with him in Taiwan in regard to his business when I was with U. S. Shoe. He was having serious financial problems brought about by his manufacturing failures in the Philippines and came to Phil Barach for help. Phil turned him over to me and we tried to work out something to save the business. At that point there was nothing we could do. When Jerry saw our Taiwan operation he stated to cry, "If I had only done it this way."

I met him later under different circumstances just by chance in Capri. Judy and I were sitting in the square and there was Jerry. He had just finished his book and reached into his sack and pulled out the book. He wanted me to read the Taiwan chapter in which he wrote about me. Jerry credited me with developing the shoe industry there and gave me the chapter to read that night. We got together for lunch the next day and he read me the last chapter. It was the Frank Sinatra song, "I Did It My Way", which he felt told his story and outlined how he lived his life. Everything was emotional with Jerry, it just had to be that way. He was crying and we consoled him. I understood why he ended his book in that manner. As I look back at that day I realize some of the similarities between us. Every time I hear the song, I think of him and, yes...me. Jerry had to be in the limelight, that was his style for he was a show man; world class. I just wanted to make it happen my way. Nothing fancy, no drama, just my way.

What about success? How has it affected me? How has it shaped my life? Have I handled it well? All these questions have been tossed around in my thoughts and actions. I believe the best explanation is in a quote from Booker T. Washington. "I have learned that success is to be measured not so much by the position that one has reached in life as by the obstacles which he has overcome while trying to succeed." I know that I have paid the price in many ways. Was it worth the time away from friends and family? Was it worth the nights alone in lands so foreign to my people, upbringing, values and mentality? Was it worth being a pioneer enduring the pain of mistakes, the unknown and the disappointments?

These are some of the questions that resonate and continually come up in my thoughts. I guess what has driven me is showing that a poor kid from "nowheresville" can find success. I learned to be competitive at an early age out of necessity, to fail was not an option. I wanted to show the world that this kid without a Dad could be that winner. I won at sports, at my paper route, at the shoe store. I wanted to show the kids from the "rich side" of town that I was a person who could compete in their league and beyond. I wanted to show my high school sweetheart that she should not have counted me out because I came from a poor family. I wanted to show my family that I could do it on my own terms. They could not control my life and who I love. I wanted to show Judy that I would bring her a life filled with love and happiness. I wanted to show all concerned that I was talented and resourceful. I wanted to show that I had the vision and courage moving to Italy for it was the future. I wanted to show my fellow shoe men that I could pioneer and build a business and better product in Taiwan and China. I wanted to show the shoe world that a brand could be built and flourish made in China. I wanted to show my critics and doubters that I could persevere even with their obstacles. I wanted to show that I was a winner for as Winston Churchill said, "Success is not final, failures not fatal. It is the courage to continue that counts."

Today life is entirely different for I am facing problems and circumstances that I have never encountered. Our branded business is being well taken care of by Ted and his staff. My involvement in the everyday running of the business is minimal as it should be. My contribution is still in the design and product development area along with our Italian office. It is still my first love.

Most of my emphasis is in an entirely different area. I am now the major caregiver for my wife who has developed Alzheimer's and needs my undivided attention. All these years she was alone raising the children and running the ship while I was gone. She put up with my straying, my ventures, my periods of self-indulgence and the maniacal driven desire to succeed. I am at her side for it is "payback time", big time. My world is now much smaller; it has come full circle.

It's learning a whole new set of skills in an area where my artistic talents do not seem to be helping. I am now being domesticated, no apron, but dish pan hands are in the cards without a question. I really never went shopping on a regular basis and never had to plan the meals, never mind cook them. Cooking was beyond me and has become even more complicated for me with electric. We now live in a wonderful condominium without a gas range so I am now chief cook and bottle washer and getting better at it daily. I've used my organizational skills to at least put some semblance to the organized chaos.

This book has been a great diversion from the everyday issues. It has made me re-think where I am today in every facet of my life. It has brought back events that have escaped my thought in years. One event triggers another and names from nowhere come into view. Most of all, it has given me a different perspective of who and what has transpired over the years that I have been involved in the footwear industry.

I started working in shoe stores by accident, having been "drafted" by an older kid to help after a football game. The manager liked my work and I've been in the industry ever since. I have been fortunate to have seen the industry evolve in every phase of development since that time. Who would have dreamed this lanky kid from Worcester would travel the world and see it from every conceivable viewpoint. The key players from my youth are all gone and their flamboyant style no longer exists. The world would be so foreign to them if they were here today. For those of us that are still "around", we are practically dinosaurs in the scheme of things.

About ten to twelve years ago when I was giving a presentation of the Caressa line to a department store group, I mentioned Phil Barach's name. After it was over, one of the buyers asked me who he was.

Phil died just about a year ago and in the minds of some in the industry, he departed this life long before. I guess I will never come to grips with this. I'm thinking it will definitely happen to me.

It's strange. I feel my skills as a designer are far better than twenty years earlier. I do not feel that I have lost a step. A designer can get a true evaluation of his skills, for it is put down on paper. I am a realist and when my Italian counterparts gladly use my contributions for their European collections, I know it's not "lip service" or, in Yiddish, we use the word "rachmonis", which is a far better explanation. It means we did it because we felt sorry.

When I sit down to work on the collection or a specific project, the fire and the creativity is there. I find the creative juices are still flowing and there is still that competitive spirit. I guess you can't change the spots on a leopard or kill someone's desire to create.

It's strange how events turn. I have gone from designing

four lines and running a business to one line. I approached a friend who is now in a position to give me some freelance work. Money is not the issue. What I need is the work and the need to "win".

I have been winning my whole life and when it is taken or let go by choice, it's difficult to retrieve in every way. Sammy Davis, Jr., when interviewed, once said, "I just love to work, so when I go to the fridge late at night and the light goes on, I do my routine!"

It's not quite that bad, but I still feel the rush that pushes me to achieve for achievement's sake. With all that is going on in my personal life, the need for this type of outlet is key. Besides, there are only a few of us in this shoe world who have the ability and experience to know how to get it done in every area, possibly four to five, no more.

I can say there is very little that I would change even if the shoe gods condoned it for I would have made a whole different set of errors, more than likely, unforgiving ones. Surely some of my decisions I would like to re-think today. Maybe the road map that I laid out was flawed with dead ends, difficult turns and unforeseen pitfalls. However, we found a way to reach our goals, at least most of them. I never expected anyone to do what I was not willing to do myself.

My blessings were wonderful, talented, dedicated co-workers and friends who lived the dream with me. All of this never would have happened without them. I can never thank them enough or repay them for their tireless contributions. What pulled me through many of the rough times was the need to make it happen. We had the responsibility to our staff, families, supporters and thousands of workers who depended on us winning. Most of it would never have occurred if Judy had not put up with my endless travel and time away from the family. There were many times when she was not well and had every right to protest. She backed me at every juncture.

I look back at the personalities that gave me that break and influenced my life. Most of them are gone but, hopefully, some of you will catch a glimpse of their experiences and personalities. Maybe you will be able to transpose yourself for a moment and be captured by their charisma. It was a different time, a different world. I know my memory tapes will always be there at a moment's notice.

To those that I have "beat up", I have only tried to bring out the truth and not just my opinion and attitude. It was part of the history and had to be told. I hold no grudges or harbor any ill will.

I would never have gone into business if Ted and Leslie had not decided to join me. Their contributions cannot be measured. What they were able to accomplish in their areas of responsibility were indispensable to the growth of the corporation. They were the stabilizers when I was off course. They talked sense when I had a crazy scheme. Without that ability to keep each other afloat, we would not be here today.

Ever since I could remember, I had a pencil in my hand. My first memories of that were drawing tanks and planes as my mother read my brother's letter from somewhere in Italy. I have been drawing ever since, not only on paper but etching them into my psyche, my being. I've drawn life from many different angles and situations. My virtual sketch book is filled with so many interesting scenarios, ideas and tales of joy and sorrow, wins and losses, happiness and loneliness, success and disappointments.

There is a part of my life that I have not discussed and I have purposely decided not to include it in this book. I just felt there was a need for more time to digest how to present it on paper. I now know it's my next project.

At the beginning of this book I asked myself the question, "Why am I doing this?" There is no one reason that can answer that question. I believe setting down the stories of one's life and how it relates to the events that shaped it is important. We always learn from any form of history for it usually repeats itself. I know I did my very best. It was what my Mom taught me.

CPSIA information can be obtained
at www.ICGtesting.com
Printed in the USA
BVOW07s1038050416

442939BV00005BA/6/P